Practicing Development

UPENDING ASSUMPTIONS FOR POSITIVE CHANGE

edited by
Susan H. Holcombe
Marion Howard

Kumarian Press

A Division of Lynne Rienner Publishers, Inc. • Boulder & London

Published in the United States of America in 2019 by
Kumarian Press
A division of Lynne Rienner Publishers, Inc.
1800 30th Street, Boulder, Colorado 80301
www.rienner.com

and in the United Kingdom by
Kumarian Press
A division of Lynne Rienner Publishers, Inc.
Gray's Inn House, 127 Clerkenwell Road, London EC1 5DB

Library of Congress Cataloging-in-Publication Data
Names: Holcombe, Susan H., editor. | Howard, Marion, editor.
Title: Practicing development : upending assumptions for positive change /
  Susan H. Holcombe and Marion Howard, editors.
Description: Boulder, Colorado : Lynne Rienner Publishers, Inc., 2019. |
  Includes bibliographical references and index.
Identifiers: LCCN 2018053713 | ISBN 9781626377950 (hardcover) |
  ISBN 9781626378001 (paperback)
Subjects: LCSH: Economic development. | Sustainable development.
Classification: LCC HC79.E5 P6755 2019 | DDC 338.9/27—dc23
LC record available at https://lccn.loc.gov/2018053713

British Cataloguing in Publication Data
A Cataloguing in Publication record for this book
is available from the British Library.

Printed and bound in the United States of America

The paper used in this publication meets the requirements
of the American National Standard for Permanence of
Paper for Printed Library Materials Z39.48-1992.

5 4 3 2 1

Contents

Part 2   Turning Development Around

Part 3   Preparing Development Practitioners

Acknowledgments

We are grateful to our students and colleagues, whose insights and practice inspired us to pursue and complete this exploration of right-side-up development and sustainable practice.

We thank the authors who contributed to this volume for their time, effort, and wisdom. Any omissions are our own.

We also acknowledge Ravi Lakshmikanthan, who provided valuable assistance in surveying our former students. Lyndsey Ellis and Ruth Warren generously provided editorial support for several of our contributors. In Kenya, Zipporah Wambua, Makueni County director for public participation and civic education, and Kapelo Powon, West Pokot County chief of staff, kindly provided information and insights for Chapter 11.

We thank the team at Lynne Rienner—our copyeditor, Michele Wynn; Nicole Moore; Shena Redmond, who guided us on style and preparation of the final manuscript; and Sally Glover, who handled communications and marketing. Lynne Rienner, our publisher, was a pleasure to work with, always available and helpful.

We have attempted to provide an alternative perspective for the future of sustainable development and for an upended model of development led by practitioners, institutions, and communities from the Global South. We hope that this book encourages dialogue and inspires our fellow practitioners, educators, and other readers.

—Susan H. Holcombe and Marion Howard

1

Practicing Development

Susan H. Holcombe
and Marion Howard

Government, multilateral, and philanthropic efforts since the end of World War II have invested financial, managerial, and intellectual resources in the mission to produce "development" and reduce poverty. More recently, attention has also been paid to fostering human well-being and dignity and to conserving the natural environment. Yet the fruits of these efforts have rarely been examined from the perspective of those living in poverty and inequality, the very people who feel the effects of this development. In this book, we argue that we've been doing development upside down. The perspectives, policies, and processes of development have been dominated by organizations and actors from the industrialized world who have built an industry centered on the distribution and management of foreign aid. But development cannot be imposed, and foreign assistance is not development. Aid can be helpful, but it can also be harmful to countries, communities, and their social, political, and natural environments—smothering or destroying capacities and assuring lack of sustainability.

Yes, there have been signal successes in reducing poverty and inequality, improving health and education, and drawing some attention to connections between environmental degradation and development that is *not* sustainable. With instructive exceptions, these gains have too often been top-down interventions that may not be effective or sustainable. The development industry's past and present are rooted in a model of delivering and receiving foreign assistance. In this model, rich-country donors of the Global North, institutional and individual, are the "doers," giving aid to the "done-tos" in the Global South. This relationship needs to be turned on its head so that impoverished communities, civil society, and Southern governments become the doers. The chapters in this book explore this

1

problem and suggest new directions for practitioners from both developing and industrialized countries.

New Directions

The idea for this book emerged from the editors' experiences. Together, we have well over half a century of development practice, ranging from the village level to large agency headquarters, as well as thirty-plus years of experience teaching midcareer practitioners from developing and industrialized countries in a hands-on master's program in sustainable international development. Using our experience gained from practicing, teaching, and learning from students, colleagues, and a variety of actors in the field, we frame the key challenges that face development practice today. We also rely on the independent voices of thoughtful practitioners with experience in both donor and recipient development organizations.

We start with two chapters that lay out the current context of international development and provide background for the many chapters from development practitioners that follow. Chapter 2, written by both of us, sets the stage with a look at the contradictions and complexities that constrain development. We argue that despite good intentions, development practice has been dominated by donors and donor-imposed theories of development. Development has become an industry focused on feeding itself, an enterprise in which survival of its organizations too often takes precedence over sincere aspirations for development.

In Chapter 3, Marion Howard explores the meaning of sustainable development and how we have organized globally to achieve sustainable development. Basing her analysis on her decades of work in recipient organizations, she looks at some of the systems within the development industry that keep us from achieving effective development.

In Part 1 (Chapters 4 through 9), the contributors explore the vision and values practitioners bring to development, as well as the nature of the gap between our ideals and practice. Seasoned practitioners, working in a variety of development fields, situations, and locations, take a strategic perspective on the changing development landscape and the persistence of poverty, inequality, exclusion, and mismanagement of the environment. Four of these authors are from industrialized countries and two are from less developed areas. All have a critical understanding of the changing landscape and a strategic vision for the future of development practice. Drawing on their decades of experience, these six authors offer their reflections on development practice in the past and consider where we might find ideas and inspiration for change for the future.

In Chapter 4, Laurence Simon offers a series of stories that plunge us into the philosophy of development and the ethical dilemmas inherent in

"First World" practitioner engagement in developing countries. His tales ask us, as people of privilege, to confront our own perceptions and to listen to and respect other perspectives. He examines what this means for training development practitioners and recounts his firsthand experiences setting up a graduate program in sustainable international development.

In Chapter 5, Vinya Ariyaratne tells the story of Sri Lanka's Sarvodaya Shramadana Movement, which, over its sixty-year history, built on traditional values of justice and community to reach more than 15,000 of Sri Lanka's 38,000 villages and improve the lives of more than 4 million people. Sarvodaya's philosophy of social equity, sharing, and governance through participatory democracy is key to its growth and impact. Ariyaratne also addresses scaling up, learning, and resilience through wars, natural disasters, and funding challenges.

In Chapter 6, Thomas Dichter raises direct, challenging questions about the aid business, examining the role that donor-country practitioners have played in the world of development and should play in development practice going forward. He looks at the industry that development has become and makes clear in his assessment that much education for development professionals is training them to maintain the business of development.

Patrick Awuah, in Chapter 7, makes the case that young Africans educated in ethics, innovation, and entrepreneurship and armed with courage and passion can challenge rampant corruption and be innovative and entrepreneurial. Awuah founded and leads Ashesi University in Ghana, which offers a world-class education grounded in critical thinking and risk taking, not in traditional rote learning. Ashesi tackles head-on the challenges of corruption to real development, emphasizing integrity in its classrooms and culture.

In Chapter 8, Tundi Agardy looks at connections between marine conservation and human well-being to remind us that a sound environment is the foundation for sustained development and that without attention to social, economic, and environmental facets of sustainability, results of economic development are temporary. Agardy considers the sometimes contradictory approaches of conservationists and development practitioners, and she discusses the movement toward holistic solutions rooted in the local situation.

In Chapter 9, Raymond Offenheiser argues that the roles of international nongovernmental organizations (INGOs) in the development industry must and are changing. Instead of delivering basic services, INGOs need to focus on changing the systems and structures that have allowed poverty and social exclusion to persist. Offenheiser uses the example of Oxfam's work on extractive industries, which linked global advocacy and local community support, to illustrate the INGO role of "leading from behind" that enables civil society organizations to take over the work and sustain it.

In Part 2, Chapters 10 through 16 move to practice in the here and now, examining how practitioners are exploring opportunities to transform development. Most contributions come from authors from the Global South who are active on the ground, planning and implementing change strategies in differing but constraining circumstances. Some contributors bring decades of experience; others are relatively young professionals working to make an impact. These authors focus on approaches that are changing the way development is done and explore where we might find inspiration and opportunities for change, and what we can do as practitioners to move these approaches in new and positive directions.

In Chapter 10, Christian Velasquez Donaldson draws from nearly a decade of advocating for systemic reform at the World Bank on behalf of civil society to look at the Bank's changing role. He delves into some of the challenges that international financial institutions (IFIs), especially the World Bank, face and how they shape ideas and approaches to sustainable development. He considers the complexities of development, looks at the constant tension inside institutions with their internal politics and power struggles, and identifies the need for empathy and dedication to the human side of development.

In Chapter 11, Esther Kamau examines positive opportunities for good governance in the devolution of authority and responsibility to the county level, assessing the accomplishments that can flow from seizing opportunities. She chronicles the experience of young, educated, committed officials in counties in Kenya who are using new constitutional provisions to engage civic participation in planning, implementing, and taking ownership of development interventions.

In Chapter 12, Agustin Madrigal Bulnes, Andrea Savage Tejada, and Joshua Ellsworth describe their ongoing work on watershed restoration and rural livelihoods in Central Mexico. They identify four practical strategies they use to improve effectiveness and sustainability of their work, each of which has worked over the long term within unpredictable and complex situations.

Elkanah Odembo, in Chapter 13, challenges African nongovernmental organizations (NGOs) to go beyond implementing projects that deliver services to communities and move to influencing and shaping policies that affect development and its sustainability. He considers the need for independent funding, transparency, accountability, and, most of all, passionate and committed leadership, if African NGOs are to assume new roles in sustainable development.

In Chapter 14, Lu Lei describes the Chinese approach to poverty reduction and its incipient attempts to protect environmental health. China is a new actor in international development and, through its own efforts, has achieved the largest reduction in poverty seen in recent times. Lu Lei describes both the top-down setting of poverty reduction goals and the local mechanisms and accountability systems used to meet change objectives.

In Chapter 15, Fanny Howard and Rixcie Newball relate how a local community and an indigenous-led regional government agency worked together to use the power of international and national law and policy to fight a major threat to their natural resource base and traditional livelihoods.

Chapter 16 includes four microcases from development practice that illustrate how committed leadership and new roles of national and international NGOs can work. Pallavi Gupta explains how a "bridging" organization helped bring an innovative women's health and sanitation project to scale in India. Sarah Jane Holcombe describes the work of one innovative individual, Thailand's Mechai Viravaidya, who succeeded in catalyzing attitudinal and behavioral changes relative to HIV/AIDS and family planning in Thailand by using culturally appropriate approaches. Lu Lei offers the example of a large centralized country, China, where national policy and localized, concrete, targeted measures successfully and substantially reduced poverty. Raymond Offenheiser offers a case study of Oxfam America's Behind the Brands campaign, which took a new approach to food production and nutritional security by working with ten global food corporations to set up best policies and practices designed to change the way they do business.

In Part 3 (Chapters 17 and 18), we bring the book back full circle to the question of upending development to turn it right side up. In the final two chapters, we synthesize the contributors' observations on the past aid industry and on present and future directions for development. We draw on all the prior chapters in discussing future roles for development practitioners, who are working in both donor and recipient agencies in the North and South, and to make specific recommendations for development studies programs in a changing world.

In Chapter 17, the editors look for lessons from the book's many authors. How can development practitioners working within organizations make change within the constraints of the development industry, as described by contributors? How can we move toward development practice that honors participation, ownership, capacity building, agency, conservation of the environment, and social transformation? And how can practitioners negotiate the ethical dilemmas they inevitably face as idealism meets reality, both in the field and within their organizations?

In Chapter 18, we draw lessons from the earlier chapters and from our own experience as practitioners and as teachers of master's-degree students in an international development program. We conclude by offering recommendations for designing development studies programs and preparing practitioners to negotiate the constraints of the development industry and contribute more effectively to sustainable poverty reduction, conservation of the environment and natural resources, and improved quality of life. We suggest that development professionals can transform development, turning it right side up, and that development studies programs can help equip them to do this.

Cautionary Notes

This book has a number of limitations, and we would like to mention several. First, there is no good way to differentiate the "doers" and the "done-tos" without using loaded language that emerged from and reinforces some of the very perspectives this book seeks to upend. In our own chapters, we decided to use the terms North/Northern and South/Southern, as in Global North and Global South. By *North,* we mean industrialized countries that are generally on the "donor" side of the development-industry equation. By *South,* we mean economically disadvantaged nations (historically referred to as Third World, undeveloped, or developing countries) and spaces and communities negatively impacted by contemporary economic and political systems that tend to be on the "recipient" side of the development-industry equation. Some of the other contributors use different terms.

Second, there are gaps in the subjects discussed in this book. Because of space constraints, some critical aspects of sustainable development practice get short shrift. The private sector has always been an actor in development, particularly in terms of resource extraction and investment. Increasingly, however, the private sector is being asked to implement parts of aid agreements, perhaps in pursuit of greater efficiency or better value for money, or perhaps in a neocolonialist approach aimed at keeping resources and control of development in the hands of the rich and powerful, whether consciously or unconsciously so. We don't know what impact these arrangements, often defined as public-private partnerships and called for in the 2030 Agenda for Sustainable Development, can have on building the local capacity necessary for sustainability or on distorting development objectives.

Nor do we focus on innovations, often in the private sector and business-minded NGOs, that Northern social entrepreneurs are pioneering in order to put assets, organizational resources, and leadership in the hands of the previously excluded. The Global Banking Alliance for Women, Root Capital, VisionSpring, Thousand Currents, and One Acre Fund are just a few examples of these innovative approaches. Labs for innovative development have sprung up—for example, the Global Development Lab, sponsored by the US Agency for International Development (USAID); MIT's D-Lab; and the Northern-led but global partnership-based UNLEASH Lab—along with a myriad of highly competitive, generous global innovation awards for teams of young social entrepreneurs and inventors. New development approaches such as those of the Doing Development Differently (DDD) community and Harvard's Problem Driven Iterative Adaptation (PDIA), while still coming from a Northern perspective, are seeking to question and change the development industry's traditional paradigms. And a range of Northern development organizations from small NGOs (Give Directly and Action Against Hunger USA, to name two) to bi- and multilaterals (for example, USAID and the European Commission) are experimenting with building self-reliance and expanding development outcomes through reforms such as *unconditional cash transfers* and *multipurpose vouchers*. We urge readers to research these and other organizations and programs. We are not assessing or endorsing any of these programs or organizations but are simply offering a few examples of currently recognized innovations in the development industry.

Likewise, gender is not the primary focus of any chapter. Development rhetoric calls for inclusion or the mainstreaming of gender analysis and gender rights into development plans and implementation; in practice, we know that this does not always happen. New actors in development are mentioned, but there is not space for an in-depth discussion of changing roles, approaches, and programs—such as the Chinese Silk Road initiative (One Belt One Road)—and what this means for developing countries and development practitioners. Although a concern for governance and its role in lasting development is evident in many chapters, none of the authors address governance separately as an issue essential to sustainability. We also pay scant attention to the role of economic growth and development. Equally, questions about the limits of economic growth and consumption, though critical to the twenty-first century, are given only passing attention.

In addition, insufficient attention is given to the role of Southern nationals working in Northern donor organizations and INGOs, whether within their home countries or elsewhere. National development practitioners working in international organizations can find themselves in a difficult position. They may have second-class status relative to international staff. Based on their status within their own culture, they may bring an elite perspective to their view of development or they may be well-grounded in the contexts of poverty, social exclusion, and environmental threats in their own country. But regardless of their experience and knowledge, they may be trained or pressured by their organizations to adopt Northern perspectives and adhere to Northern methods. And in many cases, there may be strong incentives not to rock the boat and to avoid risks.

We do not apologize for the many subjects we have been unable to examine. This book cannot be encyclopedic, and many of these gaps have been covered extensively in other books. Instead, we seek to raise questions and share knowledge about the nature of development practice and the way forward. We rely on the reflections, observations, and stories, emerging from the professional experiences of Southern and Northern practitioners, which readers can put to use more generally.

Third, we assume that our focus on Southern contributors will not deter Northern readers. Twelve of our nineteen contributors hail from the Global South and several of the Northern contributors, including one of the editors, have worked in their practice almost exclusively for Southern-based recipient organizations. The imbalance in this book is intentional. As teachers and longtime practitioners, we are acutely aware of the overt and hidden privilege, power, and entitlement that come from being a product of the wealthy North, advantages that can overpower or silence voices, knowledge, methods, practices, and initiatives from the South. We hope that our Northern readers, especially students, can use their reading here to step back, listen, appreciate, and value the perspectives of their Southern colleagues.

Fourth, contributions to this book overlap in many ways but also do not always agree with each other. As development practitioners, we all see reality through our own lenses, and the mixing of perspectives can provide a healthy challenge to unexamined assumptions. Along these lines, as editors we suspect that some of our contributors, especially those working most actively in the field today, have felt it wise to moderate their critiques of the development industry, not so much out of deference as from a recognition of the power held by donor countries and their agents. Careful reading suggests where these donor impediments to sustainable development lie.

Finally, we are not so naive as to think that a revolution will upend the development industry. We recognize that much aid serves political and economic objectives of donor countries. That is unlikely to change anytime soon. But we argue in this book that we must be concerned with the development enterprise's obsession with quantification, measurable results, top-down technical fixes, and dependence upon Northern expertise, qualifications, worldview, and decision making. Within both industrialized and developing countries, myriad obstacles (corruption, environmental challenges, social exclusion, oppression, economic inequity, and other afflictions) to right-side-up development persist. Also, economic theories that vary from neoliberalism to market fundamentalism to dependency theory remain alive and well in some quarters. The problem with theories is that their complexity and lack of grounding in reality can make them difficult to implement in real life, even if germane and appropriate. The same may hold true with the demand for unreasonable quantification in the search for necessary accountability.

We hope to generate dialogue among development practitioners, the development industry, foundations, and private philanthropists about the definition and objectives of development, about who controls and benefits from development, and about accountability by whom and for whom. Where development is not primarily politically or economically motivated (and perhaps even where it is), we hope to expand the opportunities and means for practitioners to advance the local control, capacity, and participation that enable sustainability. And most important, we hope to foster an environment in which local practitioners and the people they serve can take the lead in defining and implementing their own development, benefiting from, but not driven by, the knowledge and experience of others.

2

Good Intentions and the Reality of Development Practice

Susan H. Holcombe
and Marion Howard

We have taught more than a thousand graduate students, most of whom brought substantial practical experience to their studies. Two-thirds of them came from the Global South. Invariably, they sprang to life when we began discussions of Amartya Sen's *Development as Freedom* (1999) at the annual orientation for students. Ideas of human dignity and of one's right and capacity to take control of one's own destiny were galvanizing concepts—concepts underpinned by human capabilities stemming from freedoms to enjoy economic security, good health and education, political engagement, and freedom from physical and psychological threats because of war, ethnicity, gender, or other distinctions. Our students' idealism and optimism would soon enough be tested by the realities of implementation in the real world. As teachers and practitioners, we knew our students would always have to manage the tensions between ideals and reality. From our own practitioner experience, we knew colleagues who, in focusing on projects, lost sight of the longer-term outcomes and values. We wanted our students never to lose their ideals. Although the means of development practice may include economic, ecological, or technical methods, the end is about the well-being of humans and of the natural and built environments in which we live.

In this chapter, we highlight the contradictions and complexities that constrain development. We draw on our own experience and that of former students and colleagues to point out that despite the best intentions and commitments, the development industry has turned development practice upside down. By upside down, we mean that the focus has too often been on applying top-down, donor-designed solutions. The development industry has focused less on local leadership, capacity, involvement, and locally designed

9

solutions and decisions. It is easy to forget that ordinary people and communities bear the consequences of development projects and that failure to engage local leadership, government, and civil society can lead not only to imposed solutions and failed projects but can even shape and contribute to "development" that is itself upside down—that is, development systems that benefit elites, maintain inequitable distribution of resources, and deepen power imbalances, exclusion, and inequality.

The twentieth-century practice of international development started in optimism, underpinned by reality. The economic and political resurrection of Europe after the devastation of World War II led many to believe that interventions such as the Marshall Plan (1948) could work similar wonders elsewhere. Although this book is not a history of development and development programs, it is based on awareness that organized development has mushroomed since the late 1940s. Development started with bilateral programs and grew to include multilateral development banks, the inter-governmental system of the United Nations (UN), international non-governmental organizations, foundations, religious groups, and individual philanthropists—many from the rich North, but a growing number from East Asia and the emerging South. Development has also become big business. The amount of money in the sector, from both official and private sources, has grown enormously.

Development is about goals. If we do not know where our development practice is going, we will never reach our goals. The values we bring to development practice shape the road to development change. Our students' enthusiasm for Sen's capabilities, freedoms, and human development philosophy reflects this commitment to improving the human condition. Economic growth and modernization may be a means to reaching goals, but they are not the ends. Development stakeholders do share many globally articulated and agreed upon goals that reflect values associated with human development, such as the 2015 UN Paris Agreement on climate change or the Sustainable Development Goals (SDGs) discussed in Chapter 3. The problem is not with stated goals, but with how those goals are implemented. What we say is not always what we do, and where we aim for is not always where we end up.

Ideals and values confront the pragmatic realities of ideologies and national interests. Development ideologies and national interests have shaped the course of development in multiple ways. For years, there was tension between capitalist and socialist approaches. Market approaches were often a condition for receiving Western aid, even though data suggest that rapid opening of markets did not increase economic growth but did increase poverty in many countries (Rodrik 2002). Aid allocations may skew toward particular countries to keep a favored ally in power. Politicians may support food aid or official development assistance (ODA) because it builds markets for Northern agricultural products and other goods and services, or because it bolsters national security. Defense spokespeople may argue that development and diplomacy are cheaper than conflicts that put national wealth and lives at stake. These competing interests driving development are not new. In the United States they have continued from President Truman to President Trump. A challenge for young development practitioners is to learn how to manage tensions between the priorities of development organizations they're working with, especially funders, and their own ideals.

The glow has long been fading from the development enterprise and its manifestations in the aid industry. Devendra Raj Panday—development economist, civil servant, formerly permanent secretary of finance in Nepal, and one of Susan Holcombe's classmates—made an intriguing blunt statement. In his view, Nepal needed to stop foreign aid to allow the nation time to set its own priorities and build institutions for the modern era. When Nepal emerged from isolation in the 1950s, it was a darling of aid donors; in the decades afterward, it became highly dependent on aid for both its development and regular budget. Panday wrote about the symbiosis between donor and recipient, noting that "developing countries are regularly driven by their appetite for aid to formulate aid requests, accompanied by shifts in development strategies that are more apparent than real. The donors contribute to this process directly because they themselves have to justify their engagement in a non-performing country" (Panday 2011, p. 143). This collusion between donors and the ruling elite diverts attention from ordinary people. Ruling elites have few incentives to develop (and own) their own strategies for development, to make difficult changes such as addressing caste and class differences or accepting land redistribution, or to build modern institutions and capacities that allow a developing country to have independent and sustainable development (Panday 2011).

Although our students from the Global South mostly chose to study sustainable development out of a moral commitment, they have a declining respect for "First World" development work. They noted the large number of expensive four-wheel-drive vehicles clogging the streets of capitals, but not necessarily visible in rural communities. They spoke about the high salaries and lifestyles that separated many (but not all) expatriate experts from the realities of indigenous development. They referred to *tied* aid, in which expenditures on goods and consultants in the donor country limited the funding that actually went to countries and communities. They talked about the occasional arrogance of aid officials, fortified by their role as donors, and about their frequent disrespect and ignorance of local culture, customs, and values.

We, too, have seen this. For example, a senior UN aid administrator, development planner, and trained economist returned to his home country in the Global South to serve with the newly elected government as chair of the central bank. On a visit back to UN headquarters in New York City, he described to former colleagues the humiliating experience of hosting a delegation of junior officers from the International Monetary Fund (IMF) and World Bank and being obliged to listen to their lectures about policies he should adopt. This arrogance has also extended to international staff of INGOs, who have used their positions to abuse coworkers, women, and children. Systemic power imbalances are pitfalls in the development enterprise that can pave the way for specific acts of arrogance and abuses of power and for potentially corrupting influences such as expatriate salaries that amount to great wealth locally, perceived elite status, and perquisites of vehicles, houses, and privileged schools.

Recognizing Progress

In this chapter, we introduce some of the ways in which development today has got it backwards. Before doing so, we stress that we recognize that there have been signal development successes over the past seventy years. There has been real progress, but it is progress that has, sometimes unintentionally, been top-down and characterized by a focus on the short term—not on sustainability. Yes, some countries have moved from low- to middle-income status. Absolute poverty has been reduced substantially. However, much of that growth and poverty reduction took place in one country, China, and was the result of Chinese national, not outsider, policies and interventions. Poverty remains dire in many countries. Chronic malnutrition increased in 2016 over prior year declines (FAO et al. 2017), including in some least-developed countries that the Organisation for Economic Co-operation and Development (OECD) notes are also experiencing declines in foreign assistance (OECD-DAC 2017). According to studies by Oxfam International and the World Inequality Lab, inequality remains high and is on the increase (Lawson 2018, Alvaredo et al. 2018).

There have been laudable improvements in child and infant morbidity and mortality rates. But some health improvements are not spread equitably throughout society, whereas others are largely the result of technical interventions, a good example being immunizations against polio and measles. It is worth remembering that reductions in infant and childhood mortality in the industrialized North in the early twentieth century preceded technical innovations of immunizations and antibiotics, resulting instead from investment in widespread water and sewage systems and hygiene behavior changes. Today, immunizations can be implemented as top-down interventions, administered to people. We don't know whether such programs can be made sustainable, or if people living in poverty will be able to claim continued access to or control over such interventions. More broadly, donor-initiated innovations often do not survive donor involvement and/or are not widely adopted.

Donors want credit for their own innovations and may be disinclined to introduce or scale-up the innovations of others. In consequence, there has been a recent flurry of interest in scaling up successful innovations to the national level (Cooley and Kohl 2012, Holcombe 2012).

In education we know that today many more children, including girls, attend primary school than ever before. Our former students and colleagues tell us about quantitative success in terms of numbers of schools and enrollment. They also raise questions about quality of learning and about how education will shape children's futures. These doubts cloud achievements. Are we shortchanging sustainability and avoiding difficult, messy questions about how local communities and countries take control and become agents of their own development? The development community has been aware of this problem. The aid effectiveness movement over the past decade or so has done valuable work in identifying the importance of participation and ownership, management capacity, and two-way accountability. These are embedded in global agreements such as the Paris Declaration of 2005, the subsequent 2008 Accra Agenda for Action, and the 2011 Busan Partnership for Effective Development Cooperation and are reflected in the advocacy work of some organizations such as Oxfam International, Advocates for International Development (A4ID), Global Fund for Women, or the Doing Development Differently (DDD) community. But we would argue that it has been hard to translate these ideals into effective aid implementation, in part because of perverse incentives and systems built into the development enterprise.

In the rest of this chapter, we explore some of the reasons our successes are not always building the foundation for sustainability. First, we discuss the major factors that have inhibited and continue to inhibit the effectiveness of development practice. Second, we address several new factors that are changing the landscape of the development field in the twenty-first century.

Factors Inhibiting Development: Yesterday and Today

Conflation of Development with Aid

Oddly, development practitioners often see development through the lens of aid. Intellectually, practitioners know that the two are different—that financial, technical, and other aid may, under the right conditions, contribute to development objectives, but they also know that aid does not necessarily result in the human, institutional, and other capacities needed to sustain development goals and is not even always the purpose of aid. Nonetheless, for many decades, the development profession in the North has operated as though development and development aid were the same. We should admit that aid funding pays the salaries of many development practitioners and acknowledge that the transfer of financial and technical resources through aid is one means of addressing poverty, inequality, and sustainability. We are not urging elimination of all aid. Our argument is more complicated. Foreign aid has long constituted a significant portion of development budgets in the poorest countries. It created a system of dependency, binding donor and recipient together, as Panday has noted. We need to understand what this lens of aid as development does to our thinking. Bluntly, this conflation divides stakeholders into givers and takers.

The thinking goes that because the rich "givers" have the funds and technology, they must know better how to develop. Those who are "takers" see that they must conform to the strategies of the donor to keep funds flowing. Aid thus becomes a self-reinforcing system. Recipient countries, particularly those that have not experienced successes, have the need to develop new aid requests that correspond to changing priorities of outside donors. Donors, similarly, contribute to this process by changing strategies because they have to justify their engagement in countries that have not performed well and maintain control of the industry. Both sides are linked to each other as though on a hamster wheel. Donors, through control of funds and expertise in an aid system they created, hold power over recipients as recipients adapt strategies—or adopt strategies—to align with donor requirements. Donors keep funds flowing, as they need to show that they have ever-more-innovative strategies and tools to address development challenges.

In recent decades, the engagement of NGOs, foundations, and individual philanthropists may inadvertently link into this hamster-wheel syndrome, even as these stakeholders seek to support new solutions to old problems of poverty and inequality. To give but one example of many, a graduate student of ours did a six-month practicum with a local NGO in the Sudano-Sahelian region of a West African country. This local NGO had been approached by a large INGO to execute a community-based health project. Like most INGOs, this particular INGO received its funding from governments, foundations, and individuals and, in this case, was actually the intermediary for funds from a major US foundation. The African NGO had not previously worked in maternal, newborn, and child health, which was the focus of this project. Nonetheless, the director of the African NGO told our student that he saw this project as a way to secure funding through a new network for the purpose of organizational advancement. He directed his staff to do a good job because the INGO "is financially stable and generous, allowing [the African NGO] to be flexible with its budgeting." He noted that "the expectation from the INGO [which was relaying the funds from the foundation] is very high, and if we do good work, there is a potential that they will continue to work with us" (Saenbut 2014, p. 29). Our student noted that staff had recently gone for three months without payment of salary. Taking on the new project was a matter of organizational and personal survival. Overall, our student observed situations in which incentives drove both the local and international NGOs to buy into a system that valued the continued flow of aid money over effective development that would call for building local capacities and respecting local participation.

Critiques of the perverse effects of aid are many. Panday has written prolifically about the failure of aid to address structural and systemic inequalities in society or to build "institutional capacity for policy formulation and administration of development programs that respond directly to the need to alleviate poverty and sustain long-term growth" (2011, p. 143). William Easterly (2001, 2006), a former World Bank economist and now an academic, documented the perverse behaviors and negative incentives inherent in the aid system, which continued to invest in failed approaches. Dambisa Moyo (2009), who went from Zambia to the World Bank to Goldman Sachs, argues that aid has left Africans worse off. She criticizes aid conditionalities that required countries to adhere to rich-country-designed economic policies, at the same time as the aid helped circumvent accountability systems, encouraged rent-seeking, siphoned away local talent, and weakened pressures to reform recipient country policies and institutions. Ghanaian economist George Ayittey argued passionately in an interview about Moyo's book that "the presumption that Africans don't know what is good for them and that Americans or other foreigners know what is best for Africans is extremely offensive" (2009, n.p.).

Development as Industry

Development assistance has become an industry with an interest in organizational enhancement and growth that competes with the ideal of building sustainability derived from growing government and indigenous capacities. Young development professionals, motivated by ideals such as ending poverty, assuring justice, advancing inclusion, or conserving the environment, enter this industry only to confront the realities of survival in the aid business. If sustainability means the creation of human, institutional, and material capacities for recipient countries and communities, it implies a declining role for aid organizations. This poses an uncomfortable contradiction. The goals of sustainable development may be at odds with the development professional's aspirations for a career that offers financial and other stability, or with the aid organization's concern about survival. Incentive systems within development assistance organizations seldom reward long-term sustainability of gains. The reward is for short-term achievement of project outputs. International development personnel are regularly transferred among countries, projects, and tasks. This is not new. The 1992 Wapenhans Report that scrutinized World Bank projects estimated that more than one-third of projects failed to achieve objectives. Critics looked at the preponderance of internationals used to draft projects, serve on appraisal missions that in part persuaded governments to agree to loans, and monitor implementation. But unless the government was committed to implementation, the project would fail. Across a range of development organizations, there is today a premium on innovative approaches and plans that will distinguish one's own organization from others in the competition for funding or status. Less attention is given to scaling, replicating, or adapting successful innovations. Is this because international practitioners are programmed to move on to their own next innovation rather than to adopt or support replication of someone else's successful innovation?

Development agencies are in reality spared real scrutiny of and accountability for sustainable outcomes and goals because of the short time frame for implementation, evaluation, and learning. Evaluations at the completion of projects can rarely measure outcomes or sustainability, and they can best report only on inputs and perhaps outputs. The World Bank has matured since the Wapenhans Report. Reforms to date have focused on learning and knowledge sharing but rarely on analysis of internal-management systems and incentives that shape practice (IEG 2015). Internal-management practices and the role of incentives in implementation behaviors in development organizations often were off-limits for discussion. A study inspired by the DDD community, aptly titled "Doing Development Differently: Updating the Plumbing to Fit the Architecture," suggests this may be changing (Bain, Booth, and Wild 2016). Referring specifically to the World Bank, it identifies management factors such as incentives, norms/culture, leadership, and others that need attention. Changing development management is difficult, but development practitioners could look for lessons from the experience of some larger development organizations in the South, such as the Grameen Bank, or government accountability systems in China or Rwanda that devised performance evaluation and incentive systems focused on poverty-reduction results.

Donors and Northern Partners Know Best

Development in the aid industry has been defined by Northern theories and policies. The neoliberal Washington Consensus, a set of ten economic policy prescriptions, is probably the most criticized theory of development coming out of Western market systems. The Washington Consensus long guided the funding decisions, agenda, and influence of many Northern donors, not only the World Bank and IMF. These policies have come under assault, especially by developing countries that have suffered the consequences of rapid opening of their economies, skewed trade and subsidy policies, one-size-fits-all development initiatives and values, and international institutions inadequately structured to serve the interests of poor and less powerful countries. Now the Washington Consensus is less advertised as a donor's preferred theory of development change, but a preference continues for policies and programs of globalization and opening markets. The most succinct critique of the Washington Consensus came at the start of the twenty-first century from economist Dani Rodrik (2002). He observed that countries and regions (China, East Asia) that experienced economic growth and poverty reduction did so not because they followed Washington Consensus policy prescriptions but because they did not. Places that followed this Northern-prescribed policy advice saw only slow growth or decline. In human terms, this can be seen in reduced human well-being in Africa, where per capita income actually declined. Rodrik noted that the prescriptions of the Washington Consensus were an imperfect description of then highly developed economies, but that these countries had not followed the neoliberal policy prescriptions to achieve growth. Indeed, he has argued, it is virtually impossible to implement all ten prescriptions at once.

At the turn of the century, economist Irma Adelman observed the tendency of development economists to look for "mono-theories" of development (2001). Perhaps it is a tendency of the development industry to expect simple, prepackaged solutions that magically solve problems. Still, the misguided notion that the North is uniquely equipped to provide the South with technical solutions for poverty is remarkably resilient. The idea that outsiders could put together a package of interventions to achieve rural development was tested at several village demonstration sites by the Millennium Villages Project (MVP), a program started by economist Jeffrey Sachs. Superficially, the evidence presented by Sachs and colleagues suggested the success of their interventions. A six-month practicum by one of our former students took her to an MVP site in Africa. She spoke the local language, so while foreign representatives of the project talked to local leaders, our student talked to community members who said that although they welcomed the outside money, they did not feel empowered to continue or replicate the project on their own. Nina Munk (2013) did a deeper study of the MVP, conducting interviews in multiple locations over six years. She found that the claimed poverty reduction did not occur, projects were plagued by corruption, villagers distrusted outsiders, and local governments lacked ownership. Scaling interventions to national levels remained more a hope than a reality.

The belief that Northern agencies and "experts" know best has often been fortified by enormous discrepancies in pay and benefits between local and international practitioners. This has been particularly true of international staff in bilateral and intergovernmental agencies, multilateral banks, and even many INGOs. In some Southern country offices, most of the highest positions can be held by personnel from donor countries, who may receive amenities such as comfortable houses, cars, paid vacations, and school fees for their children on top of salaries and per diems many times higher than the salaries of the highest paid local workers. This is changing in some agencies, including multilaterals, in which local practitioners have been promoted to senior positions or country directorships are reserved for local staff. Some INGOs, as a matter of principle, are trying to limit the salary discrepancy between international and local staff, along with shrinking the pay range between the highest and lowest paid workers. In other organizations, the discrepancies remain; like the omnipresence of expensive aid agency vehicles on the streets of Southern capitals, the discrepancies stand as a visible symbol of the power disparities between the rich North and the supplicant South. Discussing such practices remains taboo within many organizations and fuels the argument that the development industry—with its wealthy foundations, donor institutions, and implementing agencies controlling the money and retaining the power—is maintaining a culture of neocolonialism or "economic apartheid." Within this world, local employees can find it impossible to question workplace inequality and wage disparity for fear of losing their jobs or surrendering the access, voice, and credibility that they do have, which allows them to work for development in their communities. In some cases, local staff can see this disparity as justification for corrupt practices, such as siphoning off resources intended for humanitarian aid.

The most destructive aspect of the deeply ingrained attitude that the "donor knows best" is that it can engender an arrogance that makes it difficult to listen to and respect practitioners from recipient countries, much less the "beneficiaries" of development interventions. It can contribute to corruption, exploitation, and a sense of impunity among personnel, particularly those posted in the field, that they can get away with abuses of power; including but not limited to the recently reported sexual abuse of vulnerable women and children by humanitarian workers. In July 2018, the report of a six-month investigation by the United Kingdom's International Development Committee, a cross-party parliamentary group that scrutinizes aid spending, found that sexual abuse and exploitation of beneficiaries by aid workers and UN peacekeepers have been an "open secret" for years, along with sexual harassment inside agencies. The sense of impunity of field staff has been exacerbated by a culture of "complacency verging on complicity" and "self-delusion" in the aid sector, a disconnect between field personnel and leadership, challenges to reporting misconduct, and a lack of institutionalized accountability, all of which contributed to what the report identified as the "collective failure" of leaders to tackle an "endemic" problem. The report went on to say that victims must be put at "the heart of solutions" (International Development Committee 2018). We are aware that too much of the development industry remains entrenched in structures and systems stemming from a North-South power imbalance, a legacy of privilege, and an elitist "old boys' network." In response to the parliamentary report, the United Kingdom's international development secretary, Penny Mordaunt, stated that "until the sector is fully prepared to address the power imbalance, cultures, and behaviors that allow sexual abuse, exploitation, and harassment to happen, we will never stamp it out" (Edwards 2018).

Obsession with Quantification and Measurement

Linked to the creation of a development industry is a growing fixation by Northern development donors and practitioners with quantification, measurable results, top-down technical fixes, and dependence upon their own expertise, qualifications, worldview, and decision-making ability. Whereas we fully agree with the need for transparency and accountability, we have many questions about current notions of quantification and measurement. What does quantification miss, and what are some of the unintended consequences of using the growing power of quantitative analysis, the resources for which reside mostly in the North? We have questions about what kind of quantification, who defines what needs to be measured and how, who has access to the results, and how they will use them. And given that development resources are limited and quantification requires time, money, and effort, are goals that are hard to measure—such as institution building, civil-society empowerment, and local policy development— pushed aside? We would even ask if, in some cases, the development industry is promoting corruption by demanding measurements from local staff lacking the time, resources, or know-how to produce them. Additionally, the will to collect donor-required data can be missing. The information the donor wants may not be needed for effective project management and outcomes, and project staff and stakeholders may not need the numbers required by the donor to improve or transform the local situation. In such cases, donor-demanded measurements can be seen as an imposed, even arbitrary, requirement that wastes precious staff time, funds, and resources, so the incentive to fudge data can be powerful. In the development industry, being compelled to deliver measurable results can lead to top-down technical fixes and dependence upon Northern-defined and -taught views of expertise, qualifications, and decision making.

One example illustrates this obsession with quantification and how it blinds us to realities and sustainability. More than a decade ago, a thoughtful evaluation study of a project demonstrated that school-based child deworming led to increases in school attendance and improved test performance (Miguel and Kremer 2004). Since then, in what has been called the "Worm Wars," dozens of articles have been published either challenging or supporting the original evaluation. Hours of costly brain power have been expended to analyze and reanalyze the evaluation process. Nowhere near the same amount of effort, time, or money was invested in action to make change or to understand the social, cultural, environmental, and political factors that influence if, how, and why local households, communities, and government agencies can take ownership of deworming. Nor have we really examined whether, and to what extent, the growing donor demand for quantitative evaluations, with their requirements for rigor and sophisticated technique, also serves to exclude participation of development managers and evaluators from recipient communities. Without local participation, local decision making and ownership of results are threatened.

Implementation Gets Short Shrift

The imposition of donor theories of change, the industrialization of aid organizations, and the obsession with quantification may all work together to deflect attention from implementation of change efforts. Panday (1989) noted that "many development projects are now implemented not by the government agencies directly but by teams of foreign consultants on a near-turn-key basis. This is because the donors would rather concentrate on 'getting things done' than on a more productive strategy for building institutional capability in the country" (p. 317). Versions of this donor dominance of implementation continue.

Looking at the cycle of planning, implementation, and then evaluation, we observe the amount of human and financial resources that went into developing the project or aid agreements and then into developing evaluation reports. Plans lay out the concrete inputs and output targets to be met during the project life. During implementation, the donor (and thus the recipient), through monitoring regimes, focuses on making sure the targets of the plan have been achieved. There are considerable incentives to demonstrate that targets have been met, but many fewer incentives to identify shortfalls that could help make midproject corrections or offer learning opportunities to improve future implementation. Involving stakeholders in implementation could build capacity and commitment to sustain the innovation, but that isn't done because involving them might slow down implementation. Post-intervention evaluations become increasingly costly as more rigorous methods are applied, so involving local stakeholders complicates the process because of the need for particular skill sets. Without stakeholder involvement, implementation may not be locally owned or evaluation learning applied to future planning and sustainability, especially as the donor moves on to other projects.

Implementation is a complex, flexible process; it needs leadership that can align the overall vision and goals with authentic adaptive practice. When intervention plans are developed overseas or in faraway capitals, inputs and timelines may be laid out, but less attention is given to building stakeholder buy-in, planning flexibility, or verifying local feasibility. Without a priority for national or local execution, it becomes too easy for donors to implement interventions using their own techniques and not allow local leadership and management to apply indigenous methods or learn new methods by doing. Some foundations, whose assets come from the successes of recent tech entrepreneurs, seek to apply methods of technology or of market organizations to solve development problems. Too often, their assistance comes as a top-down package to deal with problems and solutions that are externally selected and defined.

Enabling local governments and community groups to learn from experience, from adapting traditional methods, and even from mistakes, can build capacity to make sustainable change, but it can also take more time. Even when donor state-funded aid is aimed at laudable development goals, implementation may be constrained by the short time frame of projects and, as mentioned earlier, by the imperative for development workers to show measurable, donor-defined results. Aid administrations need to report back to their parliaments and electorates. For example, in instruments such as the Paris Declaration, OECD countries have committed themselves to transparent and equitable relations with development partner countries. In practice, as examples illustrate, a donor's equivalent commitment to quantifiable, predefined results has had pernicious consequences. As mentioned, the drive for measureable results within the time frame of the project encourages donors to do it themselves rather than take the time to allow local executing agencies and stakeholders to learn by doing and to analyze results within the local context. Often, our students would return from their six-month practicums and tell us how INGOs they'd been working with would truncate participatory planning exercises because "there wasn't time." In the classroom, they had studied the need for participatory planning and implementation to achieve project goals and sustainability, but implementation in the field ran up against challenges of donor deadlines and schedules laid out in a donor-driven plan.

Development Today and Tomorrow

Today, new issues, actors, and approaches are altering the landscape of development practice. These add to the above factors that have impacted and hindered effectiveness of development initiatives in past decades and still continue as challenges.

National Interest as a Driver of Aid Has Not Gone Away

The Paris Declaration of 2005 identifies five core principles specifically thought to improve aid effectiveness. These principles interconnect to advance a new approach to development whereby: (1) developing countries set their own strategies for poverty reduction, improve their institutions, and tackle corruption (ownership); (2) donor countries align behind these objectives and use local systems (alignment); (3) donor countries coordinate, simplify procedures, and share information to avoid duplication (harmonization); (4) developing countries and donors shift focus to development results, and results get measured (results); and (5) donors and partners are accountable for development results (mutual accountability). In spite of the fact that these principles were developed and agreed upon by donor and recipient nations and that follow-up partnership agreements pave the way for implementation (the Accra Agenda of 2008, the Busan Partnership of 2011), often (though not always) donor-state aid is driven by the donor state's national priorities and foreign policy goals, rather than geared to support achievement of national strategies identified by the recipient government, sometimes in collaboration with civil society. Furthermore, funding may be given to states perceived as necessary political allies and not granted to states that give development a high priority.

Aid, Corruption, and Governance

The discussion of whether the aid industry breeds corruption and fouls the trust needed for sustainable development is getting new attention. Some argue that aid is associated with lower corruption, or that corruption might contribute to economic growth by oiling the wheels of implementation. Others argue that corruption is a form of rent-seeking—using resources to obtain economic gain without reciprocating wealth creation—that doesn't benefit and may harm society. Panday has said it is something even worse. Referring to comments by World Bank president James Wolfensohn at an Anti-Corruption Conference in 1999, Panday noted that "at the core of the incidence of poverty is equity, and at the core of the issue of equity, is corruption." In his view, "corruption is not only detrimental to economic development, but its cost is borne disproportionately by the poor." He argues that corruption destroys the optimism of people, even in the face of gains in health and education (2011, p. 243). Corruption leads to despair and, we would add, destruction of trust.

Poor governance contributes to corruption. When corruption is present, institutions are too weak to support development that is accountable, and there is a dearth of strategies and funding to enable evolution of those institutions. Corruption has many causes, but we should not ignore the reality that rich-country multinationals involved in resource extraction contribute to the creation and sustaining of corruption and related human-rights abuses and civil conflicts—the mining of coltan in the eastern Congo being one painful example, with gold and silver mining in San Martin, Honduras, another.

Many in the development world lament what they define as weak governance in poor countries and proceed to define good governance and accountability using a Northern lens, rooted in the historical and philosophical heritage of Europe and North America. By the 2000s, it was proposed that aid should be allocated on the basis of governance, not only on the basis of poverty. So development organizations strengthened and expanded their focus on building institutions that worked as they thought best, in accord with their own standards and experience. A number of studies connect stable democratic institutions with less corruption, but links between systems of governance and levels of corruption can be reciprocal, not causal. Strengthening sociopolitical institutions will not necessarily address the root causes of corruption in any particular place. Nor is democracy a panacea for corruption. This is especially so if democracy is defined as elections and not as the presence of values and institutions of good governance such as community participation, accountability, transparency, and functioning of the rule of law. The lessons that Northern donors may perversely be drawing from their own history is that Northern institutions of good governance need to be imposed from the top down, not nurtured from the bottom up, evolving organically from the roots and homegrown systems that exist in individual societies. The use of this inaccurate Northern lens can cause development practitioners to overlook the seeds, knowledge, and customs that support establishing accountable institutions and tackling causes of corruption that already exist in different ways in Southern countries.

Suppliers of Development Resources Are Changing

Aid is only one resource affecting development efforts. Foreign direct investment (FDI) exceeds flows of remittances, and nowadays both dwarf official development assistance. World Bank data indicate that net flows of FDI to low- and middle-income countries amounted to over $648 billion in 2015, while remittances amounted to $450 billion in 2017 (World Bank 2017b). OECD reports net ODA in 2015 from its Development Assistance Committee (DAC) members at $133 billion. There are questions to be answered about where FDI goes and who it benefits, and whether remittances serve private consumption or public goods and production. The most important resources for development may not be financial, but technical resources, information exchange, and knowledge sharing, which are less easy to measure. Diasporas may play a bridging role in introducing innovations, identifying markets, and building institutions (Brinkerhoff 2008). The role of national leadership and government strategies can be obscured by the development industry's entrenched focus on aid as the lever of change. An experienced UN development practitioner told us that the role of foreign technical expertise and aid is marginal to overall development success. From Singapore, East Asia, and China to nascent efforts in Rwanda and Ethiopia, success (as measured by human development indicators) has been the result of national leadership, priorities, and efforts. Foreigners can have something to offer with new technologies, best practices, and connections to alternative sources of technical and financial assistance, but they need to learn how to support national development agendas and capacities and put their privilege, assets, and connections at the service of communities.

New Actors Are Revolutionizing
Development Financing and Implementation

In the twenty-first century, new donors and global powers are emerging, particularly the country economies that make up the BRICS association (Brazil, Russia, India, China, and South Africa), some of which challenge Northern emphases on rights or governance reforms and employ new patterns of implementation. China is a prime example of this. It focuses on partnerships, arrangements in which China invests heavily in infrastructure projects in return for a set stream of commodities from the partner country. The "One Belt, One Road" initiative invests in transport connections to build economic cooperation. The Chinese-initiated Asian Infrastructure Investment Bank represents the coming of age of alternatives to the Northern-led Bretton Woods institutions (the World Bank and IMF) and a shift in power centers. Our students have seen Chinese development successes and sometimes yearned for an enlightened authoritarianism that might have a strategic vision for development and top-down authority to cut through the corruption crippling development, allowing their own countries to experience the rapid social and economic development that they observe in China.

Another example of a state-led regime where our students have observed successes is Cuba's single-party socialist system. Implementing egalitarian policies, sometimes through authoritarian methods and even the sanctioning of repression, Cuba achieved a distinct, alternative model of development—especially in areas of social and environmental development such as the eradication of extreme poverty; a more equitable distribution of income, assets, and basic public goods (what Cubans refer to as a "generalized" level of wealth or "enough to get by"); and enviable advances in health care, education, organic agriculture, natural science, and conservation. Cuba has had substantial influence in Latin America and Africa through the provision of technical, albeit not financial, humanitarian and development support. The Cuban development model bears examining, along with the national growth of the BRICS countries and the economic boom of the "Asian tigers" (Hong Kong, Singapore, South Korea, and Taiwan). South Korea especially has emerged as an important actor in the world of international development cooperation and financial support.

Globalization Affects Development Practice

The development world needs to be clear-eyed about globalization. Openness and trade may produce benefits in the aggregate, while deepening inequality within and between countries. Detailing the impacts of globalization is for another book, but here we need to acknowledge the charges that globalization and neocolonialism (particularly through the role of multinational corporations and a handful of increasingly wealthy private foundations and INGOs) constrain sustainable national development. We see this in intensifying and unequal impacts of management, externally imposed solutions, and overexploitation of natural resources, often leading to poverty, environmental destruction, and devastating conflicts. Other global forces—such as new pandemics, climate change, and the extinction crisis—have the most devastating impacts on the poorest countries and most vulnerable peoples. Amid all of this, now we observe an erosion of rich-country support for development funding and humanitarian assistance, and a vocal, nationalist resistance to migration in parts of Europe and the United States.

We could add many others to these continuing, evolving, or emerging factors that are hindering development. There is our inability in the United States to take seriously the environmental consequences of unfettered economic growth, only one of which is climate change. We can add impacts of violent conflict and challenges of peace building; ethnic and religious sectarianism; identity politics and dehumanization; population size, migration, growth, and density; species extinction with loss of biodiversity and ecosystem services; and many other dynamic variables—all of which interact and connect with each other. Yes, development is globally linked, complicated, and messy. There are no easy solutions.

Looking Forward

The promise of the future lies with the people of developing countries. Unlike the immediate postcolonial period of the 1950s and 1960s, today there are increasing commitments and competencies in developing countries, as well as a restoration of respect for preserving and recovering traditional knowledge and methods. People are asserting the right to set their own development paths. Southern practitioners and governments need to know what they want from "development" and how to go about it. Northern practitioners and countries need to know how to support indigenously defined, led, and implemented development. Although the critique of the development industry in this book is not new, it has been difficult for organizations that dominate development to act on the critiques that even they espouse. This book is about preparing future practitioners, North and South, to upend the practice of development, turning it right side up. To find transformative solutions, we need to take a good look at the landscape of development work and at attitudes and practices hindering development today.

3

What Does Lasting Development Look Like?

Marion Howard

This chapter is about sustainable development, an integrated model of development that combines and connects multiple disciplines, sectors, and actors. Currently, sustainable development is the most widely accepted global development paradigm, so it is important to understand what it is. First, I set out to define sustainable development, because how we define development matters. Development is led by organizations, not by individuals, and organizations have a vision of development; it's essential to define that vision. We need to know where we want to go before we can design effective policy and plan and implement action. Second, I examine fundamental challenges to achieving sustainable development that I have encountered as a practitioner working with sustainable development since the 1990s. These challenges include: (1) the nature of the development industry; (2) the need for meaningful participation; and (3) the difficulty of implementing an integrated approach in a specialized world.

An Introduction to Sustainable Development

Sustainable development is well defined in international law and policy. Global agreements such as the Rio Declaration, Agenda 21, the Johannesburg Declaration, the Millennium Declaration, and the 2030 Agenda for Sustainable Development prescribe sustainable development objectives and provide guidelines. Although not a totally new approach, sustainable development came into its own in the 1990s and since then has emerged as the global model for the twenty-first century. By 2015, when 193 countries adopted the 2030 Agenda for Sustainable Development, every country in the world had agreed to orient its development work toward this model.[1] So what is sustainable development? It's an integrated approach that combines economic growth with environmental conservation and social and political development, each having equal weight or importance and reinforcing the others. The basis of sustainable development is that environmental, economic, and social stability and community well-being are fundamentally interdependent. Probably the most well-known definition comes from the World Commission on Environment and Development's report, *Our Common Future* (1987). It reads: "Sustainable development is development that meets the needs of the present without compromising the ability of future generations to meet their own needs" (UN General Assembly 1987, p. 43). This definition says sustainability means meeting needs now and in the future (intergenerational equity) and emphasizes agency. It states that people should have the ability to meet their own needs, which implies that no one else should do that for them or hinder their ability to do so—not even a team of development "experts." The definition was honed in the Earth Summits (Rio 1992, Johannesburg 2002, and Rio+20 2012) to become the "three-pillar" approach. In the 1990s, it was described as integration of the "3 Es" of environment, economics, and equity and later as linking the "three pillars" of economic, environmental, and social development.

Today, many definitions of sustainable development exist within the general consensus that it combines environmental, economic, and social dimensions. Sustainable development is driven by values, so sustainability is achieved through a holistic approach that weaves the three dimensions together with fundamental principles. Therefore, besides the three pillars that are the cornerstone of the integrated approach, most models include enabling factors or fundamental principles that support the pillars to ensure sustainability (see Figure 3.1). The model presented here includes the fundamental principles of inclusion (of all stakeholders, especially vulnerable groups), capacity development (of individuals, institutions, and society), participation (of all community members to control and influence their own development), equal partnerships (across all affected sectors and communities), good governance (processes and institutions that meet the needs of society and properly use and manage available resources), equitable distribution of power and benefits (achieving an equilibrium of power and sharing fairly in the fruits of development), and local participative management that includes functions of research, strategic planning, and ongoing monitoring, evaluation, and learning. Sustainability factors can vary from model to model. For instance, one of our students developed a model that she tested in the field, in which the customary three pillars were associated with "eight enabling characteristics" that included most of those in the model presented here but added health and meeting basic needs/alleviation of absolute poverty (Laski 2016).

Figure 3.1 Sustainable Development Model

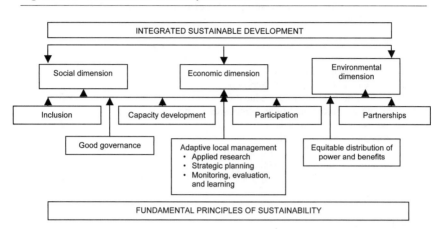

But all too often development interventions are still planned and implemented in silos that do not take into account the interrelated nature of development problems and, therefore, fail to recognize the need for holistic, sustainable solutions. Adoption of the Millennium Development Goals (MDGs) in 2000 and the Global Goals for Sustainable Development (SDGs) in 2015 institutionalized development targets to be achieved by specified years; eight MDGs by 2015 for "developing" countries and seventeen SDGs by 2030 for all countries (see Table 3.1). To promote sustainable development and attain the global goals, we need to focus on policies that facilitate or hinder well-being, strengthening the former and changing the latter.

A Focus on Development Practice

Even though sustainable development is radically different from the economic-growth theories that have dominated the development industry since the 1950s—such as the linear stages-of-growth, structural change, international dependency, neoliberal and neoclassical models—it is still haunted by mindsets and management patterns that linger from prior development approaches, so success is threatened by the same stumbling blocks that hindered development in the twentieth century. Unless these are overcome, any model of development—however innovative, transformative, and inspiring—will fail to achieve the change needed to bring about development for all. Sustainable development cannot be realized without a major overhaul of the dominant structures, systems, and values of the Global North that have underpinned the development industry since its inception. The first step is

Table 3.1   Global Development Goals: Millennium Development Goals (MDGs) and Sustainable Development Goals (SDGs)

	No. of Targets (21)	No. of Indicators (60)
Millennium Development Goals[a]		
1 To eradicate extreme poverty and hunger	3	9
2 To achieve universal primary education	1	3
3 To promote gender equality and empower women	1	3
4 To reduce child mortality	1	3
5 To improve maternal health	2	6
6 To combat HIV/AIDS, malaria, and other diseases	3	10
7 To ensure environmental sustainability	4	10
8 To develop a global partnership for development	6	16
Sustainable Development Goals[b]		
1 No poverty	169	232
2 Zero hunger		with 9 repeating
3 Good health and well-being		(as agreed
4 Quality education		upon 2017)
5 Gender equality		
6 Clean water and sanitation		
7 Affordable and clean energy		
8 Decent work and economic growth		
9 Industry, innovation, and infrastructure		
10 Reduced inequalities		
11 Sustainable cities and communities		
12 Responsible consumption and production		
13 Climate action		
14 Life below water		
15 Life on land		
16 Peace, justice, and strong institutions		
17 Partnerships for the goals		

Notes: a. MDGs adopted in 2000, to be achieved by 2015 by developing countries.
b. SDGs adopted in 2015, to be achieved by 2030 by all countries.

to upend, and then transform, deep-rooted mindsets that dominate the development industry.

In this book, we examine development from the perspective of practitioners, with authors describing and questioning the development industry, its practices and attitudes, as encountered on the ground. Development practitioners are defined as:

> people working in the international development sector—in a bilateral/ multilateral agency/international NGO, as staff member or consultant; or employed by a government department or a non-governmental organisation

in a low-income or middle-income country that receives financial aid. . . .
We are employed by organisations receiving and/or disbursing funds in
order to work with other intermediaries to achieve a contractually agreed
purpose. (Eyben 2013, p. 4)

Scholars have critiqued the development industry from varied perspectives (Frederique Apffel-Marglin, Robert Chambers, James Ferguson, Uma
Kothari, Serge Latouche, Maria Mies, Helena Norberg-Hodge, Gilbert Rist,
Wolfgang Sachs, and Aram Ziai), including prominent voices from the
Global South (Arturo Escobar, Gustavo Esteva, Dambisa Moyo, Majid Rah-
nema, Amartya Sen, and Vandana Shiva) to name only a few. We will not
revisit these valuable critiques, most of which examine the aid industry at the
macro level. Less has been written by practitioners, especially those working in recipient agencies at the micro level. As a practitioner who has only
worked in Southern recipient organizations, I will set the stage for the chapters that follow by summarizing challenges to development that I encountered
repeatedly. I will draw especially on experiences from my twenty years working with the Colombian government in the regional (subnational) sustainable
development agency responsible for managing the environment of the San
Andres Archipelago, southwestern Caribbean.

Our government agency had a clear sustainable development mandate
and a congressionally defined jurisdiction, and it was staffed by committed
workers who were eager to learn, make change, and improve the natural
environment and the community's quality of life. I lived in the islands for
decades and was contracted (and paid) as a Colombian resident. Leadership
and staff were mainly from a national ethnic minority (recognized as
indigenous internationally) that had suffered decades of marginalization by
the national government. They were part of the local community, connected
to the natural environment, and shared a development vision. Our organization had substantial power on paper, but its subnational status, minority-
group leadership, and national legacy of centralization and colonialism
meant that in reality, we struggled for power within entrenched sociopolitical systems. Perhaps our biggest constraint was that we had no regular
funds, in spite of being a government agency, so we had to turn to the aid
industry's model of donor-funded projects. This meant that while trying to
design and implement projects to impact environmental and socioeconomic
dimensions and, thereby, change the status quo, we had to deal with powerful national and international institutions that controlled the funds. The many
challenges we faced as a sustainable development agency at the subnational
level, forced to work within the international development industry, were
intertwined and are generalizable to the broader development context, setting the stage for issues raised in the contributors' chapters.

Challenges to Achieving Sustainable Development

Challenge One: The Nature of the Development Industry

As a development practitioner, a major challenge I found working in a recipient country organization is that the industry is rooted in North-South power dynamics. Not only did partners often try to impose work styles, values, and practices, but we had to grapple daily with their assumptions of superiority, structures of external control, and even disruptive actions. To give a few examples, international organizations would ignore our authority as a government agency, abuse partnerships, disrespect the community, and compel us to waste valuable time and resources. Even after we informed partners that certain actions were illegal in Colombia, they would do them anyway—for example, collect biological specimens against national and international law, gather data without permits, publish and present our work without acknowledgment, with errors, or against our wishes. There were the project managers who insisted on corresponding with our executive director rather than with the project manager who was their counterpart (imagine if our project manager insisted on talking to *their* executive director or CEO). There were the partners who held meetings with stakeholders without informing or including us, imposing their language and customs, insulting the indigenous community, and disrupting the participatory process. There was the multilateral that promised us cofunding for a project, failed to come through, and then insisted their chosen consultants be paid with funds they were implementing on our behalf, even if we had local professionals who could do the jobs better for a fraction of the cost. There were donors who had us write their final reports (as well as our own), donors who insisted on dictating who we could hire, donors who told us we couldn't use project funds to pay for water and sandwiches for community volunteers but that their per diem fees (one day could equal a month's local salary) must be paid by the project.

Perhaps most astonishingly, there was the big international nongovernmental organization (BINGO) that claimed in its annual report that it had led one of our most successful, award-winning projects, when the reality was we had planned and executed the entire project in collaboration with the local community, two small INGO partners, and a multilateral donor, and our project had no connection *at all* to the BINGO that made the claim. When we investigated what we could do, we learned there was no legal way to hold any INGO headquartered in another country accountable. A few months later, when organizers of a major UN conference wanted our project presented there, the BINGO received (and accepted) the invitation. Examples go on and on, and it is not only international partners who have been dismissive. Indeed, when dealing with a minority-led organization and indigenous local community, national partners can have the most entrenched preconceptions and the deepest biases and be the most paternalistic. Although we have stories of wonderful partners generously giving their time, knowledge, and money and trying to respect local culture and customs, sadly they are the exception.

The project approach. All of this plays out within the framework of development projects, both in the overarching structure of how development happens on the ground and also inside individual projects. International development is dominated by the project approach. A project is commonly defined as a series of activities aimed at bringing about specified objectives within a set timeline and location with a predetermined budget. Projects have been at the center of how we implement development policy for decades. Many have observed that the project model has been the method of choice, not necessarily because it is the most effective way to achieve development, but rather because projects are manageable for donors and make it easier to meet their accountability requirements. Problems with the donor-controlled project approach have long been evident. As noted by a 1998 World Bank report:

> Faced with low implementation capacity and pressure to "move the money," aid agencies have a long history of attempting to "cocoon" their projects using free-standing technical assistance, independent project implementation units, and foreign experts—rather than trying to improve the institutional environment for service provision. . . . They have neither improved services in the short run nor led to institutional change in the long run. (Dollar and Pritchett 1998, p. 22)

In spite of the known limitations of donor-driven projects, the international development industry is still dominated by this model, and practitioners are aware that this is the reality in which they must work. For example, nearly 100 percent of the funds of the World Bank's International Development Association (IDA) are still disbursed via projects. In 2006, the Center for Global Development estimated that in 2003 there were at least 30,000 active donor-funded international development projects. As many projects as this was, the figure was too low because it did not include the vast number of projects that result from dividing aid received at the national level into smaller projects that are executed subnationally, which is a common method of distributing aid within countries. In spite of the current emphasis on principles introduced in the 2005 Paris Declaration[2] to deal with criticisms such as those above from the World Bank, no evidence suggests that the number of development projects is decreasing, that planning or reporting requirements are becoming less burdensome for recipients, or that donors are being any less controlling and interventionist. On the contrary, fragmentation of aid and numbers of donors and actors (partners, implementing and executing agencies, NGOs, civil society organizations, and so on) are increasing, with the result that the number of projects, contracts, and requirements a recipient country or in-country agency is dealing with at any given time continues to proliferate.

While donors talk about larger program approaches and recipient agencies are invited to provide feedback to donors, externally controlled, time-bound projects remain the legal and contractual basis for donor funding. Even the word *aid* is steeped in power as it connotes financial assistance given from a more capable institution to a less capable institution. For instance, when we produced our first international project to submit to a multilateral donor (for what our team thought of as a grant award), someone from the donor called our executive director and asked for the names of our external consultants. Apparently, the donor hadn't considered that we could have produced the project proposal ourselves. When the director replied that an in-house team had developed the project in collaboration with the community (and that we produced all our projects that way), the donor was astonished—and proceeded to put several names from its own staff on the project document as authors with no author from our team. So even when a Southern agency produces its own projects with a great deal of effort, knowledge, and innovation and is awarded very competitive grants, the credit often goes to the donor or an international partner. When Northern organizations receive a grant, it is seen as an "award" and they are congratulated and feted, but when Southern organizations win a grant, it is often regarded as "aid" or "assistance" and is subject to heavy-handed external control. Presumably, this is because the giver is the superior partner and the recipient is not an equal partner or is not to be trusted fully with implementation, even if the recipient designed the project and the external partners know little to nothing about the local reality. But recipient organizations desperately need money to accomplish their mission and serve their communities, so they often accept demeaning terms that can accompany funding.

The project model and sustainability. Development actions must be sustainable to achieve lasting change, but projects and sustainability are an uneasy fit. In project terms, sustainability refers to the potential of an intervention to supply continuing benefits after the end of the project. By definition, projects are time-bound, oriented toward specific deliverables, accountable in the short term to donors and beneficiaries, generally narrow in scope, and rooted in simplified versions of reality. In contrast, sustainability is about complexity, expanding scope, long-term goals, multidisciplinarity, and inter- and intragenerational equity, all of which qualities are antithetical to the traditional project model. Because much effort, time, and money is wasted if projects fail to achieve sustainability, this dilemma is central to current debates about aid effectiveness. Today, the pressure on executing agencies to deliver long-term results through short-term projects is enormous, even though the project model, and by extension the aid system itself, tends toward the unsustainable. Most recipient agencies do not have the power to change or even question the methods, requirements, and timing through which aid is delivered, so they struggle daily to deliver, prove, and report on results within project constraints.

Incorporating sustainability into public administration and institutions has been a topic of interest since the concept of sustainable development gained credence in the 1990s. However, very little attention has been paid to how sustainability through projects can actually be achieved. In addition, development practitioners are rarely trained to manage projects for sustainability, in spite of being held ever more responsible for the sustainability of outcomes, resulting in an ongoing tension between managing interventions to achieve immediate, measurable results and managing to achieve sustainability. Working toward the 2030 Agenda and SDGs makes this a critical area of concern for all levels of the development industry. Achieving project sustainability calls for a significant transformation of the traditional approach to donor-funded project management, that is, a shift from management characterized by external control, rigidity, and prescribed steps to locally controlled, adaptive management that is agile, flexible, and transparent and allows for complexity and change.

Development projects happen within complex systems and changing environments, so adaptive management recognizes the need to change projects in accord with the changing situation. This is done by integrating ongoing, systematic learning into project management. Although adaptive management is not new, "the challenge in using the adaptive management approach lies in finding the correct balance between gaining knowledge to improve management in the future and achieving the best short-term outcome based on current knowledge" (van der Bliek, McCormick, and Clarke 2014, p. 32). The sustainability of development initiatives is influenced not only by the planning process and resulting design but ultimately by how interventions are implemented. Traditional management takes a narrow, siloed approach that insists management adhere to a preapproved project document, whereas sustainable development requires a flexible approach that allows for project adaptation during implementation. However, in reality, local managers are trapped in the paradigm of donor-driven, short-term interventions and generally lack the power to make decisions or changes on the ground to improve sustainability. This presents a critical challenge for sustainable development. Practitioners need to have the courage to question the fundamentals of the aid-delivery system and its requirements. Until that happens, whatever the development model and its goals, practitioners and their organizations and communities will continue to struggle to make change and achieve lasting benefits within the reality of the present system.

Challenge Two: The Need for Meaningful Participation

To upend the paradigm of Northern dominance over Southern development requires active, meaningful, empowered participation by recipient communities and their institutions. Development financing—whatever the source (multilateral, bilateral, UN, foundation, government, NGO, private sector) and method by which it is delivered (aid, grant, loan, through projects, programs, and so on)—is given to organizations, not individuals, so it is important to remember that when we speak of community participation, we are not talking only of the "target group" or "direct beneficiaries" of an intervention. Communities include public institutions; private-sector enterprises; civil, neighborhood, and religious organizations and the range of people, such as educated and uneducated, workers (homemakers, laborers, professionals), women and men, the marginalized and the privileged, the voiceless and the powerful, and so forth. Although development organizations do not usually dispute the need for participation, there is much discussion about what is meant by participation and why some participatory projects and programs succeed and others fail. Questions such as who participates, when, how, and to what extent have been debated for years, as have the pluses and minuses of participation, why it matters, and to what ends. Participation itself has tended to be rife with issues of dominance, inequity, power, exclusion, and a failure to trust local processes, respect local voices, incorporate local results, or support local decision making; even when resulting from well-designed, managed, and documented participation.

Participatory development. Sustainable development requires a transformation of society, its structures, and institutions. Such comprehensive change can only emerge from individuals, communities, and their institutions. However, in the world of post–Paris Declaration development, the participatory and rights-based approaches emphasized in the 1990s are being supplanted by a modern version of the top-down model of Northern control that originally defined aid. Some externally led projects may contribute to development, especially to prescribed visions of development that don't prioritize local visions or what affected populations want from development. For example, infrastructure can be built, vaccinations can be given, training can be provided, and aid dollars can pour in, but to be sustainable, development must change deeply embedded systems. To revamp the dynamics and distribution of power, structures of exclusion, lack of access to resources, and inequitable distribution of the benefits of development requires individual transformation and a transition to a place of agency, power, capability, and commitment to justice and mutual well-being. Practitioners must reexamine the role of participation and figure out how to use participatory methods, which often achieve hard-to-measure results, in an industry increasingly dominated by the demand for measurable results in a limited, inflexible time frame. Development workers are caught between donors and the communities they are serving; between managing to deliver immediate results or to advance structural change and transform inequitable systems; between the pressure to advance vertically defined, dictated solutions or the need to share power through collaborative, inclusive horizontal processes. Furthermore, because development practitioners themselves are not free of assumptions, biases, and the need for self-transformation, meaningful participation and effective comanagement call for reflective practice, which itself requires training and an enabling environment.

Participatory development is firmly rooted in international law and policy. According to the United Nations, participation is a fundamental human right, and all people must be accorded the right to participate in making decisions that will affect their lives. Agenda 21 calls for "meaningful and effective" public participation in sustainable development. Participatory rights are enshrined in international human-rights instruments, for example, the Universal Declaration of Human Rights (Article 21), the International Covenant on Civil and Political Rights (Article 25), and the Convention on the Elimination of All Forms of Discrimination Against Women (Article 7). Especially significant for development practice, Article 2 of the Declaration on the Right to Development says:

> The human person is the central subject of development and should be the active participant and beneficiary of the right to development. . . . States have the right and the duty to formulate appropriate national development policies that aim at the constant improvement of the well-being of the entire population and of all individuals, on the basis of their active, free and meaningful participation in development and in the fair distribution of the benefits resulting therefrom.

To meet these requirements, many countries have incorporated the right to participation in national law, some starting with their constitutions. In these countries, practitioners must know participatory theory and methods to successfully do their jobs. Also, some states—often as party to international instruments such as the Declaration on the Rights of Indigenous Peoples, the International Labour Organization (ILO) Convention 169, or the Convention on Biological Diversity (CBD)—guarantee the right of free, prior, and informed consent (FPIC) to communities that may be affected by projects.

Participation and sustainability. Participation supports lasting change through continuous community engagement, collaborative decision making, partnerships, and comanagement. Participation in development takes many forms, serves many purposes, and can improve management, projects and programs at all stages, and deliverables, products, and outcomes of interventions. At the same time, taking part in meaningful participatory processes empowers participants, builds capacity, and creates commitment, steward-ship, and ownership of development actions along with responsibility and capability for ongoing management; all of which advance sustainability. The weight put on process emerges not only from the increasing emphasis on aid effectiveness, but even more from a profound understanding that develop-ment will not happen unless people, and by extension their civic and gov-ernment institutions, are their own agents of change. But unfortunately, in my experience, even donors and international partners that support local par-ticipation do so within narrow limits.

The notion of consulting stakeholders to learn about the local situation, history, problems, and assets is often accepted. However, whether this information is considered in project design and implementation is another question—sometimes it is, sometimes it isn't, or maybe it is taken into account if it supports the donor's preconceived ideas. But rarely do donors or partners encourage, or even begin to understand, empowering the com-munity to make the decisions—select the problem to be tackled, identify the solution, and take a leadership role in planning, implementing, and/or evaluating. Participation at that level can take time. Sustainable develop-ment calls for local ownership, but often communities don't have the infor-mation, power, and resources they need to solve their problems (indeed, one might argue that if they did, they would already be solving them), and it takes time to build capacity and gather resources. In a true participative approach, stakeholders select project solutions and, if they lack the knowl-edge to do so, our role as development practitioners can be to identify options, share knowledge about alternatives, and provide education, train-ing, and empowerment to enable educated decision making. Outside experts can be invaluable to make new technologies and methods available, strengthen institutions, provide know-how, and share power but should not impose or even propose solutions. Participatory decision making greatly enhances the likelihood that a development project will be sustainable, but none of us, including the communities we work with, can make intelligent choices without being aware of the options.

Simply put, once a community identifies a development problem or issue it wants to solve, it needs information to help it decide how to do so. First, for community-based decisions to be taken seriously, there must be a legitimate participatory process. This means setting up a formal consulta-tion structure with systems to document the process. This can be accom-plished by doing a full stakeholder analysis and inventory of organizations to identify who needs to be involved. Then stakeholders can be clustered (e.g., by interest, location, affiliation, language, and so on) to facilitate set-ting up working groups. To put practitioners and the people on a more equal footing and increase participation, working groups can be locally led and control the terms of meetings (time, place, language, agenda, and so forth).

While working groups are gathering information about the problem or issue to be addressed (context, history, risks, and the like), the practitioners supporting the process can be researching how similar problems have been dealt with around the world. After gathering as much information as possible, the practitioners should share all the information with the working groups, which can then take the lead in identifying theories of change and designing their preferred solution(s). Once the stakeholders have reached their decision, a participatory project can be developed. If desired by the community during the process, the practitioner might also facilitate visits from one or more outside experts who could share their knowledge about the problem and potential solution(s) with stakeholders, visit potential project sites, and train community members.

To stop being objects of development and become agents of development, stakeholders need training, information, capacity, and the power to make informed decisions, as we all do. And then development institutions must trust the process and the people, respecting and honoring their decisions. As Brazilian educator Paulo Freire makes clear, knowledge allows all of us to transform reality through action (Freire 1970). The process of learning enables us to take what we learn and reinvent it to apply to concrete, existential situations. Communities can combine new knowledge with their lived experience to better control or change their reality, for instance, in a development context, to produce alternatives that work locally because they integrate traditional practices with new technologies. Not only are informed communities able to make their own decisions and come up with better solutions, but externally imposed solutions can be unsustainable for any number of reasons—they don't fit the local situation; they don't redistribute power, provide equitable benefits, or change the status quo; they need long-term external support and require maintenance or management skills unavailable locally; people are more invested in solutions they choose and manage themselves; and so forth.

The ability to engage in meaningful participation depends on both individual internal capacity and equitable external processes in an enabling environment. This calls for education, knowledge sharing, and capacity building. People need to know about alternatives and how they have worked in other locations, about sociopolitical structures and mechanisms of oppression, and about how to exercise power. Involving communities in strategies to create change, build self-worth and empowerment, and generate, analyze, and apply knowledge paves the way to the self-determination, collective action, and enabling environment needed for transformative, sustainable development. Unfortunately, this level of involvement is all too rare in an industry dominated by Northern hegemony and attitudes of superiority that seem to result in an inability to trust and respect the ability of Southern communities to make their own decisions and control their own development.

Challenge Three: The Difficulty of Implementing an Integrated Approach to Development

Development in the twentieth century was hindered by the failure to take an integrated approach to problem-solving. Integrated approaches aim to achieve a variety of benefits by involving multiple stakeholders and balancing actions that address the three dimensions of sustainable development (social, environmental, and economic). The difficulties we experienced implementing an integrated approach tended to stem from two quite different issues—first, our agency's understanding of and support for holistic development but our lack of capacity to carry it out; or second, the broader failure of some of our donors and partners to support, or even comprehend, holistic development at all.

Lacking capacity to implement an integrated approach. Working for twenty years in a regional government agency that struggled to advance its sustainable development mission, I observed firsthand the challenges we faced. As part of Colombia's National Environment System (established by law in 1993), the agency is the region's environmental management authority, so its primary obligation is to manage natural resources for conservation and sustainable use.[3] Everyone I worked with believed in integrated development and knew conservation wouldn't happen unless projects also produced economic benefits (poverty alleviation, sustainable livelihoods, new jobs) and social benefits (capacity development, institutional strengthening, inclusion), but to actually achieve sustainable development requires more than understanding and commitment. Typically, government is organized in sectoral entities (ministries, departments, and so on), but in practice, sustainable development requires cutting across sectors to achieve economic, social, and environmental objectives. This means that if we want to implement sustainable solutions, we have to overcome fragmentation and ultimately create new systems and structures of governance that eliminate it. In our case, our government agency

> has a wealth of ideas on how traditional livelihoods and the local economic model could be improved to be sustainable with conservation objectives but has no expertise in business or economic development. . . . The very nature of sustainable development is holistic, multidisciplinary, and integrated, which is difficult to achieve in a world in which managers and their institutions continue to have environmental or economic or social science mandates, goals, and responsibilities—but rarely, if ever, all three—and to be managed and staffed by professionals and technicians who themselves have been trained in "siloed" education systems that narrowly define fields and assign approaches, methods, and values to certain fields. (Taylor et al. 2013, p. 64)

To achieve sustainable development, practitioners need a broad base of knowledge. Ideally, a sustainable development agency would have a cadre of practitioners; each with a broad-based, interdisciplinary perspective and multisectoral knowledge and skills. But few practitioners are educated that way. So for now, our government agency has a sustainable development mission that facilitates hiring staff from a range of disciplines, putting them together in multidisciplinary project teams, and we do our best to manage diverse teams and implement cross-sectoral projects within the limits of our training and existing institutional structure. Global challenges call for innovative solutions that blend knowledge and skills from across disciplines, pulling from the social and natural sciences and the arts and humanities, and breaking down approaches rooted in narrow specializations. Fundamental to sustainability is integrating the natural sciences, which look at ecological and physical systems and processes with the social sciences, which examine social, political, and economic systems and processes.

Less understood or accepted is the notion that embracing the humanities will also help achieve sustainable outcomes. Humanists focus on subjects offering many perspectives and ways of seeing the world—such as language, history, philosophy, the arts, and culture—that link to international development in several ways. Significantly, students of the humanities acquire a broad, diverse approach to learning that can build their ability to critically analyze a variety of factors affecting a situation and to understand multiple perspectives.

In 2014, the British Council commissioned a study to understand the value of the humanities in meeting global development challenges. Policymakers, practitioners, and human-resource managers at development organizations around the world were asked to consider how studying the humanities contributes to the design and delivery of development solutions. First, participants said that to achieve development requires a range of abilities that go beyond the technical. They identified four attributes essential for effective development practice that they strongly associated with training in the humanities: critical and analytical thinking, flexibility and tolerance for ambiguity, the ability to communicate and negotiate effectively, and knowledge of local conditions and contexts. Second, because humanists are exposed to a myriad of opinions and perspectives in their studies, they can be more likely to respond creatively to rapidly shifting situations on the ground. Third, participants considered practitioners trained in the humanities likely to be more sensitive to different cultures and to write, present, and speak more effectively, especially in local cultural contexts. Overall, a clear message emerged that all development programs and organizations, even the most technical, need "humanizing" (British Council and IPSOS 2014). Sustainable development is strengthened when practitioners can draw on many disciplines and approaches to knowledge; combining technical, scientific, and humanistic methods to construct a more robust worldview and deeper understanding of reality.

Failure to comprehend and/or support an integrated approach. The existence of a well-developed global framework of institutions, laws, and policies promoting the integrated approach gives us a solid foundation for sustainable development. However, some Northern partners, in my experience especially INGOs, ignore or are unaware of the legal and policy framework that guides development in most countries of the Global South. This means that implementation is not only hindered by a lack of capacity to manage for sustainability and put sustainable development into practice on the ground but is also hampered by an inability of many partners and donors to acknowledge or even comprehend the concept of sustainable development—the equal, horizontal interplay of sectors that are regarded as unconnected or contradictory in the minds of many from the North, as reflected in traditional development models. The reality is that many donor agencies and Northern partners are not equipped to handle integrated approaches and can be unable to respond adaptively to development challenges, deal with complexity, or tolerate ambiguity.

This is exacerbated by the fact that most political systems institutionalize human-defined boundaries, jurisdictions, and sectors that are not based on natural systems. This plays out in development interventions. The social and economic dimensions have often overshadowed the importance of the natural environment, or the environment has been neglected entirely. Simply put, economic and social systems are located within nature and dependent on natural resources, so ultimately they will be controlled by natural boundaries, limits, and time frames. Besides access to economic opportunities, political systems, education, health care, and other social services, development means equitable access to a healthy environment, natural resources, and ecosystem services, so conservation and socioeconomic development must go hand in hand. To achieve the SDGs requires a multisectoral approach that reflects the complexity and interdependence of environmental, social, economic, and political dimensions. Inequalities must be addressed and an approach used that recognizes multiple actors and shared social responsibility (UNDESA and UNDP 2012).

Growing inequality and exclusion in some countries, notably the United States, and systems and structures that permit or enable this, are major obstacles to sustainable development. For development to last, a collaborative, community-centered approach is essential. This means that instead of the development industry dictating how programs will be carried out and money will be spent, the people who will be most affected must have the strongest voice. Sometimes less-educated members of the community will grasp integrated approaches more easily than specialists, already seeing the world as the interdependent system it is. This can be because they haven't been trained in narrow disciplines that break reality into artificial, man-made divisions. Specialized points of view can cause us to be enthralled with narrow, technical fixes that are not lasting or effective within complex systems. Experiencing the world as an integrated system promotes multidisciplinary, organic solutions based on reality.

Moving Forward

At their core, the challenges discussed here can emerge from different goals that motivate actors—organizations and their individual workers—in the development world. An organization with insufficient funding of its own can't work independently in the existing development industry. Generally, donors don't give money to Southern organizations and leave them to execute projects without interference—no matter how deserving the recipient organization, how exemplary its track record, or how brilliant, innovative, and effective its projects. Recipient organizations find themselves working with donors, international and national partners (that are often implementing funds from international donors), and local organizations, all with different levels of power. And all of these players can have different goals. Even as individuals (and organizations are established and run by individuals), we see development differently—some of us think the crux of development is poverty alleviation, others that it is health, others that it is democracy and governance, others that it is conservation and natural resource management, and so on. Our focus is determined by our worldview, values, and, often, by our specialized education.

Furthermore, we can have different loyalties. Simply put, as development practitioners we have three options. Are we working primarily to advance our own career? Or to support the goals of our organization? Or to serve the people who are the focus of our work? Sometimes these options are compatible, and sometimes they conflict. And at different times in our lives, often for good reason, we will prioritize one over the other. In my experience in partnership projects, we would be working together smoothly toward the same goal, generally as defined in the project's purpose and objectives, until we hit a bump in the road. At that point, our loyalties would diverge. As an indigenous government agency, our first loyalty was to the people we served, especially the most vulnerable. But the donor and partners were responsible to different constituencies (often their own funders) so, naturally enough, their first concern was not the development, transformation, and ultimate liberation of our oppressed community. Then, as project executing agency, we would find ourselves trapped between our commitment to the community and pressure from funders or partners to serve their needs, which we had to try to do because we couldn't serve the community without the donor's money. This played out in every project I worked on, to some degree. It led to what we called "the donor dance," in which we did our best to appear to be following the donor's lead while, in reality, we were prioritizing actions we (and those most affected by the project) believed were needed for local development.

When properly understood, sustainable development can resolve or, at least, minimize these dilemmas. First, sustainable development takes an integrated approach that seeks to balance the social, economic, and environmental and is rooted in values of inclusion, equity, good governance, participative management, and so on. A holistic perspective to development inherently reconciles and harmonizes the different priorities that each of us may believe are the heart of development; this is because all are likely to be equally important in an integrated model. If all development actors understand integrated development and are committed to its objectives, that puts organizations—and the individuals who work in them—fundamentally "on the same page" from the beginning. Second, the 2030 Agenda and SDGs, which all UN countries have signed onto, and other global instruments that define development law and policy, which most UN countries have signed onto, provide a unified framework of goals and objectives toward which we can all be working.[4] This doesn't mean we won't have differences as we work to translate shared macro-level goals into local actions and then determine how best to implement these actions, but if we agree on where we are going and who should benefit, differences will be easier to resolve.

Sustainable development also provides guidance on methods. Besides the need for an integrated approach, it calls for active participation and local agency, involvement of multiple stakeholders, empowerment and capacity building, and evidence-based decision making, characteristics that help determine how we work on the ground. And, if we share common goals and a vision of where we are going, whether we are serving our own need for a job and career advancement, the objectives of our organization, or the people seeking development, fundamentally these interests will converge.

As stated at the beginning of this chapter, definitions matter. If we share a "true north"—or a "true south" to upend our orientation—that will guide us in developing congruent, harmonious policies and projects, and in planning and implementing sustainable actions, and will provide a yardstick or standard against which to examine the effectiveness of our development decisions and interventions. In the following chapters, authors working in a variety of spheres, countries, and organizations shed light on development practice.

Notes

1. There are 195 countries in the world today—193 UN member states, all of which signed the 2030 Agenda, and two nonmember observer states, the Holy See and the State of Palestine. Not included as countries are the Cook Islands and Niue, Taiwan, dependencies, areas of special sovereignty (autonomous territories), and any other areas not recognized by the UN as self-governing.

2. The Paris Declaration on Aid Effectiveness (2005) has five core principles. These principles interconnect and are geared to ensure that it is now the norm for aid-recipient countries to develop their own national development strategies (ownership), for donors to support these strategies (alignment), for donors to work to streamline their efforts in-country (harmonization), for development policies to be directed to achieving clear goals and for progress toward these goals to be monitored (results), and for donors and recipients alike to be jointly responsible for achieving these goals (mutual accountability).

3. Conservation is a complex concept of environmental management that combines elements of protection and preservation (such as restoration, recovery, and safeguarding natural processes) with management of natural resources and ecosystems to ensure sustainable use.

4. The fact that the United States, compared to other donor and recipient nations, is signatory to few global development, human-rights, and environmental instruments can pose a real challenge in development work. It means that the United States, a major player in the world of development, is fundamentally an outlier and can be working from a different perspective and toward different goals than many of its partners (whether from industrialized or developing countries). Furthermore, the United States may be unconcerned or unaware that this is the case.

PART 1

Reflecting on Development Practice

4

The Journey from Practice to Learning

Laurence Simon

My father never mentioned *tikkun olam,* the Jewish concept of social action to repair the world, or talked with me about humility, but both were woven into the fabric of my upbringing. As a young adult I ventured into developing countries, hoping to carry these qualities with me as I went to experience worlds other than my own and to gain some of the insights and skills needed to become less of a burden and more of a help. Perhaps this story of the journey from practice to learning should begin here—with the ethical uneasiness of the outsider.

Tales of an Outlander

The First Tale: The Umbrella

Before I came to Brandeis University in 1992, where I founded a graduate program in sustainable international development in 1993 and served as its director until 2014, I was working in Sri Lanka for a national poverty-reduction program under a technical assistance contract with the United Nations Development Programme (UNDP). Often I walked down the small lanes where I lived. One night I was on my way to a hotel for dinner when clouds rolled in. The sky opened with such heavy rain that I took refuge in a doorway. After some time with no end to the deluge in sight, a man approached from the dimness of an open area next to where I stood. He motioned me nearer, where I saw his family huddled under a tarp. A rural family; they had come to the city to sell vegetables in the open market and would spend the night here. Communication was essentially nonverbal, as my Sinhala was limited to greetings. They were polite to the point of timorousness, not nervous, but observant of the social and cultural distance between us. I had experienced such awkwardness before. In sub-Saharan Africa, I often felt first interactions in small shops or village gatherings were guided by leftover colonial habits of obsequiousness—perhaps toward a white man or maybe respect for someone from a rich country or simply the politeness due a foreign guest. But here a different scenario was unfolding. The father's hands were outstretched, offering an umbrella. At first I demurred, so very aware of their circumstances. He persisted, continuing to hold the umbrella toward me, gesturing at the torrential rain. I accepted the umbrella, although I had no way to say I'd return it that night on my way home.

I left, had a delightful dinner, and two hours later when the rain had stopped, approached the place where my benefactors were ensconced. Then I saw an open shop. I ducked inside, thinking to thank this family with a new umbrella. But then I wondered what they would think. True, their umbrella was in poor shape, with a broken spoke and hardly able to remain open over one's head. But might the gift of a new umbrella, though likely welcome, also be an embarrassment that reflected not their generosity but their poverty? I considered a large box of chocolates, which I thought would be a treat for the children and might better protect the dignity of their gift to me, for they had no way to know I would return. But then would I be ignoring the practical necessity of a new umbrella? Or should I give both? This dilemma reminded me of ethical problems debated in the Talmud, the rabbinical teachings on Jewish law and their interpretations over six centuries, applying Jewish logic and values to living a committed life. I wondered what the sages would say. I won't tell you what I did because I've thought of this so often in the decades that followed that I actually can't remember if I gave them a new umbrella, or chocolates . . . or both. Whatever I gave them, I do recall that the family greeted me shyly, but with smiles upon the return of their umbrella and the tangible offering of my gratitude.

During my career in development, I've approached many such interactions with Talmudic deliberation. For me, the challenges of development have always followed an ethical discourse, one that could consider a human ethic broad enough on which to build a philosophy and practice of development, one strongly empowering enough to overcome the true causations of poverty and preventable suffering. For many of us in development, this discourse acknowledged that development was not just a technical fix or merely growth in gross domestic product (GDP) but a fundamental reordering of society and of humanity's relationship with the natural world. For this reason, the model of the new development studies program I began at Brandeis had to be rooted in such discourse. Our students, most of whom came from developing nations, found such a pedagogy to be a validation of their own search for answers and a pathway to discover their own unique voices.

The Second Tale: The Archbishop and the Saint

In August 1976, I traveled to Philadelphia to hear the Brazilian archbishop Helder Pessoa Camara speak at the International Eucharistic Congress. A few years before, while on the staff of Fordham University at Lincoln Center, I was asked to escort the archbishop around New York City. Even as an archbishop, Dom Helder wore a plain brown cassock and wooden cross. Yet his aura of goodness emanated not from his outward appearance or from the kindness of his countenance, but from his words, spoken gently but firmly, about the injustice of poverty and oppression. The poor called him the Bishop of the Slums; the military rulers of Brazil called him the Red Bishop. He lived simply—as Dorothy Day, activist leader in the Catholic Workers Movement, would say—so that others may simply live. Dom Helder was often quoted as saying: "When I give food to the hungry, they call me a saint, but when I ask why they are hungry, they call me a communist." If Father Gustavo Gutierrez of Peru is the acknowledged father of liberation theology, the late Archbishop Camara is surely the activist priest whose life was on the line for his advocacy. In Philadelphia, he spoke in a session on social justice with Mother Teresa, the Albanian-born nun whose "calling within a calling" was to live among the poor of Calcutta and serve the needs of "the unwanted, the unloved, the uncared for." Mother Teresa, who in 2016 was canonized by Pope Francis, spoke about her congregation of the Missionaries of Charity, which she had founded in 1950 and for which she had rightly received the praise of a world awed by such selflessness. Charity for Mother Teresa was channeling God's love to bring peace into the lives of the destitute, whereas for Dom Helder, social justice was the embodiment of God's love.

Dom Helder spoke of Mother Teresa's devotion and then, in the softest of tones, began the most passionate but oblique critique of charity, which has been repeated innumerable times in his writings, homilies, and heartfelt pleading for what a radical revolution of love really means. Charity alone, an act even of genuine kindness but that might ignore the cause of the suffering it was meant to heal, aided the perpetuation of injustice. For Dom Helder, God's love called him to go beyond charity, to repair the breach of justice that could not happen without reordering humanity's social reality. With tears in his eyes fixed above the audience, Dom Helder ended his talk that day with the words of an old Brazilian folksong: "When one man dreams alone, it is nothing but a dream, but when two or more dream together, it is not merely a dream, but the beginning of a new reality." These thoughts resonated powerfully with my own upbringing—with the values of social justice that for my father were the true meaning of our Jewish heritage, the takeaway of our people's suffering and of our lives' work to repair the breach.

The Third Tale: The Philosopher and the Holocaust

But how would I, or others with the freedom to choose a career, make even a dent in the needless suffering of much of humanity? And how could we equip ourselves with the understanding and skills to build a better world? These questions have plagued me and many of my students. Hannah Arendt once told a story to my graduate seminar in political philosophy at the New School for Social Research about two families she knew in Germany at the outbreak of World War II. One was a well-to-do Berlin family whose sons had the advantages of wealth, a refined milieu of great music, philosophy, and literature. The other was a rural family whose sons' formal education was limited by their station in life and by the relentless demands of farming.

As the war heated up, the sons of both families were conscripted into the German army, but only the sons of the wealthy family went. And here Professor Arendt posed the unanswerable questions: Why did the sons in Berlin go willingly to the army, while the farm lads refused and died in prison? What makes for a moral compass or the courage to refuse to participate in the machinery of oppression? Was it a fine education or a family culture grounded in basic decency? Years later the questions continue: How do we or can we even intervene from outside? Or is the world so interconnected that oppression and poverty anywhere are linked everywhere—even to the modest bank account of a professor or his graduate students?

Each tale I've related here poses its own ethical dilemmas and also connects to the others. The first prompts us to ask, How can we best manifest simple relationships of caring, of shared humanity, of human dignity in our interactions across barriers of cultural geography? The second speaks to broader questions, stimulating us to dig deeper into the roots of the first tale and ask, Why was that umbrella so tattered and that family sleeping under a tarp, while I was strolling to enjoy a delicious dinner in a fine hotel? And the third compels us to go deeper yet and ponder our own connection to oppression, and ask, How do we acquire and transmit the ethics of compassion and then follow that star even into sacrifice? We in development are taught the need for competence, and many of us are drawn to our careers through an innate calling to reduce suffering. But the challenge I took on in 1992 was to institutionalize these values and questions in training the next generation of development workers.

Building a Program of Sustainable Development

Coming to Brandeis

After an early career with Oxfam America, the American Jewish World Service, and that stint with UNDP, I came to Brandeis University and soon proposed we launch a master's degree program called Sustainable International Development (SID), through which aspiring professionals could gain insight and skills to contribute to the development of communities and nations. As I pursued this idea I met Jack Shonkoff, dean of the Heller

School, who quickly saw the advantages of moving the program into Brandeis's first professional school. My thoughts of the Sri Lankan family, Dom Helder, and Hannah Arendt were ever present as I pulled together a team, and we developed the vision and basic competencies we hoped to impart. We focused on three realms of program development: first, designing a financially sustainable program that would attract and be available to a diverse group of students, including many from poor, underprivileged communities; second, creating a welcoming, safe learning environment for students from around the world; and third, building a curriculum to give students access to philosophical and practical skills that would enable them to bring innovation and change through their own practice.

Seeking Sustainable Financing and Recruitment

Recruitment was key, but first we had to find financially viable ways to support our students. By design, we wanted two-thirds of our students to come from abroad, mostly from low- and middle-income countries, and to be largely midcareer practitioners with several years of work experience in development. We wanted US students to experience working on teams and projects with peers from countries where they wanted to work, and students from developing countries to work closely with peers from the world of privilege and power.

A viable financial plan posed a challenge to our values. Tuition at highly ranked US private universities is beyond the reach of even most US students without financial aid. So how could students from low-income countries afford to pay even a share of tuition? And even if we could offer full scholarships, living expenses would cost multiples of annual family income for our target applicants. Would we be able to attract only the sons and daughters of national elites, however committed? To recruit students from low-income countries, and even deserving US students, we needed financial options to attract them to apply to SID and then enable them to attend. We had two advantages. First, Brandeis and the Heller School supported SID's vision. They welcomed the contribution the program would make to increasing student diversity and to the university's mission to advance social justice. Second, we were willing to work hard to build relationships with a range of donors who could provide part or full tuition and living expenses for increasing numbers of students.

Over the years, we created long-term ties to funders, including scholarship programs of the World Bank, the Ford Foundation, the Fulbright Program, the Open Society Foundations, the Trace Foundation, AmidEast, and the Tibet Fund. For example, in our first twenty years, Ford funded 125 of our 1,800 graduates. The US Agency for International Development (USAID) occasionally supported students from its country missions, as did the UN World Health Organization (WHO) for a sister program we started in global health. We made annual visits to embassies in Washington, DC, and held information sessions in developing countries organized by our alumni. Using faculty ties to nongovernmental organizations (NGOs), we developed channels to groups such as the Aga Khan Foundation and Oxfam. We received significant help from BRAC, the world's largest NGO, headquartered in Dhaka, Bangladesh, to attract students from its ranks and to train the many members of its staff who attended the SID program. In gratitude for his extraordinary career, we created a named scholarship to honor BRAC's founder, Sir Fazle Hasan Abed. Hundreds of applications poured in for this scholarship and for other regional scholarship competitions (including one in the US Mississippi Delta) we created and advertised with development agencies around the world. Our efforts to build ties with funders expanded outreach to the kind of students we wanted for the program.

Individual donors also responded generously. Bobby Sager provided significant scholarship assistance for students from countries in conflict. Moses Feldman provided two endowment funds, one for student scholarships and another to support engaged scholars from developing countries. Seymour Bluestone provided a bequest that now, eighteen years later, is a memorial to his hope for one world. We were painfully aware of the significant sacrifices made by many students' families. For example, families in Africa sold land and livestock so a daughter or a son could study in the United States.

Individual supporters often filled critical funding gaps for students, including awards to subsidize the required practicum. Supporters offered social, as well as financial, support. The Osher Lifelong Learning Institute at Brandeis (BOLLI,) provided host families for many new students. Some stayed in their homes until they settled into housing, and many of the retired BOLLI members maintained strong relationships with their students throughout their time at SID and beyond. For example, one BOLLI family virtually adopted a woman from East Africa who needed weekly trips to Massachusetts General Hospital for treatment. Brandeis faculty also served as hosts. Two students, one from Zambia and another from South Africa, lived without cost in the home of a physics professor and his family. What more loving experience can we imagine for students than this care given so far from home? Most months, our large forum at Heller was filled beyond capacity by BOLLI families, faculty, and others for cultural nights, organized by the students themselves who wanted to give back by showcasing their regional food, skits, music, and dance.

We still needed to show the university we could do more than break even on program expenses. For the first twenty years, even with expanding operating budgets and growing faculty and staff, SID contributed about 20 percent overhead above expenditures to cover our share of university fixed costs. When SID achieved scale, most years we had students from forty to sixty countries, representing all of the world's major faith traditions and regions, and for over two decades we maintained roughly the proportion of students from low- and middle-income countries we had envisioned. One year, the program grew so large—over 125 new students—that we began to scale it back. Thus, we were contributing to the university's global footprint, expanding curriculum across disciplines, and more than paying our way.

Creating an Environment to Enable Learning

Preparing students for development practice meant more than opening the door to the classroom. It meant modeling inclusive, participatory practices that aligned with SID's vision of sustainable development. It meant welcoming students to a diverse community and easing obstacles to learning.

Orientation. If you had left your home in Asia or Africa twenty-four hours earlier, had several long flights in economy class, and were hurtling toward an unknown land and unfamiliar culture, you often arrived having had little sleep, stressed, and exhausted. Some at the school felt it was unnecessary to meet grown students arriving from other countries. Our admissions director and I did not. We felt that exhaustion, coupled with culture shock, produced anxiety for these students that was just as potent as what a young American arriving alone and for the first time in the poorest developing nation might face. New students were not just grateful to be met; they felt the human touch that welcomed them to a new place and new segment of their lives. We not only met them at the airport but made sure they had sheets, towels, and soap for their first night in a strange land. When funds were available, we offered a preorientation course for students in academic English.

Orientation was not the usual half day of administrative briefings before classes started. Our orientation started the week before classes and aimed to prepare students to learn effectively, interact collegially, and come together as a supportive community despite their disparate backgrounds and resources. All their professors were at orientation and had roundtable discussions on pressing issues of development. These discussions were the first occasion where new students could speak from their experience and learn about ours. This was empowering, especially for students from educational environments in which faculty always spoke and students only took notes.

A focus at orientation was to delve into why we do development work and what values we bring. In my welcoming address, I would tell them development begins with deep respect for each other and that if you come with experience of struggle, you bring a priceless qualification to our community. I would often tell them that prospects for development were far more hopeful than when I was their age, but that we were far from victory over hunger and poverty, environmental degradation, preventable disease, and violent conflicts.

The silliest part of orientation was an invitation for volunteers who could stand on their heads. It had purpose, too. I introduced an upside-down map with the South at the top (which is just as valid as the familiar geographic alternative) because this was a simple way to start our mission for the year. We wanted our students to begin to look at the world differently, even to the point of being disoriented, to shed the familiar, and to consider new worldviews. Orientation stimulated disorientation, to emphasize that we are all in search of new meanings. We introduced the theme of revolutionary thinking, devotion to scientific inquiry and its difference from dogma. If Copernicus had lived long enough, he would have been astounded that his simple observations toppled the Ptolemaic universe. The very word *revolution* comes from the Copernican view of the rotations of the earth around our sun. For us at SID, it meant critical thinking that could envision a new world society as fundamentally different from ours as ours is from feudalism. If we had lived in Europe between the ninth and fifteenth centuries, most of us would have been serfs who had been taught that feudalism was the natural order of society, as ordained by God. I suggested to our students that perhaps many of us are just as strong true believers in our contemporary social order. I asked if our descendants will look back on our time and wonder how we could think ourselves civilized when we have a billion people so deeply impoverished that they cannot guarantee the survival of their own children against malnutrition and diseases that are entirely preventable. If they would be astonished to discover that we spend trillions of dollars on military expenditures and weapons and only about $40 billion on official development assistance ($34.6 billion in 2017, which was 0.18 percent of the US gross national income [GNI]). If they would be saddened to learn that even the world's richest country, the United States, has a large population living in poverty, and jails one out of every 100 adults. And I'm sure they would be flummoxed by our notions of race.

Each year, I asked students to raise their hands if they came from Africa. Some did, of course, but I would admonish the rest that scientific knowledge suggests the human genome is nearly identical in all people. Markers in our blood show our common ancestor in Africa, the "mitochondrial Eve" as James Shreeve calls her (Shreeve 2006, p. 62). Shreeve says: "What seems virtually certain now is that at a remarkably recent date— probably between 50,000 and 70,000 years ago—one small wavelet from Africa lapped up onto the shores of western Asia. All non-Africans share markers carried by those first emigrants, who may have numbered just a thousand people" (p. 63). At orientation, these revelations about migration across continents and adaptations that emerged for skin pigmentation, as well as characteristics of culture, challenged our students. We all grow up with origin myths. "So when I ask you in the next two years how many come from Africa," I would say, "all hands should be raised in human solidarity." With this simple exercise, each entering class would begin its journey to become a one world community.

The learning environment. My favorite event soon after orientation was the poster session at the Brandeis Faculty Club. The first-year graduate students developed posters to showcase their work before coming to SID. Students set up their posters around the perimeter of the large dining room and other students, faculty, staff, and often the Heller dean and Brandeis provost would make the rounds. The diversity of the incoming students and of their work was always extraordinary; they arrived at Brandeis having already dedicated three, five, or even more years to the development field. The poster session validated students' lives and experience, ensuring that they, along with the faculty and administration, knew that they did not come to us as babes in the woods to be brought up in our image, but rather that they arrived with vision, know-how, and answers to share with the Brandeis community.

The SID learning environment needed to nurture agency and put values of respect into practice. The diversity of our student body became a platform for learning. Students from the United States would work in close quarters with their peers from developing nations. Students from developing nations would not find themselves isolated in a program geared to US attitudes and ideology. The advantages to learning were many. Students were immersed in a new pedagogy of dialogue and exploration. This was different for most, who came from educational cultures where knowledge was transmitted by teacher to student with scant possibility of self-discovery; what Paulo Freire critiqued as the "banking concept of education." At first, many students were reticent to express themselves but soon found that the faculty we had recruited respected contrary and novel views. For some students the challenges were different, especially those from the United States, who had advantages of language and self-confidence. Their challenges might be learning how to make space and give voice to others, question their privilege, and work together collaboratively rather than competitively. Sometimes they had to be constrained from dominating class conversations with their own assumptions or from automatically assuming leadership when working in diverse teams.

Most students, regardless of their origins, had never lived in a truly cross-cultural environment. They relished the experience of forging partnerships with students of vastly different life experience. However, sometimes there were tensions. For example, one year a clique of three young US students exhibited intolerant behavior and resentment, disruptively treating African students as unqualified to be at SID. We tackled the problem immediately through the mechanism of a New England town meeting. Town meetings were a useful, participatory forum to raise and address student concerns, and to model methods of practicing development. We called a meeting of all students-in-residence to talk about professionalism and civility in community. At the outset, I stressed that everyone needed to realize the degree of sacrifice and struggle it took for many of their fellow students to get to SID. For example, few of us had experienced, or could even imagine, growing up in one of the world's worst slums at Cité Soleil in Haiti, or life as a child shining shoes on the streets of Liberia. The life and work experience of many of our students can be beyond the grasp of others. I asked who could understand the life experience of the student who was jailed for trying to free young Vietnamese girls who had been trafficked into prostitution in China. Or of the Palestinian student who was incarcerated in an Israeli jail for violence during the Intifada and had his moment of pacifistic awakening in conversations with an Israeli Jewish conscientious objector. Or of the Pakistani woman who couldn't return home because her family might kill her for marrying outside her branch of Islam. Or of the US student who as a teen escaped with his younger sister from an abusive family and lived in the back of a car for a year.

What all these and hundreds more who have been our students and friends over these years have in common is a deep sense of privilege for being at SID, a deep sense of humility for the promise of their future careers, and a deep sense of respect for everyone who has known sacrifice. I went on to speak about civility, and that the word for us connotes the social glue that holds society together. I asked them to

> please remember that the best development workers are not necessarily those who had the benefit of the best academic preparedness prior to arriving here. We choose people for this program because we see, or hope we see, a strength of character, an abiding commitment to the cause of just development, to fairness in everyday life, to sensitivity to the misfortunes and limitations of others, an empathy for those ill or deprived or poor, and a quality of humility that is more important than the logframes you learn, all the straight "A"s you earn, and all the ambitions that will be frustrated without this code of conduct.

I concluded by asking everyone to celebrate with me the uniqueness of everyone in the room, their humanity, and their future.

We backed up our words with interventions—like town meetings, team trainings, mentoring, and intense group work—designed to nurture respect for others and the ability to work across differences. Many international students had never left their own countries or regions before coming to Brandeis. They may have come from nations with an internal diversity of languages and cultures, but for some, coming to the States caused culture shock that also had the potential to be liberating. To give an example, many gay and lesbian students had never declared themselves prior to being at Heller, whereas others who were straight had never met an openly gay person or had a gay friend. The stigma in some countries was so great, and the threat of arrest so intimidating, that it took time for students to realize that in the United States, sexual orientation is a protected category against discrimination and that even some of their teachers were gay. Many felt more comfortable after meeting classmates who were openly gay, accepted in our SID community, and increasingly in US culture. Others struggled with deeply held, often religious, convictions that being gay was wrong. Exposure to gay students and faculty and open discussions led many to question their assumptions.

Another advantage for international students studying in the United States was simply to experience a genuinely open society. Many students had not experienced a functioning democracy and could not imagine a vigorous free press, freedom of assembly, and other personal freedoms, or an environment where we spoke openly of contradictions of US history and of racial and other tensions present in US society. A Dalit student from India told me that being at Brandeis was the first time he didn't have to constantly think about caste. Yet we were aware of dangers, too. I often wondered what the impact of living in an environment of free expression would be on students when they returned home to repressive societies.

Designing a Living Curriculum and Culture of Sustainable Development

When shaping an emerging field of study, universities don't launch a new degree program without due diligence to researching its need, market competition, institutional capacity, and budget requirements. There were already master's degree programs around development studies in the United States, United Kingdom, and Europe. Most, however, were discipline- or sector-bound as degrees in development economics, public health, or agriculture; with others that were less about development than training in environmental sciences.

Envisioning a new curriculum for sustainable development. With a few exceptions (notably, the Institute for Development Studies at Britain's University of Sussex and the Netherlands' Institute for Social Studies), few if any of these master's degrees met the criteria I sought for Brandeis: interdisciplinary, focused on issues of sustainability, and integrating the science of ecology with political economy, social theory with ethics and philosophy, and modeling curricular values in extracurricular events and community. We were to train development practitioners and we were to help develop their critical thinking, fluency in environmental knowledge and political economy, and practical skills of planning, implementation, monitoring, and evaluation. We saw our program as furthering the emergence of the still new field of sustainable development, as one that spanned local to global.

Proponents of sustainable development refuse to entertain the hitherto accepted tension between environmental conservation and economic growth. *Our Common Future* (World Commission on Environment and Development 1987) presented global challenges as "interlocking crises" that required integrated strategies to dissolve compartmentalized responses within broad areas of concern (environment, economics, social) and sectors (energy, agriculture, trade). Coming from the real world of development practice, I shared that vision. Disciplinary learning was essential to train specialists for sectoral work. Yet many development agencies, from local Southern NGOs to international Northern-based NGOs, were run mostly by generalists, whose expertise was more visionary and programmatic than scientific. In contrast, the largest multilateral agencies were dominated by development economists and specialists. Our students needed to be comfortable with both.

When SID began in 1992, no professional degrees were offered in this new field. Universities compartmentalized the study of developing nations and left concerns about subjects such as environment, climate change, culture, and gender to specialized departments. My own discipline of geography, perhaps alone, stood at the intersection of natural environment and society. Geographers are trained in the physical environment and consider impacts of human activity. Subfields of geography focus on human, economic, and cultural aspects of place, natural resource use, and demographic change. An early master's program in development was at Clark University in Massachusetts, with strong ties to its renowned Graduate School of Geography, where my training took place. This influenced my thinking as we shaped our new program.

The SID curriculum was always a work in progress; evolving over the years with student and faculty input and experience. We proceeded with caution. If problems of underdevelopment could be approached as an epidemiologist would in identifying the cause of a disease, our work would have been vastly easier. But development is a contested field, following ideological constructs, influenced by personal commitments and vested interests that perpetuate those constructs in an epoch of history. Workers in a particular epoch had no valid perspective in the eyes of the established order and were ignored, or worse, by men in top hats. This posed the fundamental fallacy of scientific and economic inquiry for Michael Polanyi and his brother Karl, working in different fields. Michael Polanyi rejected the notion of absolute objectivity in science because we are creatures of the universe we are observing. Perhaps we too are such creatures of the worlds in which we grew up, that it is hard for us to see beyond our own ideologies and image. Karl Polanyi argued that the progress of society relied on our ability to resist oppressive and overwhelming social constructs of unbridled capitalism and that "progress could only come through conscious human action based on moral principles" (Block and Somers 1984, p. 1). For me, this meant that we all start trapped in the blinders of our youth and natural loyalties to our families. I think of this when I see children at demonstrations with their parents. If I agree with the demonstration, I think the children are being taught ethics. If I don't, I fear for the children's minds. Because we are rooted in our own contexts, we believe in the universal validity of our experience, our faith traditions, and our cultural and social adaptations to both oppressive and existential reality. In our program, we needed to be ever vigilant that our curriculum, although rooted in an ideology of sustainable development and social inclusion, was not imposing a single worldview or dictating solutions to the world's pressing problems.

Core competencies. We developed a set of core competencies, which we knew would evolve with the field of development and needs of our students (see a summary of the core competencies in Chapter 18, Box 18.1). Over the years, a curriculum takes on the look of a patchwork quilt, with courses developed around faculty and student interests, and courses constructed to test the teaching of new tools such as geographic information systems (GIS) and participatory methods. Periodically, working with graduating students, we mapped our courses against the core competencies to evaluate how and where the students developed their capabilities. The competencies were grouped around the "3 E's"—environment, economy, and equity. Ideally, courses would be structured around critical debates, so our economics courses were hardly the kind taught in many business schools.

The 2008 statement written by our faculty was grounded in development values: "Development objectives, and the systems and methods used to achieve them, are influenced by values that are not always explicit. The SID Program has an explicit set of values and expects its graduates to be explicit about the values that underpin their professional work and conscious of the implications of values in their assumptions, theories of change, and implementation methods and practices." We spoke of values rooted in the social justice tradition of the Heller School and Brandeis University, and identified principles on which to base our teaching and learning. We had high expectations for the careers of our graduates. We worked to train SID students to become agents in transforming conditions that give rise to persistent poverty and to build a global society free of poverty, preventable disease, and environmental degradation.

The practicum. From its founding, the program required most students to spend the second year in a six-month practicum and to write a case-study master's paper based on their observations. For less experienced students, placement in a professional development organization in a country of their interest provided work experience and a grounding of learning in the real world. For those who were more experienced, the practicum proved just as important through placements providing higher professional responsibilities and rare opportunities.

The practicum became one of the program's major attractions. We invested in practicum coordinators who had maturity of judgment and experience in the field of development practice. They, along with faculty, helped students consider how best to use the practicum. Students of all nationalities needed more field experience. It was a challenge to decide whether to concentrate on deepening their experience in a known area of the world or to diversify their experience geographically and culturally. Some advanced students from developing countries wanted to gain experience in headquarters of donor organizations. For example, a student from Pakistan was placed in the office of the administrator of UNDP in New York City and a student from Mauritius at the United Nations Environment Programme (UNEP) regional headquarters in Jamaica. We required formal job descriptions, written and approved by the host institution, student, and program prior to signing off on a practicum. Periodic evaluations of students were done by their host organization supervisors. Students served in small and large development organizations. Some were hired after their practicum, for example, the student who as a child arrived in the United States as a Vietnamese refugee. She did her practicum with the United Nations Children's Fund (UNICEF) in Thailand and has had a rich career with UNICEF ever since, serving in several senior postings, including Darfur in Sudan.

The faculty. A curriculum can only be as effective as its faculty. When SID began, there were few development specialists at the university. We could draw upon a pool of expertise of biologists, anthropologists, human-rights specialists, and others, but we needed to recruit our own faculty—people who, given their own origins or years of experience in developing countries, understood the world of our students and of development. As our revenues increased, over some years we recruited a full-time faculty of ten scholars and practitioners, reflecting the interests and diversity of our international student body. We also invested in building a cadre of adjunct faculty drawn from prominent development organizations headquartered in the Boston area. These included, among others, the heads of program evaluation and of microfinance at Oxfam America, an oceanographer from the Woods Hole Research Center, and World Education's vice president for Africa. The senior investigative reporter for WGBH, a Boston affiliate of National Public Radio, taught communications skills. Adjuncts were critically important to our curriculum—providing state-of-the-art experience, global contacts, and always the generosity to mentor students far beyond the classroom.

Did We Get It Right? A Call to Social Responsibility

In constructing the SID program, we believed that it needed to be guided by moral, cosmopolitan principles of a shared, equal humanity. We were on guard against a curriculum that served to reinforce entrenched power relationships and the status quo. SID alumnus Rhoderick Samonte of the Philippines put it best: "SID is not a passport to privilege, but a call to social responsibility." Samonte came from the Roman Catholic liberation theology movement. The founder of that movement, Father Gustavo Gutierrez, provided a key to our mission as an education program:

> But the poor person does not exist as an inescapable fact of destiny. His or her existence is not politically neutral, and it is not ethically innocent. The poor are a by-product of the system in which we live and for which we are responsible. They are marginalized by our social and cultural world. They are the oppressed, exploited proletariat, robbed of the fruit of their labor and despoiled of their humanity. Hence the poverty of the poor is not a call to generous relief action, but a demand that we go and build a different social order. (Gutierrez 1983, p. 44)

Brandeis looks to its roots in Jewish values. SID students came from all faith traditions. The curriculum was not an endorsement of any tradition or social doctrine; rather, it was about the common quest to solve severe problems of unsustainable, unjust development and help students acquire the critical thinking and practical skills to develop their own theories and practice.

In a globalizing world, we needed to listen more than lecture. Freire said the great struggle unfolding in all societies was to counter the forces of dehumanization: "The oppressors, who oppress, exploit, and rape by virtue of their power, cannot find in this power the strength to liberate either the oppressed or themselves. Only power that springs from the weakness of the oppressed will be sufficiently strong to free both" (Freire 1970, p. 44). I think he meant that only power that springs from humility is strong enough to counter the arrogance of power. Humility enables self-reflection and questioning of the seemingly fixed reality enveloping us all. No matter how wrenching it is to question the familiar, it is the essential step to enter a world of possibility that finally disperses the social illusion that paralyzes the mind.

In 2014, after twenty years as SID founding director, it felt time to step down. I remained on the faculty teaching in SID and Heller's PhD program, and I founded the Center for Global Development and Sustainability to enlarge our capacity for applied research. Over the years, SID attracted several thousand students and a world-class faculty. The financial model we created was sustainable and yielded excess revenues for the school. But the pressures are there. Other programs in sustainable development have grown up in recent years, but I believe the model we created can remain a beacon in the field of development studies. The cost of US private universities, and even public ones, still remains out of reach for most students. Will universities in developing countries be able to create SID communities of learning without the lessons of living in open democratic societies? Today, the most important lessons for development are not coming out of the advanced economies. They are emerging, despite national problems, from places such as Bangladesh, Sri Lanka, Brazil, China, Costa Rica, and Rwanda. Perhaps the future SIDs are by right in these countries.

On April 10, 2013, I made a pilgrimage of sorts to view the Cyrus Cylinder on loan to the Smithsonian Institution's Arthur M. Sackler Gallery in Washington, DC. Of course it was impossible to read with an untrained eye, but its tiny Babylonian cuneiform script baked into the clay had an outsized influence on world culture. The Jewish Bible refers to Cyrus the Great as "the anointed" of the Lord, who, as king of all the Persian Empire, permitted conquered peoples in 538 BCE to return from exile and rebuild their holy sanctuaries, including the temple in Jerusalem. The words inscribed on the cylinder are revered by the people of Iran, by the people of Israel, and by the founding fathers of the US republic, for these words laid the foundation for a new kind of society, multicultural and tolerant of all faiths.

The cylinder was on a spotlit pedestal in the middle of a darkened room. I felt a bit awkward standing there for so long and found myself lapsing into a meditation on how little I knew of the roots of my culture and, as a development practitioner, how ignorant and perhaps arrogant I must be to work in cultures with histories about which I know so little. Over 2,000 students came to SID over two decades, most from ancient civilizations. You can't survive on past greatness, and ancient communal hatreds still poison many societies, but what a strong foundation they have upon which to build new relevance in the world and follow the lodestars of their own cultures.

5

On Learning and
Practicing Development

Vinya Ariyaratne

*This . . . model is what I call development from tradition, which simply
says we don't automatically assume that true human development consists
of economic growth, even economic growth redistributed in a reasonably
just way or even economic activity pursued with a view to satisfying the
material basic human needs. . . . I develop this in my study of the Sarvodaya movement in Sri Lanka. Here we see a living community which is
very conscious of having a rich philosophy of life. It defines human needs
more broadly as cultural needs, affective needs, social needs, spiritual
needs, and needs of expression. . . . In the "development from tradition"
approach you don't necessarily reject the goals of [other] approaches;
however, you treat these instrumentally. People who define development
this way view modern technology or modern rationality systems or the pri-
macy given to improving consumption or physical comfort in a radically
different way from those who assume that these things are unconditionally
good in themselves and not subject to the scrutiny of another set of values.*
—Interview with Denis Goulet 1990

In 2018, the Sarvodaya Shramadana Movement completed
sixty years of evolution as a constructive force contributing to nonviolent
social transformation in Sri Lanka. The movement has survived fourteen
government changes, two bloody youth insurrections that were met by hor-
rendous suppression, and a civil war that engulfed the island nation for
nearly three decades. On two occasions—in the mid-1970s and late 1980s—
the Sarvodaya Movement was subjected to systematic government harassment and suppression of its operations. Today, the movement stands as a
well-recognized and respected development entity with an unparalleled
island-wide grassroots network, a strong national presence, and international

outreach. In the six decades of its existence, Sarvodaya has reached over 15,000 of 38,000 villages in Sri Lanka through a variety of participatory development interventions, touching the lives of over 4 million people.

I served as executive director of the Sarvodaya Movement from 2000 through 2010 and have been general secretary since 2011, but my involvement really started the day I was born. The movement was founded in 1958 by my father, so I grew up in the environment created by the movement. I started going to villages in the 1960s. In this chapter, I recount the journey Sarvodaya has traversed, examine the effects and nature of international development assistance on the organization, discuss one intervention in some detail, and take a peek into the future. The story of the Sarvodaya Shramadana Movement offers a vibrant example of a people's movement in the Global South.

Philosophical Vision

Sarvodaya means "the awakening of all" in society, and *shramadana* means the "gift of labor." The Sarvodaya Shramadana Movement—or just "Sarvodaya," as it is known—seeks the personal and social awakening of all beings through the sharing of labor and other voluntarily gifted resources. The vision of Sarvodaya is a no-poverty, no-affluence society, and its mission is the creation of a social order based on the values of truth, nonviolence, and self-denial, and governance through participatory democracy. The devolution of power and resources, upholding basic human rights, satisfying basic human needs, protecting and nurturing a healthy environment, and tolerance for religious, cultural, ethnic, and linguistic differences have pride of place in such a social order.

Those of us in Sarvodaya have always believed in the inherent capacity of even the most impoverished communities to surmount their plight if the barriers that prevent them from unleashing their potential are removed. The process that Sarvodaya evolved is known as awakening—starting with the individual, the family, the village, the city, the nation, and the world. Based on Buddhist and Gandhian thinking, for six long decades Sarvodaya has weathered many a social, economic, and political challenge to still survive and thrive as a unique people's movement that promotes a holistic model of development. In this model, social and economic needs of poverty-stricken communities are fulfilled through an integrated development process built on spiritual, moral, and cultural values. This kind of democratic participation and organization enables the people to be innovative and adaptive to new technologies while upholding value systems, nurturing progressive traditional norms, and freeing themselves from psychological dependencies from outside. Social, economic, and political emancipation becomes a realizable target for the village people.

The Sarvodaya Journey

The Beginnings

Sarvodaya was born ten years after Sri Lanka (then known as Ceylon) gained independence from the British in 1948, following nearly four centuries of colonial rule. Sarvodaya began in 1958 with A. T. Ariyaratne, my father, leading a group of students from Colombo who volunteered their time and labor to help in a rural village. Its emphasis in those early days was on values of service and community participation. As shramadana activities became widely known, Sarvodaya inspired people throughout the country. In 1969, it began its One Hundred Villages program to bring integrated development to a broader rural base. The organization began to expand from hundreds of unpaid workers to thousands of villagers participating in their own communities. Post-independent Sri Lanka's development discourse was affected by significant demographic, social, cultural, and economic changes, and Sarvodaya weathered those changes as a truly indigenous grassroots development movement.

The Third and Fourth Decades

Economic development and Sarvodaya. The election of a new center-right government in 1977 marked a significant shift in the social, economic, and political landscape of Sri Lanka. Most notably, the introduction of a neoliberal market economic model and an executive presidential system led to far-reaching consequences for every aspect of people's lives. The state-dominated, welfare-oriented, agro-based economy started to change, with the private sector becoming the driving force in the economy and government policies being changed to attract foreign capital and investment. Sarvodaya, which sought an equitable, self-sustainable rural economy, was confronted by this massive onslaught of a market economy that was forcefully initiated by the private sector and supported by state machinery and popular media. Even though there were subsequent changes in government and several social safety nets introduced to address some negative consequences for the poor, the core structures of an open economic model remain in 2018. The executive presidency, too, remains intact, even though many presidents have been elected during the last two decades with a mandate to abolish the system of executive presidency.

The basic thrust of Sarvodaya's economic policy is to eradicate poverty and ensure the basic needs of all people are met. Accordingly, the village economy should be structured to achieve these two objectives. The resources available in each village should be scientifically surveyed and utilized with resource conservation in mind. The most modern and appropriate technologies that can be placed under the control of the village people should be employed for the purpose. Although Sarvodaya recognizes the reality of the open-market economic system dominant in Sri Lanka and internationally, it will only work with those aspects of the dominant system that support and can be integrated with village, division, and district economic structures. Those aspects of the open economy that do not lend themselves to such support and integration are rejected by Sarvodaya. For example, Sarvodaya completely rejects the current economic structures that make a few urban-based people richer while increasing the relative poverty of the majority of the people. Sarvodaya envisages instead an economic system in which village, division, and district-level economic structures under people's control can compete in the open economy to provide people with fulfillment of their basic, secondary, and tertiary needs. To begin with, this requires placing the necessary resources and technologies, together with managerial skills, at the disposal of the village community. The next step is to establish structures at the next level (division or subdistrict) to bring together the village communities in a particular area. Secondary economic needs can be satisfied at that level, but tertiary needs must be supplied by district-level economic structures.

Sarvodaya's economic policy gives priority to raising the living standards and productivity of rural farmers who are engaged in the cultivation of rice, minor food crops, vegetables, tea, rubber, coconut, and fisheries, and especially providing women with opportunities in home-based cottage and small industries. To realize the revolutionary economic vision of Sarvodaya, a new program emerged in the mid-1980s, the Sarvodaya Economic Enterprise Development Services (SEEDS), discussed later in this chapter.

Armed conflict and Sarvodaya. The other factor that deeply affected the country and Sarvodaya is the armed conflict between the government of Sri Lanka and the armed Tamil rebels, particularly the Liberation Tigers of Tamil Ealam (LTTE). The conflict started in 1983 and had escalated into a full-blown civil war by the end of the 1980s. Therefore, while continuing countrywide work with disadvantaged communities on a comprehensive development model, Sarvodaya also had to initiate a major program to address effects of the armed conflict, including assisting the affected communities and large numbers of internally displaced people (IDPs) in the north and east of the country. It also had to work to address root causes of the conflict at all levels. From the mid-1980s to the early 1990s, Sarvodaya received generous external donor support for its development programs and was able to expand its portfolio of activities significantly.

The latter part of the 1990s saw the war's rapid escalation, with no resolution in sight. Sarvodaya implemented its 5R program: relief, rehabilitation, reconstruction, reconciliation, and reawakening. We adopted a people-to-people approach with an emphasis on harnessing the spiritual energies of citizens to bring about a shift in consciousness while working on satisfying people's basic needs, meeting the needs of conflict-affected communities for socioeconomic development, and promoting the concept of community self-governance to devolve power to the grassroots. People from different ethnic and religious communities came together to take part in massive peace marches and meditations held almost every month in various parts of the country. The intention was to build a critical mass of consciousness to counter violence and stop the war. Sarvodaya action created a sense of hope among the most affected communities trapped in war. These communities can be an integral part in the peace-building process in Sri Lanka. We believe Sarvodaya's mass mobilization for peace contributed to the ultimate willingness of parties to the conflict to accept the need for a cease-fire and sit down for negotiations.

The Fifth Decade

The turn of the millennium brought tumult and challenge to Sri Lanka. The century began with the signing of a cease-fire agreement (CFA) in February 2002 between the government of Sri Lanka and the LTTE. In December 2004, the Asian tsunami wreaked havoc in many Sri Lankan villages. Elections in 2004 and 2005 brought a new Sinhalist national government and president to power. By 2006, the CFA broke down and hostilities resumed between the government and the LTTE. Finally, the end of the war came in 2009 after government forces defeated the LTTE. During this time, Sarvodaya launched an organizational transition, a strategy that included a new funding model with a few new development partners, and a second generation of leaders took over operational responsibility of the organization.

Community health and Sarvodaya. With the 2002 cease-fire, Sarvodaya was able almost immediately to embark on a program to reach conflict-affected communities in Northern and Eastern Provinces and also assume greater responsibility for promoting peace and reconciliation. With the cessation of hostilities, access was opened to communities that had been closed by conflict. Sarvodaya offices in some districts in the north were reopened. Major programs in child development and community health were initiated. One of the key interventions was a joint program with the Ministry of Health to control malaria in Northern and Eastern Provinces, supported by the Global Fund to fight AIDS, tuberculosis, and malaria. Sarvodaya was the principal recipient for the nongovernmental organization (NGO) sector and was instrumental in delivering long-lasting insecticide-impregnated bed nets in LTTE-controlled areas in Northern Province. The program continued for ten years until Sri Lanka was declared malaria free by the World Health Organization (WHO).

Humanitarian disasters and Sarvodaya. The Indian Ocean tsunami of December 2004 devastated the shores of Sri Lanka. Sarvodaya directed efforts to bring the 5R program to the survivors, particularly in the worst-affected provinces. District offices in affected areas were able to provide information to Sarvodaya headquarters, where a special Disaster Management Operations Center was set up. Sarvodaya's immediate response meant nearly all regular activities came to a halt, as its entire available staff focused on disaster response. Staff from unaffected areas were sent to assist in the immediate relief of those in affected regions. The national and international response was significant. Financial contributions from ordinary Sri Lankan citizens, from partners abroad, and from thousands of international citizens enabled Sarvodaya to help 40,000 families in all fourteen affected districts. Initially, this money was used to distribute emergency items—food, water, shelter, and medical supplies. In 2005, Sarvodaya was honored to receive the United Nations Habitat Scroll of Honor in special recognition of its response to the tsunami.

Over the long term, the physical reconstruction of affected areas was only part of Sarvodaya's vision for a recovered Sri Lanka. Another part was repairing the intangible personal and social damage the tsunami caused. We continue to aim for a personal and social transformation of all—an awakening of the nation, known as *deshodaya.* The permanent Sarvodaya Community Disaster Management Center was established. It is now the focal point for disaster response, working closely with the Government Disaster Management Center. It is formulating strategic evacuation plans, offering skills training, and becoming involved in flood-management projects.

The tsunami affected LTTE-controlled areas as well. The areas demarcating the government and LTTE battle lines were washed away in many areas. It this case, a natural disaster occurred on top of an ongoing, man-made disaster. It offered the rare opportunity for the parties in conflict (LTTE and the government) to come up with a negotiated settlement, as the CFA was still intact. However, leaders on both sides of the divide didn't have the vision or commitment to use this rare window of opportunity. If the conflict had ended then through a negotiated settlement, several thousand lives would have been saved. But the CFA was called off in 2006, and a full-blown war restarted. Again Sarvodaya had to focus on relief programs for IDPs and protection of civilians. After three more years of intense fighting between the LTTE and government forces, the war came to an end on May 19, 2009, with a comprehensive victory for the government. War left a heavy toll on civilians, massive population displacement (over 300,000), and significant destruction of property and vital infrastructure, including schools, hospitals, and government institutions.

Even before the war's end, Sarvodaya was at the forefront of providing relief to those displaced by fighting. In July 2008, we began coordinating relief programs in the north and east. We provided services in twenty-three of thirty-two IDP camps. For the initial relief effort, Sarvodaya used its network to bring food and other services to those in need. Many items were donated by Sarvodaya societies in less-affected areas and sent to camps that housed those who fled the war zone. Thanks to generous donations, over 7 million rupees (Rs) were collected. Thanks also to the work of hundreds of volunteers, by January 2009 well over 1 million meals had been provided by Sarvodaya and over 100,000 people benefited from our provision of clean water, sanitation, and medical supplies. By 2010, through the work of rehabilitation and reconstruction, one-third of IDPs were able to return to their homes, many of which had been badly damaged by the war. Sarvodaya was one of only a few organizations with direct access to affected parts of the country and still works to rebuild communities destroyed by the war.

The Sixth Decade: Planning a Future Without War
In 2008, Sarvodaya celebrated its fiftieth anniversary. Once the war ended, the movement was able to plan its future without war being a factor. Today, Sarvodaya is a well-established organization with proven impact throughout Sri Lanka. It is a diverse organization with a network of affiliated divisions and entities specializing in sectors of community and human development ranging from governance and advocacy to community health, water supply, sanitation, agriculture, education, child development and protection, law, and microfinance. As a movement, Sarvodaya goes well beyond provision of services by helping communities establish their own locally based organizations, known as Sarvodaya Shramadana Societies (SSSs). To date, such societies are active in an estimated 5,400 communities and are helping their members improve their capacities to implement and direct their own development initiatives. Of these communities, nearly 3,000 are classified as *gramaswaraj* (self-governing villages), having attained high levels of self-sufficiency and community-level organization. We envision that gramaswaraj communities will become models for other Sri Lankan communities and then for communities throughout the world, thus actively leading the way forward in promoting holistic, sustainable development.

Funding the Movement: Sarvodaya and Development Assistance

The Early Years
The first two decades of Sarvodaya's evolution, from 1958 to 1978, were completely based on voluntary sharing of labor, material, and local donations. A significant increase in the number of villages accepting its development approach across the country resulted in rapid organic growth as a volunteer

movement. However, this rapid expansion required external assistance to scale-up organization and support demand. Local resource mobilization alone was not sufficient to respond to this need. Therefore, while promoting self-help, community participation, and local resource-based development, Sarvodaya did not shy away from receiving development assistance from a variety of external funding sources.

During the latter part of the 1970s, the movement received donations from smaller charitable organizations and well-wishers in Europe who learned about the movement through articles that appeared in popular international publications such as *Reader's Digest.* There was a personal connection between donors and recipient communities in which donors and/or donor representatives directly participated in village development activities, often living in the community with Sarvodaya workers and working side by side with villagers. The process was one of mutual benefit in the true Sarvodaya spirit of sharing and was a transformative process for both donors and communities. External assistance received was based on needs of communities with no strings attached. Using this method, Sarvodaya demonstrated how external financial and technical assistance could be channeled in a way that does not create dependency but enhances community self-reliance and leverages local resources.

Formalization of Development Assistance: The Third and Fourth Decades

In the mid-1980s, with rapid expansion of Sarvodaya's services to a significantly larger number of communities and the escalation of ethnic disturbances, Northern donors who supported Sarvodaya proposed creating a donor consortium to better coordinate and enhance effectiveness. The perceived advantages of a consortium—the possibility of longer-term planning because of stable budget support, better remuneration for full-time workers, scope for technical assistance to improve human-resource capacity and institution building, and a comprehensive monitoring, evaluation, and reporting mechanism—were attractive and compelling reasons for Sarvodaya to agree to a donor consortium. At its inauguration, the Sarvodaya Donor Consortium brought together over twenty-six development partners from around the world on one platform. However, as time passed, the bigger donors dominated the consortium's decision-making process, leading to serious disagreements between Sarvodaya and the consortium (Perera 1995). It was evident that, despite some beneficial impacts, the consortium model did not work well for Sarvodaya.

At the same time, when the cold war ended, international priorities changed, switching to macroeconomic development strategies. Large projects and macrointerventions began to dominate the donor landscape. Sarvodaya, which had attracted attention originally because of its broad-based, grassroots philosophy, was no longer the kind of organization donors were focused on funding. By 1991, 85 percent of our external aid had dried up and the movement was forced to go back to its roots. From then on, we relied on pioneering villages (those that had reached a higher level of development in the Sarvodaya development process) to provide support for the surrounding communities requiring development. In addition, we reduced the number of paid staff and counted on the commitment of Sarvodaya's long-term supporters to keep the movement on course. With the donor scenario being completely changed, the donor consortium was formally disbanded in 1995, and we had to develop a new funding strategy. In part, this was a blessing in disguise. Sarvodaya was forced to return to its core value of self-reliance for its own organizational and operational structure, though it had been successful in building self-sustaining communities.

By then Sarvodaya had tried diversifying its support base for village-development programs. Early in the 1990s, we established an important partnership with the government on a World Bank–funded poverty-alleviation project, the Janasaviya Trust Fund. This project can be seen as a response to mitigate the impact of structural adjustment policies on the poor. For the first time, World Bank funds were available to NGOs for poverty-alleviation programs through the government. Sarvodaya was actively involved in the design of the project, and we used our experience with microfinance in SEEDS to develop the Janasaviya Trust Fund model, and later to become an implementing partner along with other NGOs. This was an unprecedented development in terms of government opening up doors for NGOs. Around the same time, there were other projects such as the Community Water Supply and Sanitation Project that opened up opportunities for national NGOs and community-based organizations (CBOs) to receive financial and technical assistance for water and sanitation projects.

Post-Donor Consortium Development Assistance: The Fifth and Sixth Decades

A movement that functioned without any external financial assistance for nearly two decades, and later within a framework of development cooperation with like-minded organizations, had become one of the largest participatory development organizations in this region and in the world by the end of the third decade of its existence (late 1980s). Ironically, it was our philosophy of starting on a small scale that resulted in Sarvodaya's tremendous growth. The appeal derived from our fundamental belief in the wisdom and abilities of the village population—people who see each other every day and depend on each other—to decide their own fate, and not global corporations, financial institutions, or national political parties. The momentum of the movement's growth was such that by the early 1990s, in spite of harassment by the government and political violence, it had achieved enormous outreach.

Sarvodaya's work included peace building, conflict resolution, appropriate technology, and programs for children at risk, elders, and those with disabilities. It maintained its holistic approach to social mobilization, seeking empowerment of people beyond mere economic development.

The challenge was to sustain this outreach while limiting our dependence on fluctuating donor support. Although we faced serious resource constraints, by the mid-1990s Sarvodaya still had a large full-time staff and a physical infrastructure that enabled the network that was critical to maintain a grassroots presence as a national movement. Sarvodaya managed to move toward greater financial independence through a focus on using its infrastructure and human skills to generate income that supported services, and also by renewed reliance on volunteers. We made a careful assessment of all physical facilities, evaluating the capacity of each to earn income through local projects or by hiring our services out to other organizations when they were not being used for Sarvodaya's internal programs. Residential and training facilities were upgraded to attract more investment through local projects, volunteers, and use by other organizations. The district centers and educational institutions were categorized according to their potential to generate income to cover the district operational costs of Sarvodaya's services to villages and societies within each district. Staff restructuring resulted in a smaller number of core staff, and they would be supported by a team of volunteers at each center or program. The Sarvodaya headquarters was also restructured, putting emphasis on strengthening existing national income-generating projects and social enterprises such as educational toy and furniture production units and export of village products.

A new funding mix emerged with the restructuring of the organization and programs. Although the donor consortium disbanded in 1995, several of the donors that were members of the consortium (the Norwegian Agency for Development Cooperation [NORAD], the Canadian International Development Agency [CIDA], Helvetas) continued to support Sarvodaya. A few donors that were not part of the consortium (Nippon Foundation, Rishho Ko Seikai) continued to fund selected programs in targeted districts. Between 1995 and 2000, Sarvodaya attracted several new donors, including the Novartis Foundation for Social Development, which committed funding for five years in collaboration with other key development partners. Others, such as NORAD, also provided support in longer time frameworks. During this period of funding transition, a district-based strategy was adopted that channeled donor funding on a geographic basis, relying on a common-core program that was still tailored to the needs of each district. Despite significant reduction in donor funding, Sarvodaya used its restructuring, encouragement of independent funding, and channeling of donor resources to maintain its presence and core services to the villages.

The restructuring was painful but resulted in a Sarvodaya model that was financially more resilient, while still being true to the original mission of the movement. We were able to avoid undue reliance on a single donor or funding source and thus developed a healthier mix of funding. The Five Year Sarvodaya Strategic Plan for 2000–2005 aimed for maximum internal-income generation, building on Sarvodaya's existing social enterprises such as its commercial printing press, export business based on international fair trade principles, woodwork production unit, and revenue from facilities. The strategic plan also gave high priority to building human resources for the future by calling for investment in a comprehensive program to develop the knowledge and skills of existing workers, recruit new staff, and nurture second and third layers of leadership.

Strengthening Sarvodaya's internal revenue capacity and diversifying its donor support were critical as the CFA signing in 2002 and tsunami in 2004 led to changes in the donor scenario in Sri Lanka that were not favorable to indigenous NGOs. The CFA created a new space for international NGOs (INGOs) and the international peace lobby. A plethora of international "Peace NGOs" claiming to have expertise on conflict resolution, peace building, facilitation, and negotiation landed in Sri Lanka overnight and began working, often ignoring Sri Lankan NGOs and CBOs that had long been working on peace and reconciliation, albeit with meager resources. The CFA also resulted in a gush of funding for peace-and-reconciliation programs, mainly from the European Union and bilaterals such as NORAD, the Swedish International Development Cooperation Agency (SIDA), and USAID. The largest share of this new funding was channeled to INGOs that brought in international consultants and experts. Although local organizations such as Sarvodaya also gained from this post-CFA resource influx, the amounts received were proportionately much smaller and saddled with significant conditionalities such as caps on capital, and operational, administrative, and other overhead costs. Conversely, INGOs brought in highly paid expatriates as project managers and received substantial coverage for overhead costs. Some of the best staff working for national NGOs were recruited by INGOs and were offered disproportionately high remuneration. Moreover, the government, having established direct links with the LTTE, ignored civil society organizations (it would pay a high price for this neglect of indigenous organizations when a few years later, the governing party was voted out of power). This situation prevailed until 2005, when a new president was elected on a nationalist agenda. The country was drifting back to war when the CFA was abrogated in early 2006.

The Indian Ocean tsunami of December 2004 was the other critical event that influenced the development and donor scenario in Sri Lanka. The devastation caused by the tsunami and the international attention and sympathy it generated were followed by the largest ever volume of international financial assistance flowing into the country. Similar to the situation after the CFA, another wave of INGOs and newly formed charities from around the world arrived in Sri Lanka to find an environment where government could provide little coordination or regulation of aid activities. For some INGOs that were already present in Sri Lanka, the tsunami was a double bonus. Individual contributors and governments from their home countries chose those INGOs as the organizations of choice to deliver relief and assistance for rehabilitation. There was little accountability, and serious allegations of corruption, misappropriation, and wastage were reported by Sri Lanka's auditor general, among others.

Sarvodaya also benefited from this surge in funding. Given its permanent ground presence, Sarvodaya was able to respond almost immediately with a massive relief program. Friends and well-wishers from around the world lost no time in making donations and contributions. Sarvodaya differed from most organizations because of the large volume of funds it received from individuals as well as from established development partners such as foundations and bilateral donors. For tsunami relief, the bulk of Sarvodaya's funding came from more than 5,000 individuals around the world, starting from small donations of $5 to $10 up to several thousand dollars. We had to manage these funds in a responsible manner with the highest degree of accountability. A committee was formed under the chairmanship of the former governor of the Central Bank of Sri Lanka (CBSL); several independent professionals from the corporate sector were included to manage the funds. The total portfolio was approximately $15 million. With this funding support, as mentioned earlier, Sarvodaya was able to mount a systematically planned, executed, and award-winning relief and recovery program over a period of five years. Sarvodaya's post-tsunami response provides a model of how to channel the generous response of individuals to a natural disaster through an indigenous organization and also build the local organization's capacity to provide emergency relief in the future.

The Sarvodaya Economic Enterprise Development Services

The SEEDS program provides a good example of a Sarvodaya initiative. By the mid-1980s, several thousand SSSs had been established in rural and semi-urban settings in which people's participation was the critical factor in community development. However, by then it had become evident that without proper capital inputs, ordinary members of society—such as the small farmer, fisherman, petty trader, artisan, craftsman, and others—were vulnerable to the vagaries of the open-market economy. This was largely due to their lack of credit, business skills, and access to market information. Working with advisers who had both the technical expertise and a thorough understanding of the Sarvodaya philosophy, we conducted a careful study. Based on the results, we asked the advisers to develop an operational mechanism to implement Sarvodaya's economic policy to complement its community empowerment programs. In October 1985, the team recommended setting up an independent unit within Sarvodaya to help its members become financially self-sufficient by launching viable economic enterprises, thereby reducing dependency on donor funds and external assistance. This resulted in the formal launching of SEEDS in September 1986. Its mandate was to "create a dynamic rural economy and enhance the quality of life of impoverished individuals and communities through the provision of financial and other inputs." Thus, it aimed to alleviate poverty by promoting economic empowerment for a sustainable livelihood and training in entrepreneurship, business activities, preparation of reports, and so on. Ultimately the SEEDS credit-plus approach combined credit with business development services and capacity building— a strategy widely acknowledged by development professionals as a means to reach pockets of poverty.

Commencing operations as a pilot project in February 1987, SEEDS initially limited its activities to 250 SSSs in the five districts in the country. The core microfinance interventions were carried out by the Rural Enterprise Program. The Management Training Institute and Rural Enterprise Development Services, established in 1987 and 1990, respectively, were responsible for in-house training and creating an enabling business environment. The decision to initiate a multifunctional approach was taken on the understanding that no single intervention could adequately meet the varied needs of an emerging village economy. Hence, in addition to providing productive capital for generating and sustaining microenterprises, SEEDS also devolved its nonfinancial activities to district-based enterprise promotion centers and regional training centers.

By virtue of its outreach, spread, knowledge, and experience gained over the previous twenty-five years, SEEDS had emerged by 2011 as one of the leading microfinance practitioners in the country. SEEDS added value to its loan portfolio through micropawning and microinsurance services, introduced innovative savings products to create a capital base in the rural sector, trained and mentored countless micro- and small-business entrepreneurs to run their businesses effectively, helped strengthen the SSS network, and contributed to national efforts through strategic alliances with state and nonstate partners. With wide recognition by its counterparts at national, regional, and international levels, SEEDS then sought to become a development-finance company to broaden its capital base and serve a wider section of needy and disadvantaged people.

The first thought was for SEEDS to become a specialized development bank, but financial and other restrictions prevented this approach. After reassessing its role in the economic landscape, SEEDS decided to form a new finance company under provisions of the Finance Companies Act No. 78 of 1988 to support the growing financial needs of the populace, especially in rural areas of the country. With provisional approval from CBSL in 2009, SEEDS converted its credit and project finance operations to Deshodaya Development Finance Company, Ltd., which was rebranded Sarvodaya Development Finance (SDF) in 2015. This move was intended to consolidate SEEDS's legal status within the country's financial regulatory framework, and also to enhance stakeholder confidence and widen its customer base.

However, the transition of SEEDS from a nongovernmental, nonprofit microfinance institution into a regulated financial institution was a painful, challenging, complex process. The exemplary integrated rural finance model built on SSSs and SEEDS partnerships with financial and nonfinancial inputs was disrupted when CBSL withdrew the approval given to SSSs to mobilize savings from its members. This had a disastrous impact on the unique model Sarvodaya and SEEDS had built over two decades with great commitment, sacrifice, and effort. The number of SSSs receiving services from the newly formed entity, the SDF, declined sharply. Since 2014, several innovative measures have been taken to mitigate the damage caused by the decision of CBSL, and a new model based on technology has been built.

Today, SDF proudly stands as the only finance institution in the country owned by a charitable development organization. As of March 2018, SDF had a customer base of over 300,000 individuals and over 500 SSSs, with a savings base of Rs.4.4 billion ($26 million) and a loan portfolio of Rs.5.5 billion ($36 million) supporting micro-, small, and medium enterprises throughout the country. While helping realize the Sarvodaya economic vision of creating an alternative economic order, we hope that SDF will sustain the movement's welfare and development programs and free it from the need for external donor support.

The Future: The Sixth Decade and Beyond

As it celebrates its sixtieth anniversary, Sarvodaya can look back on years of community service aimed at building growth and resilience at the local level. It is grounded in a strong organization that has demonstrated capacity to grow, confront adversity, and adapt to changes in the environment in which it works. Today, its main legal body is Lanka Jathika Sarvodaya Shramadana Sangamaya, Inc., which serves as the backbone of all Sarvodaya operations, maintaining the island-wide physical and human-resource infrastructure and assuring support services to village SSSs.

The Changing Landscape

Sri Lanka (and also the *world,* for that matter) is a very different place from what it was when Sarvodaya was founded in 1958. Although today Sri Lanka is considered a low-middle income country according to the World Bank classification, significant poverty, social problems, and economic challenges remain. Governance is in a deplorable state. Exports have been increasing and overall income has risen, but economic wealth has not reached the population evenly. While the cities and upper classes have seen great progress, the quality of life in many rural areas has not improved. Many in the agricultural sector continue to live at or below the poverty level. Industrialization has created a new urban underclass whose earnings have increased but who cannot afford to feed themselves. The results of this unbalanced development can be seen in the country's internal conflict, which has affected the country for over twenty-six years, and increasing violent crime and alcoholism. Left out of the growing prosperity that they see happening elsewhere, many people feel powerless to help themselves. In many cases, they have become desperate, self-destructive, and even engage in violence.

During its sixty years, the movement's workers have helped villages organize for self-governance, carry out basic-needs projects, and establish savings banks, credit programs, preschools, training centers, and other facilities to uplift and empower all. As Sarvodaya observes its sixtieth anniversary, we are formulating a new strategic plan at a historic transition time in Sri Lanka. As we move forward, we will remain governed by ideals of participatory democracy with decentralized power and resources. We will continue to advance our holistic, sustainable approach to development that combines the ability of villages to meet basic needs with the spiritual awakening and capacity building central to the Sarvodaya approach. At the same time, we will build on our sixty years of learning to adapt and strengthen the movement to meet new needs of the twenty-first century.

Once again, Sarvodaya faces challenges in funding and working with donors. The funding environment for social investment is changing, with funding often flowing through international foundations and for-profit industries and not so much as foreign aid channeled through national government or bilateral agencies. Some of this funding continues to reflect the international donor's own domestic concerns and revisits the concept of "tied aid" (foreign aid that must be spent in the donor country providing the aid). An example is the case of a major international partnership project that requires purchase of surplus grains from the donor country. Not only does this reduce the project's direct benefit for local food producers, but it can also displace local agricultural production, introduce processed food that supplants the local diet, and create an alliance with Sri Lankan businesses that may benefit from managing imports and, therefore, encourage ongoing importation. The face of the donor community is changing with the entry of new actors, especially China, which has become the biggest lender to Sri Lanka. Such changes require Sarvodaya to have strong negotiating skills with donors, good access to information, politically and socially conscious workers, and an empowered constituency in order to remain true to our principles of socially just development.

The Interconnected Vision for the Future

Looking forward, Sarvodaya has three interlocking strategies that will enable it to effectively meet twenty-first-century challenges and advance to another level as a social movement. These strategies are: (1) preparing the next generation of leaders in sustainable development through higher education, (2) developing alternative economic models that promote a shared economy, and (3) building a national political awakening (deshodaya). These strategies have emerged organically from the movement's first sixty years and are in keeping with Sri Lanka's evolving situation and level of development.

Work on the first strategy began in 2008 with establishment of the Sarvodaya Institute of Higher Learning (SIHL), with the intent that it would evolve into a university focused on sustainable development and building a particular kind of leadership. Education at a greater depth and over a wider range is necessary if people are to solve their own problems—a fundamental principle of Sarvodaya's development work with communities. For some time, we have been concerned that the educational services the movement provides need to go deeper. To offer one example, training people at the community level to run a savings-and-credit initiative is no longer enough. All of those involved need operational skills, but some also need to understand the economic forces that influence the rural economy, how local and national markets operate, what world markets and globalization are, and how they affect communities. The educational vision is also rooted in bringing together international and national students and educators in exchanges inside and outside the country to expand the horizons of young Sri Lankan leaders and also to help build a new generation of Northern development practitioners who will experience on-the-ground training in Sri Lanka.

Expanding local knowledge of global economic forces and building leaders in sustainable development connects with the second strategy, which is to develop alternative economic models that enable a shared economy and provide sustainable livelihoods without excluding impoverished populations, including the growing urban poor. This strategy builds on the success of SDF, which already supports small and medium enterprises and empowers grassroots communities with financial solutions. The goal includes expanding services, such as technology, and broadening the scope of SDF into a full development bank to support sustainable, equitable growth and financially inclusive communities.

The third strategy, deshodaya, takes Sarvodaya's community awakening work to the national level, seeking governance that addresses the structural causes of poverty and roots of the conflict that has divided the country. As noted earlier, deshodaya means awakening the nation, and the purpose is to promote a culture of democracy, good governance, reconciliation, and sustainable peace. Participation of ordinary citizens and principles of consensual politics are used to strengthen the people's sovereignty. Community-level participation is connected to the national level—enabling engagement with governance, accountability, and the process of peace building and reconciliation that needs to follow Sri Lanka's long civil war. For example, addressing the alienation of youth who were drawn into the conflict means advocating for economic opportunities, supporting youth entrepreneurship, and offering proper education. Combining all three strategies will allow communities and their leaders first to understand structural and economic issues that deepen inequality even as the economy grows, and then to hold government accountable for delivery of social services.

Although Sarvodaya can justly celebrate its accomplishments, as we move forward, we find ourselves reflecting on persistent economic and environmental problems, examining exclusion and inequity, and seeking new ways to work together to mobilize twenty-first-century solutions to address our country's structural and communal challenges. We need to do this while remaining true to our core approach of shramadana (the sharing of one's time, thoughts, labor, and energy) and our sustaining faith in the capacities of all Sri Lankans.

6

The Business of Aid

Thomas Dichter

Dear Dr. Dichter, I have recently completed my Masters in International Development with a focus on Policy. I am currently exploring employment opportunities that expose me to different areas of International Development. I would love the opportunity to sit down and discuss the ongoing or upcoming projects and programs you are currently working on. I am also seeking advice and mentorship as a young professional trying to break into the field.

I often get an email like this from people in their twenties wanting to "break into" international development. They seek work in any of the hundreds of international NGOs, international contractors, or multi- and bilateral institutions that form today's aid industry. Most have degrees in various aid specialties, a relatively new phenomenon. In the 1960s, there were degree offerings in international relations or area studies, preparing people for work in the diplomatic field, among other types of employment. There were few programs in international development, much less such subspecialties as development practice, project management, or development policy. These new types of degrees are offered by yet another part of what has become the aid-industrial complex, the assemblage of aid agencies, public and private, their contractors, and subcontractors—the fifty or so US universities that fill the job pipeline with career-oriented aid workers.

Among those institutions, the better known ones are American University's School for International Service, Brandeis's Heller School, the School of Advanced International Studies (SAIS) at Johns Hopkins, the Fletcher School at Tufts, and the School of International and Public Affairs (SIPA) at Columbia. There are development-degree programs also at the University of California–Berkeley, Georgetown, Duke, Brown, Cornell, Dartmouth,

Harvard, Princeton (Woodrow Wilson School), and Yale. Lesser known programs include those at the University of California–Los Angeles, Fordham, University of Denver, University of North Carolina, Northwestern, George Washington University, Syracuse, University of Texas, Tulane, and others. They offer master's degrees in such areas as international development policy, development practice, sustainable development, global human development, with many subspecialties such as human rights, conflict resolution, microfinance, and so on. More and more of these programs stress the hands-on practical aspects of development work.

A colleague of mine recently spent a year interviewing candidates for jobs at USAID, many of them young people with degrees from these programs. USAID, with over 9,000 employees, was then on a staff replenishment phase aimed at rebuilding the agency, which had gone through a painful reduction in force several times in the 1990s and 2000s, starting with cuts pushed by Congress during the Clinton administration. My colleague, a retired USAID officer with over thirty years of field experience, had one question that she posed at the end of each interview: "In your view, what are the causes of poverty?" Too many of her interviewees, she reported, were stymied. If they had something to say, they coughed up quasi-tautologies—people are poor because they are without jobs, or because they lack access to credit, nutrition, education, health care. . . . If she pressed them, "OK, but why do they lack access to these things?" there was silence.

Part of why her question proved hard may have to do with the pragmatic nature of the degree programs many of these candidates came from. Take the case of the young lady whose email I quote above. I looked into one of the key programs from the school she came from, its "Masters of Public Administration—Development Practice." Here is the course description:

> Core skills and competencies of a development practitioner. The curriculum provides students with a solid background in theories and methods of development, food systems, public health, economics, ecology, infrastructure, and environmental sustainability. All coursework includes skills training components which focus on equipping students with the management, communication, quantitative, and analytical skills needed to work fluidly across disciplines and regions. Graduates of the MPA–DP degree will possess the knowledge and skills needed to demonstrate competency in these 7 core areas:
>
> • Problem Appraisal—[including] Diagnostic Tools and Frameworks, Needs Assessment Design, . . . Visioning and Goal Setting
> • Program Design—[including] Outcome Mapping, Technical Strategy Design, . . . Value Chain Analysis, Budgeting
> • Implementation and Management—[including] Proposal Development, Program Startup, . . . Progress Reporting, Risk and Crisis Management
> • Monitoring and Evaluation—[including] Evaluation Design and Sequencing, . . . Participatory Rapid Assessment

- Communications—[including] . . . Technical and Policy Writing, Public Speaking, Marketing, . . . Agenda Setting, . . . Data Visualization
- Capacity Building—[including] Participatory Methodologies, Institutional Analysis, Training and Workshop Design . . .
- Cultural and Interpersonal Skills—[including] Cross-Cultural Communication, Self-Reflection, Ethical Behavior, Empathy, . . .

This is billed as "A New Approach to Development Education" and a response to the conclusion of an expert commission "that there is significant and growing demand for skilled individuals trained in a set of cross-disciplinary competencies that prepares them to address the increasingly complex challenges of development." This program description (and the fact that it is to be accomplished in twenty-two months) is an indication of how thousands of young people are being prepared to take over the development industry as it moves into its eighth decade.

A Mismatch Between Problems and the Skills Being Taught to Solve Them

My own experience in development aid since the 1960s suggests strongly that there is no greater mismatch between a set of problems and a set of skills designed to solve them. There are at least two highly questionable assumptions behind the curriculum noted above and common to many of the current degree programs. The first is that good development professionals need to master an array of tools, methods, and techniques, all of which enable the "doing" of development, the designing, implementing, and monitoring of projects. The second is that the students and the agencies they intend to work for (that is, "we" in the North) will be managing these projects. Not surprisingly, these assumptions, as well as the curricula in many development-degree programs, mirror the existing canon of development in the major official aid agencies and large international NGOs. There appears to be little that encourages humility (e.g., the history of development suggests that it is not a process that can be engineered) or reflection on development aid's many failures and unintended consequences. Nor is there much that penetrates the enormous complexity of the historical, geographical, social, political, and cultural conditions that engender poverty. In brief, such curricula foster the perpetuation of the business of development: the getting and execution of two-, three-, and five-year contracts to implement development projects in poor countries. Too many candidates are being prepared to work within the day-to-day bureaucratic framework of development that has been around for years.

Instead, were prospective students helped to understand how complex and context-specific the process of development is, how little of long-lasting value is dependent on donor money, how poor the track record has been, and how much that poor track record is a function of short-term, time-bound, targeted direct-to-the-poor projects, and above all, if they were to get the message that local people are better equipped to lead development in their countries than we are, they might think twice about a career in the aid industry. But promoting such an understanding would not be in the interests of the institutions that run these programs (and for which, incidentally, they are key profit centers).

Nor would it be in the interest of the hundreds of agencies big and small that do the work of development, that partake of the $200 billion or so spent annually ($135 billion of which is official development assistance, or ODA). This industry needs a regular turnover of personnel, and one of the main clearinghouses in the marketplace for the thousands who hold development degrees is a for-profit firm called Devex, whose trademarked motto is: "Do good. Do it well." Devex, with offices in the United States, Spain, and the Philippines, claims over 800,000 registered members within the international development industry—for-profit and not-for-profit development organizations, donor agencies, suppliers, and aid workers.

Devex recently sent me this email:

> Hello Thomas, I wanted to reach out to you directly because I think that you would benefit from having access to more of the career tools we offer on devex.com.
>
> Upgrading to a Career Account would give you full access to the 2,500+ new positions posted to our jobs board each month, and make it easier for the recruiters looking for candidates to join the leading development organizations worldwide to find you, as your profile would be featured in their search results.
>
> Beyond finding a job, a Career Account is a smart way to manage your professional growth regardless of whether you are just starting out or progressing toward the executive-level. Through exclusive online events and insider news coverage, a Career Account connects you to practical insights and professional development advice from the best and brightest in our industry.
>
> You can learn more about all the Career Account has to offer here, but I wanted to make sure you at least had it on your radar. If you have any questions please feel free to reply and our team will be in touch.

On a randomly chosen date (January 10, 2018) I went to the Devex website (devex.com) to see what was on offer. On that day alone there were 1,294 jobs posted. Here are highlights from a posting for a "Chief of Party for a Catholic Relief Services" (CRS) project in Niger.

Job Responsibilities:

• With key CRS and consortium member program staff and other stakeholders, ensure program's strategic objectives and results are fully accomplished and while meeting expected technical quality standards.

- Oversee periodic technical reviews, ensuring best practices are followed and managing changes in program direction and focus.
- In collaboration with program staff, provide guidance and technical oversight to consortium members to ensure that lessons learned are documented and disseminated.
- Oversee the project monitoring and evaluation system, using data analysis as the basis for measuring performance. Ensure that M&E, accountability and learning are incorporated into evolving program plans.
- With program staff, ensure the delivery of quality training, technical assistance, and administrative and financial support to all partner agencies and government, including the selection and coordination of sub-grantees and consultants.
- Oversee the development and timely submission of high quality project performance deliverables as required by the donor, including, though not limited to, regular monthly reports, quarterly reports, evaluations and other donor required documents.

Management and Administration:

- Manage program budgets, including tracking of financial and material resources and expenditures in accordance with donor regulations and requirements. Ensure forecasting and project spending are accurate and timely.
- Ensure accurate and timely reporting of program finances and progress status, review actual financial performance against the budget, and explain variances on a regular basis.
- Ensure staff compliance with all CRS administrative and operational procedures and policies, as well as applicable donor regulations.
- Approve expenditures, budget adjustments, and cost modification requests to donor.

Representation and Advocacy:

- Provide leadership and oversight to the consortium, ensuring that sub-grantees adhere to their assigned scopes of work and sub-award terms, and ensuring that all members of the consortium work cooperatively and productively to achieve project objectives.
- Act as primary project contact to donor, taking responsibility for addressing all program matters, collaborating with the CRS Regional and Deputy Regional Directors, Country Representatives, and HQ on overall donor relationships.
- In collaboration with CRS Country Representatives and Heads of Programs, manage relationships with the respective national governments of the target countries.
- Oversee program communication strategies, in collaboration with CRS Country Representatives and Heads of Programs, including compliance with donor's branding and marketing requirements as well as CRS' marketing and communication procedures.

Human-Resource Management:

- Lead, manage, and supervise a team of CRS and consortium staff to meet program objectives across two country programs.

• Manage recruitment portfolio for the program, in collaboration with Country Representatives, the Regional Office and the donor as may be required, to ensure optimum service delivery through recruitment of competent and qualified staff.

Background, Experience, and Requirements:

• Master's degree in International Development, International Relations, with preferred focus on Climate Smart Agriculture, Agribusiness, Governance, Disaster Risk Reduction or related fields. PhD desired.
• 7 or more years relevant management and technical experience.
• 5 years' experience managing donor funds, with a preference for experience managing multi-country grants. Strong knowledge and experience in budget management.

It is significant that the project to be led here is not named in the job post. Is this perhaps in keeping with the generic nature of much of development work, void of context, void of deeper understanding? The focus instead is on execution, meeting the project targets and "deliverables," usually set by the funder; it's their money after all. And CRS, a venerable, sincere, and well-meaning NGO like many NGOs in the industry, has in recent years got in the habit of bidding on contracts such as the Niger project. In 2014, for example, CRS did $206 million worth of business with USAID, up from $179 million the year before.

Is it too much to hope that new development professionals might be prepared differently, with much more emphasis on the cultural, social, political, and economic contexts in specific developing countries? Might they be encouraged to take a more humble approach, a more open-ended and slower approach? As long as development contracts are part of an organization's business plan, as long as the competitive quest for development funding is the driver, preparing people for a less hands-on, more backseat, humbler role would be ill-suited to the agencies they want to work for.

In my experience the ideal future candidate for development would be someone who says, "I'm not sure at all what approach to take, or what should be done, because I don't even understand deeply enough what we are talking about. I'd need at least two or three years in the field just to begin figuring things out, listening to people, building relationships. I would not be able to promise that any of the project objectives could be met, and certainly not within a specific time frame. I could not promise to deliver the 'deliverables.' In fact I might question whether they are appropriate, and even if 'we' ought to be taking this on at all."

Clearly no one would hire this person. It would be too risky. It would be asking the development industry to cut its own throat, to become smaller, to involve less money. Hence the paradox—a less-is-more mindset would mean fewer jobs. But if "country ownership," a universally agreed core principle in the development community going back to the 2005 Paris Declaration on Aid Effectiveness, were to be taken seriously, a diminished role for "us" in the North would be the future. And rhetorically, it has been the "future" for some time now. It's just that we do very little to act on it. Here is (then) USAID administrator Brian Atwood twenty-five years ago, in 1993:

> Development assistance works best when it contributes to efforts that people in the recipient society are already attempting to carry out. . . . The fact is, unless development assistance is informed by local realities and the people who experience them daily, it will very rarely succeed. . . . The reason for this is quite simple. It is their country, not ours. It is their community, not ours. We can advise, we can assist, and we can choose not to assist, but the decisions about development priorities and policies must be reached by that society at large, not by us. It is they who bear the risk; they must make the commitment. Providers of development assistance— whether a well-meaning private voluntary group inadvertently imposing an inappropriate cultural style, or whether a panel of prestigious international experts prescribing policy changes from a vantage point far removed from the particular political and social environment—fail if we forget that it is their country, not ours. (Atwood 1993)

What Kind of Development Professionals Will Be Needed?

To unpack the challenge of preparing people for a future where people from the North are going to be less central to developing countries' progress, we need first to look at what makes future young professionals tick, what kind of skills they should have, and how they should acquire them. And equally important, is there a particular kind of personality and character they ought to have?

From the early days of the volunteer-sending organizations (the US Peace Corps founded in 1961, the British Voluntary Service Overseas [VSO] founded in 1958, the UN Volunteers founded in 1971) to today's "voluntourism" fad, the desire of Northern young people to work in the developing world has encompassed a variable mix of selflessness and selfishness, covering the spectrum from a naive impulse to save the world through a heartfelt desire to help less fortunate others, to the need to do something more meaningful than merely hold down a wage-earning job, to expectations of adventure and romance. The influences behind this motivational continuum include the 1960s reactions to materialism and corporatism, the civil rights movement, popular books and films such as *The Ugly American* and *Lawrence of Arabia,* and many others.

During the heyday of the Peace Corps in the 1960s, to go from Kansas or Minnesota to work for several years in the mountains of Peru or a village in Morocco, or to be sent to teach school in Uganda or Ethiopia, was indeed a life-changing adventure. Many volunteers recalled feeling somehow more alive, more aware of everything from the taste of a grapefruit fresh off its tree to the colors of the sky. And after mastering a new language, they could form relationships with people who had different ideas about life and the world, and even learned to eat different things in different ways. And the people with whom they worked and lived expressed their gratitude. All of this was a heady experience.

Fifty years on, the professionalization of development work has not significantly altered these underlying motivations. Any number of twenty-seven-year-olds from the North are still likely to yearn for the life abroad in a field purported to do good, to help others, and indeed to save people's very lives. And there is a kind of adventure, if not glamour, in learning a language and living in different places, in say, Egypt, Honduras, Burundi, Haiti, Mali, and Cambodia, over a possible twenty- to thirty-year-long career.

It is entirely human to see such a career in a positive light. Even after decades of work, aid veterans who have been exposed "in the field" to aid's problems, contradictions, and limits might at worst accuse themselves of naïveté, of being overly optimistic. They are unlikely to conclude that they had in some ways been an obstacle to development or caused harm, much less been part of a neocolonialist project, or think that their work embodied a patronizing approach to the "locals."

Since the 1960s, there have been a dozen or so books written in a personal vein that do draw such conclusions. Among them are Pascal Bruckner's *Tears of the White Man* (1986), Leonard Frank's essay "The Development Game" in *Granta* (1986), Graham Hancock's *Lords of Poverty* (1989), Timothy Morris's *The Despairing Developer: Diary of an Aid Worker in the Middle East* (1991), and Michael Maren's *The Road to Hell: The Ravaging Effects of Foreign Aid and International Charity* (1997). Here, for example, is a gentle but pointed comment on the transitory nature of the development project, a by-product of aid having become a business:

> We are six on the mission to the North-west Frontier: an old Japanese, a Korean, an American, a Bangladeshi, a Dutch girl, me. . . . None of us have been here before. . . . The Korean who brought us together does not know us either. He got my name from an Indian I once worked with in Manila. . . . How did the world get this way? . . . OK: the Japanese, because Japanese money is becoming important; a Bangladeshi, because they are cheap and brown; a Korean, because the mission organiser is Korean; an American to punch statistics; a Dutch girl sociologist for the soft and warm. A mix of people because this time it's an international agency. I'm in charge; I make the big decisions. We've got four weeks to come up with a project for, say, thirty million dollars. Routine. (Frank 1986)

Inside many large NGOs (Save the Children, CRS, CARE, ActionAid, World Vision, and other such) and scores of firms that bid on aid contracts (Chemonics, Development Alternatives, Inc., Creative Associates, ABT Associates, Tetra Tech, and so forth) hundreds of degreed development professionals spend much of their day in exactly this kind of "coming up with a project" routine. They do not ask Brian Atwood's implied question: Whose job is it? And for the most part they do not reflect on whether what they are doing is counterproductive. Or if they do, they do so on their own time; it is not what they are paid for. But that is not to say that quite a few employees in the industry do not see through the game of getting contracts and delivering the deliverables and are aware of the shortcomings of their employers. Here, for example, is a review of a major USAID contractor by a former employee that appeared on www.glassdoor.com:

> I worked at [name of the NGO] full-time. Pros—Good place to start out if you are looking for a job in international development. Provides you with a helpful foundation for how the development industry operates in the current climate. Great place to start if you want to be a technical expert. Cons—Very little engagement/autonomy with the field teams, and much of the project design and implementation is driven by technical experts in DC, not from the teams operating in the field. Strategic planning is supposed to come from HQ in DC, and not from the teams on the ground. Priorities are mostly around revenue generation and around people keeping their jobs, and not on genuine, good development.
>
> In my own work over the last five years, during which I had occasion to review aid projects and aid agencies in 13 countries and in talks with over 300 individuals, it was striking how many aid workers feel an uncomfortable (and embarrassing) gap between what they hope to achieve and the imperatives of the agencies they are part of. Yet these doubts do not translate into meaningful change in the way things are done. Such is the strength of the long habit of competing for the pieces of the aid pie and wanting to manage the projects it pays for.

Is the Developed World Ready for Country Ownership?

And yet the reality today is that we are not in a zero-sum situation. It is not so much a question of whether it should be "us" or "them" working to foster development. Although it is absolutely clear that developing countries must strengthen their ownership of their countries' progress, this does not mean that outsiders have no role to play at all. The world has become too international, too globalized, for poor countries to be entirely "on their own" in the development process, nor do they want to be. The cross-border movement of ideas, information, and people, from refugees to professionals, continues to accelerate and will only increase in future. But the argument for "us" to take a back seat and take on a very different role is a compelling one, and the time is now. If the fundamental conflict of interest in the current aid industry—its current business plan depends upon a continuing central role—can be faced squarely and honestly, a redressing of the balance can begin to take place.

What is needed first is a deep change in underlying assumptions and attitudes. We need to recognize that the nature of development as a business has in itself become an obstacle to country ownership and to intelligent long-term development, because structurally it favors "us" and continues to put "them" in a subordinate role. Such an honest acknowledgment would open the door to movement toward "working ourselves out of a job" over the long term. And it would enable us to be much more transparent with our funders, both those in the public and the private sphere. We would, of course, have to commit to a smaller footprint, and thus to less funding.

Released from having to "sell" development aid and to push for more and more money for our projects, we could present a more sober view of the prospects of poverty reduction, even admitting that the notion of an "end of poverty" anytime soon is counterproductive because it substitutes immediate Band-aid-type solutions (microloans, bore holes, cash transfers, and so on) for long-term change, the far less sexy and more intangible efforts to help change the institutional arrangements that are often the key constraints to development. We could even debate what role aid money plays in development at all and consider the late British economist Peter Bauer's thesis of 1974 that "aid is clearly not necessary for progress nor is it sufficient. If the personal and social conditions of progress (capacities, motivations, mores, and institutions) are not present, aid will be ineffective. What holds back many poor countries is the people who live there, including their governments. A society which cannot develop without external gifts is altogether unlikely to do so with them" (Bauer 1974, p. 17).

Bauer understood that the key variables for development lie in the cultural, social, and political realms:

> Economic achievement depends primarily on people's aptitudes and attitudes (e.g., interest in material success) and their social institutions and political arrangements (e.g., in encouraging people to take long views). Societies, groups, and individuals differ widely in these matters. . . . External contacts, market opportunities, and natural resources play a part, but a much less important one; and, again, their effective use depends on personal and social factors. (p. 17)

We might also be free to acknowledge that some fundamental cultural and societal problems might take generations to change (e.g., caste in India, a major obstacle to progress). And though we ought not to be too Cassandra-like in our pessimism, we need to be less Pollyannish in our optimism. This includes being humble about what we in the West and North know about our own development and acknowledging the possibility that we are not always the best models; indeed, as some have recently pointed out, we in the North have serious poverty problems in our own countries. Finally, we could be more forceful in reestablishing a distinction that has been—perhaps deliberately—lost in the quest for aid money, that between economic development and humanitarian aid. These have become too often conflated, not just in the mind of the uninformed public but among many who work in aid.

These changes in attitudes and assumptions, of course, need to be carried over to the curricula for those who would study development. The core of such curricula should focus on institutions, on culture, social structure, and the political economy. It should involve also a critique of development history from the days when we naively thought, in Rostovian terms, about "take-off" industries; through the heavy emphasis in the 1960s on airports, dams, and roads; and in the 1970s to a growing disillusionment about trickle-down and a new urgency about poverty, to the formulaic imposition of structural adjustment policies; and so on. During the course of reviewing the history of aid, we might recall a time when knowledge and ideas were a more important currency than money, and how it is that we moved from teaching and technical assistance to "doing" development for others.

Conclusion

The development industry was never meant to become a business or to continue in perpetuity. Development aid is not, after all, a commercial venture meant to maximize profits. To acknowledge this basic fact is to accept an eventual contraction and a future role for us in the North as supporters rather than leaders. The future leadership of development must come from the people in the developing countries; people who are energetic, dedicated, and thoughtful. In a more country-owned future for development, those fewer people from the North who should be involved need to be people with innate collaborative traits, people who are empathetic, patient, and naturally able to listen. If there are to be partnering kinds of agencies involved, they need to focus their recruitment more on who their candidates are as people, and not just on what courses they have on their resumes.

7

Courage Is the Cornerstone of Progress

Patrick Awuah

Africa has a web of visible needs: better sanitation, health care, infrastructure, education, and jobs. But one necessity is less obvious: Africa urgently needs a new generation that cares about these challenges, that has the courage, persistence, and skills to address them.

Ashesi University in Ghana was founded to test the hypothesis that young Africans, educated at the university level in a way that nurtures ethics, innovation, and entrepreneurship, would become a force for change. In 2002, when our first class of just thirty freshmen entered our makeshift campus, we wondered if, in just four short years, we could prepare them to be brave enough and skilled enough to create meaningful progress in Africa.

The name Ashesi (Ah-SHESS-ee) means "beginning" in Fante, one of many native languages spoken in Ghana. Our goal was to create a new beginning for our students, challenging them to forge opportunities for themselves and others. Over time, our graduates would spark many new, diverse beginnings across Africa.

In Ghana, there is a saying in the local pidgin, "You're too known!" It means, you ask too many questions and challenge the status quo too often. Parents, teachers, shopkeepers, and neighbors use the phrase to scold a child until the questions stop. At Ashesi, we believe that for young Africans to stand up to corruption and bureaucracy, they must ask questions. To be innovative and entrepreneurial, they must stop memorizing old answers, instead analyzing problems in fresh ways, and creating new solutions. In traditional African universities, students often sit in huge lecture classes. They take classes only within their major, and often they learn by rote. In contrast, Ashesi would feature a multidisciplinary core curriculum designed to foster ethics and critical thinking, in addition to in-depth majors.[1] Instead

95

of traditional lecture-only classes, we would offer a mix of small seminars, workshops, and hands-on learning through labs, community service, and senior capstone projects. Students would tackle problems based on complex, real-world scenarios. Ashesi aspired to be as demanding as a high-quality university anywhere in the world, with a curriculum designed for an African context.

At first, we could only afford to offer two majors. We chose business and computer science, fields with high potential to drive growth and innovation and a shortage of highly qualified graduates. Soon, in response to student demand, we added management information systems. Years later, when we had the resources, we added engineering.[2]

Would Ashesi succeed? When this first class graduated, would its members be more ethical than their peers, and more capable of tackling complex, real-world problems? Or would they succumb to the prevailing norms and feel incapable of creating change?

Ashesi's earliest graduates have now been out in the world for over a decade, and their positive impact has surpassed our highest hopes. They have touched the lives of thousands and spearheaded the development of technologies used by millions. In 2012, 12 million Ghanaians successfully voted by using a biometric voter ID system developed by a team with an Ashesi alumnus, Nii Amon Dsane, as the lead software engineer. This innovative system flags duplicate registrations and fraudulent voting. By reducing opportunities to compromise the vote, it fosters greater trust in elections.

Personal triumphs inspire systematic change. One alumna quietly refused a demand to falsify financial data, in the process turning down an enormous bribe. She and other Ashesi graduates work diligently to help African businesses operate more efficiently, with stronger safeguards against fraud, changes that help prepare ventures to raise capital, expand, and create more jobs. Another alumna, Yawa Hansen-Quao, launched a successful leadership program for women in government and business that caught the attention of UN Women, a UN entity that then hired Yawa to adapt the program for women in East Africa. Yawa funds her nonprofit girls' mentorship programs with earnings from her core business.

Our graduates' successes have sparked interest in the Ashesi model. Consistently, 90 percent of Ashesi graduates stay in Africa, where 100 percent of them start businesses or find quality placement. Of course, we've made mistakes and continue to learn from them. In our early years, we almost shut down for lack of funds and, in addition, had an abrupt wake-up call about academic dishonesty. However, after sixteen years in operation, Ashesi has long been financially sustainable, and our ethics programs have earned the fierce support of students and alumni. Our conviction is stronger than ever that integrity, entrepreneurship, and innovation can be taught in Africa and, in fact, must be taught. Here are a few things we've learned.

Fighting Corruption Requires Ethical Courage

Africa needs leaders who will do the right thing, even when no one is watching, and who will refuse to tolerate wrongdoing in others. But ethical courage can rarely be imposed; it is fostered through an honest exploration of values. Discussing real-life examples often brings clarity to the consequences of corruption. Would you want your sick mother treated by doctors who had cheated through medical school? What are the myriad costs of bribe seeking and fraud to society? If students tolerate cheating now with their peers, how will they stand up to corruption in the future? We tell Ashesi students, if you want to lead, develop your own ethical courage; then help others find theirs. Of the many ways we foster ethics, we are most known for the pioneering Ashesi Honor Code.

The Ashesi Honor Code

"I will not cheat, nor will I tolerate cheating by others." These simple words form the heart of our honor code, the first of its kind in Africa. Students sign a pledge not to cheat and to report any cheating they witness. Exams are not proctored. This code represents an intimidating departure for many students. In too many Ghanaian schools, cheating is a part of life. Sometimes teachers even encourage it. "During exams," one Ashesi student recounted, "my teacher sat me between the two worst students in the class and said I had to make sure they passed." Many Ghanaian students come to believe that letting friends copy their answers isn't cheating, but simply helping others. Also, in the predominant learning model, jokingly called "chew and pour," students memorize material, often word for word, then "pour" it back on exams. After years of being rewarded for exact recall, students are sometimes confused when we teach them that plagiarism is wrong. In Ashesi's early years, before we started our honor code, we had a few instances of cheating, but we felt the situation was under control. Then a visiting lecturer confided that one-third of his students had copied from each other and, in the process, had all copied the same misunderstanding of the material. Clearly, more students were cheating than we had realized.

These students sincerely loathed the fraud and bribery around them but resisted seeing the connection between Africa's serious corruption and academic dishonesty. We challenged them to look inside themselves and admit that pretending someone else's work is your own, or passing tests well by cheating, is fraud. Corruption in government officials shows up as electoral fraud or resource theft. Corruption in students takes the form of cheating. Most dishonest adults have a rationale to justify their behavior. They might claim to be only taking bribes to help their family or to reward supporters, but that doesn't make it right. Student-led honor systems are used in US universities such as West Point and Haverford College, but we found no examples in Africa. In fact, the most common argument against Ashesi adopting this kind of code was, "But this is Africa!" The assumption was that young Africans could never earn this level of trust.

In 2008, after eighteen months of debate, two Ashesi classes voted to embrace the honor code. Today, each new freshman class debates the issues surrounding the honor code and then votes as sophomores to join or decline. So far, every class has voted to join. Each year, a few students are reported by their peers for infractions, which shows that students are developing the courage to speak up. A committee of faculty and students investigates each report; violators found guilty are sanctioned. Initiating this honor code represented a radical step in Africa. People worried about the risk: What if we adopted it and a few students cheated and destroyed our reputation? However, taking smaller steps might not have inspired such a powerful new mindset.

Students realize that once they graduate they are likely to rise to positions of responsibility; with limited oversight, they will need to rely on their own ethical compass. And when students practice dealing with any unethical behavior in their peers, however awkward that feels, they prepare themselves for the world beyond Ashesi. In the words of one student, Robert Boateng-Duah,

> I used to believe that dishonesty and cheating could only be curbed through strict invigilation. But coming to Ashesi, I realized these actions could be more effectively curbed when confidence is inspired in people that they can do the right thing even when no one is watching. This is what the continent needs—the confidence, integrity, and understanding that doing what is right is not just about avoiding trouble, but also carries that magic within it to transform Africa.

Giving Voice to Values

Ashesi graduates inspire current students. In a six-week workshop called "Giving Voice to Values,"[3] graduates confide real-life stories to freshmen. They reassure young students that "a reputation for integrity will be your secret career weapon, because colleagues, customers, and managers want to work with someone they can trust." Graduates speak of the value of the emerging Ashesi University brand, which has come to stand for trustworthy, highly competent employees. They warn current students, "If even one of you becomes known as a cheat, you will wreck it for all of us." Graduates motivate freshmen to hold themselves to Ashesi's high ethical standards.

Graduates also explore the factors that help them handle ethically challenging situations. Our early alumni tended to quit a job when they encountered corruption. This preserved their personal integrity but did little to improve the workplaces they left. In response, we encourage graduates to share techniques for finding ethical allies at work, and to confide in fellow graduates or mentors. Together, current students and graduates brainstorm ways to resolve ethically fraught situations through finding mutually shared values. For example, a graduate might appeal to a senior manager's long-term desire to retain customers or avoid bad publicity, rather than seek short-term gains from questionable practices. Students create skits to practice possible approaches to moral dilemmas.

Africa Needs Diverse Voices at the Leadership Table

Our students and graduates want to be more ethical than the world they grew up in. But often they don't yet see themselves as leaders. We remind them that Africa needs ethical, entrepreneurial leaders, not just in government but also in engineering, business, and finance, and in our communities.

It's critical that our students learn that leadership is service, not entitlement. To this end, we weave community service into our curriculum. For some students, this is their first immersion into impoverished communities. For others, it is a chance to return to communities they know well and create change. For example, four Ashesi students grew up in a poor area where the public water pumps had been broken for years. They weren't engineers, but they took the initiative to raise money, recruit help, and bring clean water to a school in their own neighborhood. Service projects develop confidence and inspire a commitment to the greater good.

Preparing Women, Minorities, and the Poor for Leadership

Only 6 percent of youth in sub-Saharan Africa attend college. By definition, this 6 percent will become Africa's future leaders. Transforming how this small cohort thinks and acts can have huge benefits. If Africa is to experience inclusive economic growth, we must recruit more women, minorities, and the poor to our universities. We need their perspectives to help shape Africa's future products, policies, and infrastructure.

It takes commitment to ensure diversity. We've raised the percentage of female students from 27 percent to 48 percent by engaging more effectively with girls in high schools. In every Ashesi class, faculty help ensure that women students develop the confidence to speak up, and that all students treat each other with respect. We are committed to gender parity in engineering. The women on our faculty, for example, Ayorkor Korsah, reach out to young women, telling them that "to be an engineer is to be a creator, and it impacts a lot of people when you create the technology that powers our lives." To feed the pipeline of young Africans in technology fields, Ashesi holds an annual summer workshop for equal numbers of high school boys and girls; both genders excel in lively technology and entrepreneurship activities, under the mentorship of Ashesi students.

Mixing students from greatly varied economic, religious, ethnic, and national backgrounds helps develop a more inclusive vanguard of future leaders. Thanks to the MasterCard Foundation and other partners that share this vision, Ashesi can afford to recruit and offer scholarships to students from diverse low-income communities across Africa.

Homegrown Entrepreneurs and Innovators

Ashesi students and graduates want to be entrepreneurial—to earn money through hard work and innovation rather than through connections and corruption. We teach them that entrepreneurial talent is not an isolated quality but is intertwined with innovation and ethics. All three qualities reinforce each other, and all three require courage and skill.

Africa urgently needs more innovators and entrepreneurs. Our population is forecast to double by 2050, yet much of Africa's infrastructure is inadequate even for today's citizens. If we rely only on existing strategies, we will not meet our growing demand in an environmentally sustainable manner. The size of this gap can be daunting. However, when we look at this challenge through an innovator's eyes, we realize that most of the infrastructure Africa needs has yet to be designed, funded, or built. There are vast opportunities to create new, better solutions.

Ashesi graduates are excited by Africa's mix of challenges and opportunities. They are eager to create products designed specifically for our diverse communities, develop more inclusive financial services to help ordinary Africans afford a better quality of life, and test new distribution methods to deliver services the last, difficult mile to rural citizens.

In the next decades, hundreds of millions of Africans will reach working age and will need jobs. With sufficient economic opportunity, this demographic bulge of Africans of working age will be a source of general prosperity; without opportunity, it may fuel mass emigration and conflict. No single solution will improve Africa's entrepreneurial ecosystem enough to create sufficient employment. Young Africans will have to persist in many creative ways to address gaps in the legal, civil, financial, and human resources of our countries.

The world outside of Africa cannot be the sole driver of the innovation and entrepreneurship that Africa needs. New products, even if developed in the West, must be adapted and improved. Infrastructure must be maintained, updated, and extended. Unless every global organization working in Africa intends to stay forever, much of Africa's ongoing progress will have to be African-led. And unless wealthy nations intend to subsidize Africa indefinitely, many of tomorrow's solutions will have to be delivered through entrepreneurial, financially sustainable, homegrown channels.

Mindset and Mastery

Visit most African cities and you may see plenty of initiative and inventiveness among the children, as they transform junk into toys and hustle to sell goods. Unfortunately, one unintended consequence of the traditional African educational model is to teach students to devalue their own sense of initiative. Students become more risk-averse. Teachers reward pupils for memorization, not exploration. Some teachers still cane children who give a wrong answer, so that making a mistake is painful and humiliating. Poorly funded schools often have neither computers nor labs for hands-on learning, and when they do, they often allow only step-by-step, carefully prescribed use, because teachers have had little or no training themselves with the tools and often fear that students might break the expensive equipment. Sadly, some Ghanaian academics don't believe their students will ever become innovators. When we designed the Ashesi curriculum in computer science, we were quietly advised not to expect our students to advance much beyond workmanlike programming skills.

We do not accept this limitation. Nearly all Ashesi students long to create something new, but like incoming college first-year students anywhere, they don't know how to begin. One way we jump-start students' transition from passive note-takers to creators is to plunge all freshmen into our Foundations of Design and Entrepreneurship (FDE)[4] class. In this yearlong workshop, freshmen teams learn to apply design thinking to everyday local challenges, then launch and run start-ups. They are thrown quickly into a world with no right answer. Visiting an FDE class, you will hear excitement and confusion as teams, seated around a worktable, learn to brainstorm ideas and figure out the necessary steps to bring those ideas to life. Students are challenged to try something that may or may not work. They learn responsibility to their team members, to manage money, and to correct course as needed. For the first time, students learn that failure is not a source of shame, but rather a chance to learn and try again.

We strive to foster an entrepreneurial mindset across our entire curriculum. In seminars, students debate both sides of issues, reinforcing the idea that there is no one right answer. They are challenged to look for connections between seemingly unrelated topics, which encourages creative insights. Discussions around ethics, as well as visits from entrepreneurial graduates, build motivation to persist in the face of difficulty.

Confidence Comes from Preparation

However, projects and discussions are not enough. Ashesi also challenges students to understand the foundational concepts in their fields. Mastering concepts provides a base from which to deconstruct problems and create something new. For example, computer science majors don't just learn the latest programming languages. They study calculus, statistics, and algorithms to prepare themselves for lifelong learning and new explorations. To prepare young Africans to be modern, world-class innovators and entrepreneurs requires more than a few months in a business incubator. Our students grow throughout their four-year immersion at Ashesi, which starts them on a lifelong journey.

"When my software development team at work was cut in half, Ashesi prepared me to persist and continue to lead," says Ashesi graduate David Darkwa. "I encouraged my team to believe we could still succeed in creating West Africa's first cardless ATM technology. We met our goal, and now citizens without a bank account can still leverage the banking system to safely access their money." The system David's team created is being used by multiple banks across West Africa, offering potential benefits to millions of people who have no other access to the formal banking sector. "We are proud that it was created by Africans." David warns students against blind confidence, "We must try, fail early, correct. Confidence comes from intensive preparation."

At Ashesi, we teach that innovation requires mastery and hard work, as well as creativity. In their internships, community service, and senior projects, students are often humbled by the complexity of the real-world problems they hope to address. We encourage them to recruit younger students to their teams, seek out local partners, and persist over several years.

What's Next?

Looking backward, we cannot prove how many of Africa's problems might have been mitigated with better leadership. But looking forward, Ashesi has demonstrated that young Africans can learn to approach challenges with greater courage and skill and be more effective. Now, we plan to broaden our impact across the continent.

Growth and Excellence

Over sixteen years, the Ashesi student body has grown from thirty students to just under 900, with plans to reach 1,200. From our earliest years, a few global organizations have urged us to grow much more quickly, and also to save money by dramatically increasing class size. However, our priority has been to grow carefully, while strengthening our unique campus culture. We recruit more students only when we can add the facilities and faculty to accommodate them. We weigh every proposed change against our commitment to providing an immersive, transformative education. Our future plans include investing more deeply in faculty and staff development. And as we grow, we will continue our commitment to diversity, which requires us to continually strengthen our scholarship programs.

A Widening Circle of Influence

Change is coming to African higher education. Across the continent, a few pioneering universities are moving away from the traditional African educational model of rote learning and are exploring diverse ways to better educate Africa's next generation. Ashesi's Education Collaborative, launched in 2017, brings together university leaders and stakeholders from across Africa to share best practices. We learn from each other, and universities wishing to adapt elements of the Ashesi model into their own curriculum have our full support.

A few universities and high schools in Ghana have begun to carefully launch honor codes like Ashesi's. And the Ghanaian National Accreditation Board, which once perceived Ashesi's core curriculum and community service requirement as "a waste of students' time," has evolved its views. The board now asks other Ghanaian universities to add general studies classes and community service to their curriculums to foster critical thinking skills.

Growing Graduate Impact
As Ashesi becomes more pan-African, our influence spreads. Our international students come from over twenty countries; when they graduate, they return home to launch their careers. By 2020, there will be 2,000 Ashesi graduates across the continent who are working to strengthen Africa's private sector, bring more efficiency and transparency to nonprofit organizations, and improve civil society.

What We Ask the Global Community to Consider

Be Ethical
Some international nongovernmental organizations (INGOs), driven by a sense of urgency, pay bribes. This emboldens bribe seekers to harass the next INGO and further victimize local citizens. Paying bribes is not harmless. When you give local gatekeepers a bit of "dash," you help sustain a corrupt machine that uses those funds to keep itself alive.

How can you avoid paying bribes? At Ashesi, we publicize our zero-tolerance rules. Those on our staff rarely pay cash and must receive detailed receipts when they do. Bribe seekers soon realize that every individual Ashesi employee is backed by the entire Ashesi organization, with a consistent ethical stance. We also invite each person we interact with to be their best self, and to join us in helping create a better, shared future for Africa. We remind bribe seekers that Ashesi is a not-for-profit university, that we offer scholarships to many poor students, and we invite their ethical support. Sometimes this works.

There is also a difference between rewarding cooperation and yielding to obstruction. One Ashesi graduate worked to dramatically speed up cargo handling at Ghana's largest port. Instead of continuing the practice of bribing port workers, he helped his company reward efficient cargo handling with a transparent, predictable pay table.

If all else fails, every organization has one surefire method to avoid paying a bribe. Walk away. Take your project elsewhere. After we spent three years struggling to raise the funds to build a new Ashesi campus, we faced unethical demands. After months of refusals, we reluctantly planned to return every donation to our global supporters. We would stay in our crowded, makeshift, rented quarters. Ultimately, our refusal to yield was respected. We built our beautiful campus, proudly using African architects and contractors. They completed the project on time, on budget, and without paying a single bribe.

Paying bribes is like littering. It may seem minor, but it adds up to a wasteland. Is this the legacy your organization wants to leave behind?

Look Beyond Poverty Reduction to Broader Economic Progress

Global organizations often focus on reaching large numbers of people in poverty. However, poverty reduction will not by itself transform and modernize the economies of African nations. To do that, we must better educate, broaden, and retain our middle classes. Africa needs homegrown professionals, engineers, and entrepreneurs who are highly capable and ethical. We need a leadership cohort that includes both talented students from families of relative privilege, as well as women, minorities, and the poor. We need students from economically successful families to eschew entitlement and narrow self-interest, and for their peers from marginalized communities to develop courage and confidence. When young Africans from diverse backgrounds work together and form lifelong bonds, nations benefit. "Together at Ashesi," said one graduate, the daughter of a seamstress who worked in a roadside stall, "we develop a radar to notice problems, and a restless desire to solve them."

It is difficult to measure the long-term impact of a project to develop future leaders. How can we calibrate the value of ethical courage and innovative thinking? By some metrics, Ashesi is still a small institution. But Ashesi is changing the conversation about higher education in Africa, and our impact is spreading well beyond our campus.

Be Sustainable, Which Will Force You to Align Your Mission with Local Aspirations

Sometimes donors are blinded by their own enthusiasms and miss seeing cues that the community they hope to serve is only warily interested in their project. Project designers don't always ask if citizens are motivated to embrace their proposed new resource. Will the project solve a problem the community cares about? Will the benefits be enough to overcome the extra expense, effort, or hassle that comes from learning to do things in a new way?

In one village in Ghana's Eastern Region, when the well installed by a nonprofit stopped functioning, the local citizens went back to drinking from the nearby *E. coli*–infested stream. When workers from a new NGO arrived to help address the village's sanitation needs, they were met with cynicism and resistance. The broken well was not the core problem. The bigger challenge was that the community had never been convinced that the infested stream, which didn't look particularly dirty, was connected to infant ill-nesses. They did not yet view their new well as worth the effort to repair. When community members were given the chance to look at samples of their stream water through a microscope, they saw "disease" in the form of wiggling microorganisms, which changed their mindset.

In the late 1990s, I believed that Ghana urgently needed an alternative to our overcrowded public universities with their emphasis on rote learning. However, just because I could envision strong advantages to a new kind of African university did not mean that Ghanaian families would necessarily embrace Ashesi as a valuable alternative. To test local attitudes, we inter-viewed parents from Ghana's striving middle class. We probed their inter-est in the Ashesi model, and their potential willingness to pay tuition that was steep by local standards. We also interviewed business leaders, asking, "Are there employee qualities your business needs that are hard to find?" Employers told us they could not hire enough trustworthy employees who showed initiative, and who had strong leadership and communication skills. They needed the very qualities we planned to nurture. If we could prepare graduates to help African businesses grow, a positive activity in job-starved Africa, those graduates would embark on worthwhile careers, which would in turn motivate more families to invest in an Ashesi education. We had found the intersection between the Ashesi mission and local aspirations.

Despite our commitment to financial sustainability, we knew it would take years to fill our pipeline with enough tuition-paying students to cover operating costs. Until then, we would need subsidies. And we could never set tuition so high as to pay for our significant first-year start-up expenses because that would have put Ashesi out of reach of almost all families.

Fund-raising was extremely hard. Every established foundation we applied to turned us down. Consequently, we relied on a small community of individual supporters who were willing to take a chance on Ashesi's unproven model. We kept expenses low, paying Western and African staff on the same Ghanaian salary scale, which avoided expensive expat premiums and incidentally forged an atmosphere of fairness and respect. Nonetheless, Ashesi nearly closed for lack of funds. We temporarily shuttered our US fund-raising office in order to focus all our energy and limited funds on pro-viding a transformative education for our students. When 100 percent of our first graduating class quickly found quality placement, Ashesi's reputation began to rise, and our finances improved.

Finally, in 2008, after six challenging years, Ashesi achieved financial sustainability: tuition from students who can afford to pay covers annual operating costs, even as we offer scholarships to low-income students. We are proud to show the world that an African institution can sustain itself without constant infusions of donations. Donors propel us forward with their contributions, while Ashesi is able to cover day-to-day expenses. Like most US universities, we rely on donors to fund construction of new buildings, subsidize the development of new programs, and fund much of our financial aid.

Not every project in Africa can realistically achieve sustainability. However, challenging ourselves to rely on earned income from African families has kept us closely attuned to the aspirations of Ghanaian families and the needs of African businesses. If every project in Africa were based on a deeply researched understanding of local priorities and attitudes, perhaps we would see fewer misfires. If global organizations would involve local citizens at the beginning of their project design cycle, rather than recruiting Africans only to help deploy the "finished" model, we might co-create more successful products. Involving African partners from the beginning has many benefits: these partners become project advocates and understand the technologies involved. Sustainable projects in the community rely on a viable financial model, sufficient skills, and a clear motivation.

Look for Islands of Excellence, and Help Them Spread

Not every project needs to be born in a Western university, lab, or corporation. Africans themselves have begun to address local challenges and develop new opportunities. These homegrown islands of excellence engender African pride and deserve global support. There is value in ordinary Africans learning to see themselves as capable of solving problems. As one Ashesi graduate said, "I'm not waiting for some superman to fix things. If Africa is to have a better future, it's up to me." Sometimes, global organizations might do more lasting good if, rather than directly addressing a local challenge, they instead helped Africans to take the lead in solving it for themselves.

There are many ways the global community can help foster progress. We welcome partners, mentors, teachers, and codevelopers. At Ashesi, we are grateful to the forward-thinking universities and institutes that contributed to our curriculum, and to the funders who support our growth. Global capital can finance infrastructure and help promising African projects grow. We ask only that partners reinforce the nascent belief in young Africans that they, themselves, must take an active role in moving Africa forward. Outside aid and technology can be helpful but must seek to supplement, not replace, homegrown leaders, innovators, and entrepreneurs.

Without courage, the forces of inertia will win. With courage and skill, sustained progress is within our reach.

Notes

1. Ashesi University's original curriculum was developed with generous pro bono support from faculty at Swarthmore College, the University of Washington, and the University of California–Berkeley.

2. Ashesi University's engineering program was shaped by input from the faculty at the University of Waterloo, Olin College, Swarthmore College, Miami University of Ohio, Dartmouth College, Case Western Reserve University, and Arizona State University, as well as from engineering professionals and faculty from across Ghana.

3. The program "Giving Voice to Values" was developed by Dr. Mary Gentile and launched by the Aspen Institute and Yale School of Management and is now based at the University of Virginia Darden School of Business (with interim support at Babson College).

4. This Ashesi course, Foundations of Design and Entrepreneurship, was developed with support from Babson College and Northwestern University's Farley Center for Entrepreneurship and Innovation.

8

Environmentally Conscious Development

Tundi Agardy

The concept of sustainable development is rooted in the union of environmental conservation and economic development. It connects the science of ecology, the politics of economy, and the ethics of society. Our quality of life and that of our families and communities depends upon the availability of the natural resources we need to survive and thrive, and also upon our access to these resources. Environmental concerns and the management of the planet's natural resources are not divorced from our everyday well-being. The methods and language of natural science may feel distant and even alien to some, but strengthening the interface between science, society, and policy is critical for lasting development. In this chapter, I delve into these connections, and into some of the environmental and ethical concerns raised by these connections, by focusing on our planet's largest ecosystem: oceans.

Oceans cover about 71 percent of the earth, are estimated to be home to about 80 percent of all living organisms, and are critical for global and national economic and social well-being. More than 40 percent of the world's population lives within 100 kilometers (about 62 miles) of a sea or ocean. Even landlocked nations are connected to oceans and seas through rivers and streams. The world is increasingly looking to the sea for drinking water, energy, food, and strategic minerals, alongside important nonextractive uses. How this bodes for humanity's—and the planet's—future is open to question, as the global population is expected to reach about 9 billion by 2050, and attendant demands for food and energy will be nearly double what they are as I write this in 2018. Underdeveloped parts of the world are on trajectories to intensify their economic development, while developed countries continue to consume at per capita levels more than ten times those of the poorest countries. Intense conflicts over scarce surface water and aquifer water resources have already started, and the spectacular growth of energy-demanding desalination in response to water scarcity threatens access to and availability of seafood resources. At the same time, offshore energy development displaces fishers from productive fishing grounds, and catastrophic oil spills harm or even shut down fisheries.

To date, siloed thinking about how to plan economic development that allows for effective protection of the resource base, including management of marine resources and ecosystems delivering vital services, has resulted in uncoordinated fisheries, energy, mining, and marine-use policies that do not allow the consideration of trade-offs and do not capitalize on the synergies that taking a nexus approach would provide (Agardy 2017). At the same time, the allure of the "blue economy" may be pushing development of oceans even more quickly toward short-term gain and long-term unsustainability. A recent paper describes two competing discourses about oceans: one as areas of opportunity, growth, and development, and the other, of threatened and vulnerable spaces in need of protection (Voyer et al. 2018).

This chapter rests on the certainty that a sound environment is the foundation for sustained human well-being—that without attention to development-related environmental degradation, decreases in poverty and increases in both individual revenues and GDP that result from development can only be temporary. And although the connections between marine environmental health and biodiversity, productivity, water quality, or human well-being have only recently been quantified (Agardy and Alder 2005), the coastal case does provide insight on the environment-and-well-being link in clear and compelling ways (Agardy 2017). I begin with a historic look at how the concept of sustainability has been applied to the coastal and marine context, anecdotally appraise the current situation, and peer into the future as economic development in the marine arena goes full steam ahead.

A Historical Perspective on Environmentally Conscious Development

Admittedly I am neither historian nor development expert, but from my perspective as a conservationist and planner, the status of the environment as a central consideration in development has historically waxed and waned. Simplistically speaking, the focus on environment seems to have occurred in three phases: (1) an initial awakening to anthropogenic environmental degradation caused by population growth and infrastructure development; (2) a realization that in addition to the negative impacts of large-scale infrastructure (dams, roads, factories), consumption patterns also influence the environment negatively and undercut opportunities for sustainability; and (3) a recent and growing recognition that natural ecosystems are linked to human well-being through the provision of ecosystem services (the benefits people obtain from ecosystems). Thus did the Brundtland Commission's 1987 report, among other initiatives, steer the world toward thinking not only of how to achieve sustained economic growth but also at the same time long-term social and environmental sustainability. The term "sustainability" emerged to capture the idea that bettering the human condition today should not compromise opportunities for betterment in future generations (Katona et al. 2017).

In light of this new demand to think to the future, development agencies began considering how development, and in particular large-scale infrastructure development, could negatively affect natural systems and their ability to deliver the goods and services needed for humankind to survive into the future. Reform of the Bretton Woods institutions, especially the World Bank, was led by activist nongovernmental organizations (NGOs) in the United States and supported by the US Congress (Bowles and Kormos 1999). Environmental concerns and their importance for human communities largely took a back seat during the global growth period of the 1980s but reemerged in force in the 1990s. World Bank reform continued, and other development banks and financing institutions began to show more environmental accountability in projects focused on economic development and poverty alleviation.

However, the focus on the possible environmental impacts of development was not confined to large-scale infrastructure. The Millennium Ecosystem Assessment (2005) recognized consumption as another driver of environmental degradation. In this phase of environmentally minded development, multilateral financial institutions began to appraise large-scale infrastructure investment more carefully and also began to analyze how resource-use policies and subsidies could cause equally significant damage to ecosystems. Recent investigations continue to track natural capital drawdown and human consumption, pointing to glaring inequities between developed and developing countries (Balatsky, Balatsky, and Borysov 2015) and also to alarming trends in resource use beyond sustainable limits and in resource waste.

Following the realization that consumption patterns needed to be evaluated alongside infrastructure development in order to understand the negative impacts of development on the natural resource base that sustains life—and hence the prospects for sustainability—academics, conservationists, planners, and financial institutions created a new focus on the nexus of environment and development, in which the environment was seen less as a casualty of economic growth and more as an engine of sustained human well-being. This attention to the environment-and-human-well-being link-age continues to this day, as the numerous benefits that nature provides us (collectively termed ecosystem services) are being assessed, quantified, and described for their economic and social values.

These phases of environmental considerations in the development field unfolded in the arena of oceans and coasts as well, albeit more slowly and with less fanfare. Thus, one might say that although development had undergone a rapid transformation in the twenty years following the UN Conference on Environment and Development (UNCED), held in Rio in 1992, the importance of understanding the limits to growth of marine and coastal economic sectors was slow to take hold. Enlightenment about sustainability in the marine realm emerged almost prematurely in 1951, when Rachel Carson published *The Sea Around Us,* but after that, such concern lay largely dormant. Nonetheless, the issue of how consumption (and the development agencies' enabling of ever-increasing consumption) could undermine coastal and marine ecosystem health received little attention. But by Rio+20, when the focus was all on the green economy and how development could improve human lives without compromising the environment, an opportunity emerged to extend this paradigm of the three pillars of sustainable growth (economic, social, and environmental) to marine resources and maritime industries as well. Thus, the concept of blue growth emerged (Howard 2018). Michelle Voyer et al. (2018, based on analysis by Silver et al. 2015) describe the way four potentially competing perceptions of marine development were in evidence at Rio+20: (1) oceans as natural capital, (2) oceans as good business, (3) oceans as integral to human well-being in Small Island Developing States (SIDS), and (4) oceans as small-scale fisheries livelihoods.

Yet it seems odd that concerns about how development affects coastal and marine ecosystems have only recently reached a level similar to that for terrestrial ecosystems. This belated concern is odd because coastal areas the world over have been the focus of much development, as these portions of the planet are where human populations are most densely concentrated and where population growth rates are highest (Agardy and Alder 2005). Many coastal areas also serve as the gateways to inland cities, agricultural lands, and industrial areas and, at the same time, serve as launching points for maritime trade. And though we do not live in the sea, much coastal development involves the building of infrastructure that causes losses of important coastal habitat or impairs the functioning of environmental systems. The sustainability of such development has only recently been called into question (e.g., Gelpke and Visbeck 2015, van Bochove, Sullivan, and Nakamura 2014). At the same time, consumption may be an even more insidious driver of biodiversity loss and environmental degradation in coastal areas than in other regions (Creel 2003), because the favorable attributes of coastal land attract high-income communities whose residents expend significantly more energy, rely on expensive imported products, and often deny others access to coastal shores and resources. As newcomers move in and the cost of living goes up in such developed coastal places, residents may become caught in a poverty cycle that drives them to overexploit the resources they do have access to, causing further ecological impairment (see Figure 8.1).

On the ecosystem services front, the well-being of coastal communities, as well as the economic prospects of coastal nations, has been directly attributed to thriving coastal ecosystems and intact biodiversity of coastal and marine systems. Anecdotal examples of how biodiversity loss and environmental degradation inhibit development have been accumulating, and now systematic assessments of the valuable benefits that natural capital provides are being undertaken at all spatial scales. Most notable is the work of the Intergovernmental Panel on Biodiversity and Ecosystem Services (IPBES), which has attracted the interest of development banks, governments, businesses, and communities alike. Robert Watson, chairman of IPBES, recently declared, "Biodiversity loss is not a conservation issue, it is a development issue" (NPR 2018). Maria Damaki, former European

Figure 8.1   The Link Between Coastal Degradation and Human Well-Being

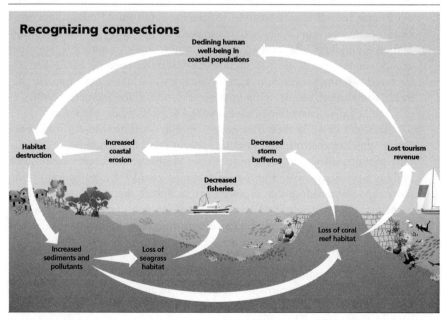

Courtesy of Tracey Saxby, Integration and Application Network, University of Maryland Center for Environmental Science, 2016.

Union commissioner of fisheries and maritime affairs and now marine policy director at The Nature Conservancy, said, "Billions of people depend on the ocean for their livelihoods, and that demand will rise as the world population grows and concentrates in urban centers near coasts. Sustained blue growth is needed to meet this demand" (Howard 2018, p. 376).

Although Carson long ago drew attention to how human fate and ocean health were inexorably intertwined in her prescient book, and despite various press-getting statements and summits in the many years since, the costs of damaging the coastal environment are still not widely understood by society or accepted by decision makers. Anecdotal evidence of the slippery slope that results from careless development—including increasing vulnerabilities to natural disasters, declining opportunities for livelihood expansion through tourism or value-added marine commodities, and greatly decreasing food security—has brought short-lived alarm, all too soon forgotten.

Sustainable Development in the Coastal and Marine Realm Today

There is both good news and bad news concerning the sustainability of development in coastal areas around the world today. The good news is that there has been significant, sustained demand for transparency and accountability among the multilateral development banks and, to some extent, the bilateral aid agencies. Monitoring lending programs and their social and environmental outcomes has led to clearer appraisal of effectiveness as classification systems and standards make data gathering easier, and information technology makes ever-more-complex analysis possible. Another aspect on the positive side is that NGOs have become more heavily involved—acting as watchdogs, calling out unsustainable development, but equally important, also training government institutions and communities to manage negative environmental and social impacts of development.

The bad news is that it is never enough—and the opportunities for human greed and corruption to outmaneuver careful management for long-term sustainability only seem to increase. Multilateral agencies want quick and high-profile results, and they sometimes avoid the kind of long-term, slow capacity building that is necessary to ensure that development decisions and policies do not undercut the environment, or the people whose lives depend on it very directly. Development aid can funnel to places perceived as potential success stories, in some cases creating too much of a good thing. The case of Mafia Island, Tanzania, offers a powerful example of how success can undercut sustainability (see Box 8.1). And generally speaking, development remains sector-specific and siloed, constraining the type of ecosystem-based management that could ensure a durable resource base and value-providing environment.

Box 8.1 Reflections on the Case of Mafia Island, Tanzania

Although less well known than Zanzibar, its Indian Ocean neighbor to the north, Mafia Island, Tanzania, has similar diverse and beautiful coral reefs, lowland jungle, and ancient ruins that support the four small villages on this remote and underdeveloped island, as well as serving to attract intrepid adventure tourists to its shores. In the mid-1990s, community members became concerned about outsiders dynamite fishing throughout their reef areas, and they contacted their member of parliament (MP) and sought the help of World Wildlife Fund (WWF) Tanzania.

After a series of stakeholder consultations that began in 1990, plans for the Mafia Island Marine Park (MIMP) emerged from a consensus of all interested and affected parties (including women fisher-gatherers who were reticent to attend meetings in this Muslim society). The communities had collectively defined the problems they faced, articulated a vision for how to deal with those problems, and created a community-based marine protected area that would safeguard their environment and their livelihoods. The goal of the MIMP is to ensure that "the ecological and economic sustainability of Tanzania's coastal and marine ecosystems is improved and maintained."

This process took several years, despite the fact that the communities were on board and good information existed on the ecology (especially because a United Kingdom eco-volunteer company, Frontier-Tanzania, had amassed a lot of information that made it possible to map the coral reefs and determine the location of the most ecologically important places). There was also sufficient political will to help Mafia Island achieve sustainable development. The park had the support not only of the Mafia Island MP, but also of renowned, high-profile marine scientists such as Magnus Ngoile, an international conservation luminary who headed the Institute of Marine Resources at that time. One hurdle that needed a significant investment of time was the fact that the Republic of Tanzania did not have any legislation in place to make marine-park implementation possible. Therefore, the WWF hired a legal expert to help Tanzania craft the necessary marine-park legislation, the Marine Reserves Act of 1995, and get it through parliament.

Then Mafia Island became a symbol of successful public-private partnerships, of the catalyzing effect of environmental NGOs, and of the importance of champions to drive sustainable policies and attract

continues

Box 8.1 continued

funding support. Development agencies began to fund restoration of reefs (that had been destroyed both by blast fishing and also by removal of coral for building material), market diversification of fisheries to create more stable revenue streams, ecotourism, and other projects. Investing in Mafia Island was suddenly seen as a win-win. The tidal wave of interest generated an influx of vast amounts of development aid, which unleashed social strife and attracted external players interested in capitalizing on the investment interest.

Mafia Island recovered from that temporary instability, but observers have commented that the ecotourism catalyzed by development aid amounts to an asset grab, in which capital accumulation by the most powerful actors takes place (e.g., Benjaminsen and Bryceson 2012). And the goal of the MIMP is again at risk as East African countries commit to an intensive blue-growth agenda that includes large-scale commercial fisheries, minerals, oil and gas, and other exploitation.

Multilateral Banks and International Aid Agencies

The environmental performance of international financial institutions and development-aid agencies has certainly improved since the time of the Brundtland Commission in the 1980s. By this I mean the consideration of environmental factors in planning development-aid interventions, as well as the eventual environmental outcomes of aid, and the commitment to rigorous monitoring of economic, social, and environmental outcomes of development. Our ability to appraise this has improved as well, as the Bretton Woods institutions and regional development banks have increased transparency.

It may surprise some to discover that multilateral environmental aid is a highly concentrated sector with the vast majority of such assistance coming from just five agencies: the World Bank, the Asian Development Bank, the Inter-American Development Bank, the European Union's aid institution, and the Global Environment Facility (GEF). The World Bank alone provided $38 billion in environmental aid over the 1980s and 1990s, plus nearly $3 billion of GEF funding administered by the bank (Roberts et al. 2009). However, direct environmental aid is only one side of the economic-social-environmental nexus of development. The murkier side is nonenvironmental assistance, and there are questions about the extent to which environmental degradation and loss of ecosystem values are truly minimized when economic development occurs.

Thus it is that the world repeatedly reacts with surprise and shock to reports such as the World Bank's *The Sunken Billions: The Economic Justification for Fisheries Reform* (Willmann, Kelleher, and Arnason 2009). This report showed that billions of dollars' worth of potential net economic benefits from marine fisheries are lost every year because of poor fisheries management—including overfishing and overcapitalization, which are often fostered by aid and perverse government subsidies. In regard to overfishing, depleted fish stocks mean fewer fish, so the cost of catching is higher. As for overcapitalization, simply put, more fleets and fishers are equipped, resulting in "too many fishers chasing too few fish," which also reduces economic benefits (Willmann, Kelleher, and Arnason 2009, p. xix). Yet the world retreated into its stupor and was surprised again in 2017 when the World Bank published *The Sunken Billions Revisited: Progress and Challenges in Global Marine Fisheries,* which showed that for global fisheries as a whole, nearly $83 billion was foregone in 2012, compared to a more optimal scenario, largely because of continued overfishing, much of it catalyzed by sector-specific development aid, not environmental assistance (World Bank 2017a). Therefore, it is important to know how the outcomes of development aid for infrastructure and services can be directly contrary to environmental assistance that seeks environmental and social sustainability.

One relatively recent mechanism for tracking such outcomes is the Project-Level Aid (PLAID) database (Roberts et al. 2009). This database corrects misleading sector coding by development agencies by categorizing development projects based on their published project titles and descriptions to give a clearer picture of donor agencies' actual spending patterns and priorities (Roberts et al. 2009). This is something that was called for as early as 1995 (Bowles and Kormos 1995), because, for example, sustainable forestry and selective logging projects could receive the same donor sector code as clear-cutting and deforestation projects (Roberts et al. 2009). Each project in the PLAID database is classified according to whether it would likely have a positive, negative, or negligible impact on the natural environment (see Box 8.2). Also, environment projects are divided into two types—green, which address global issues such as climate change, and brown, which address local environment problems such as water pollution.

The Role of NGOs and Academia

Not all development assistance is in the domain of bilateral development agencies and multilateral financial institutions. Increasingly, some NGOs are trying to help steer development projects in a socially and environmentally sustainable direction, not only at the local level but sometimes even at the regional level. NGOs have been involved in: (1) raising public awareness, practicing advocacy, and pushing for policy reform for environmentally responsible development; (2) setting priorities at the regional or even global

---

Box 8.2 Project-Level Aid (PLAID) Categories

- *Environmental Strictly Defined* projects have an immediate positive impact on the environment with clear, measurable goals and criteria for success. Examples include biodiversity protection, renewable energy, soil conservation, watershed protection, reforestation, access to clean water, and air pollution mitigation.
- *Environmental Broadly Defined* projects include those that have less definable, longer-range environmental effects than the Environmental Strictly Defined projects have or are preventative in nature. Examples include energy efficiency, industrial reforestation, family planning, desalinization, and genetic-diversity projects.
- *Neutral* projects include those projects that have no immediate or direct environmental impact and projects with positive and negative effects that roughly balance out or are minimally damaging. Examples include projects designed to fund health, education, telecommunications, disaster relief, free-trade promotion, balance-of-payments support, small- and medium-enterprise assistance, or export promotion.
- *Dirty Broadly Defined* projects are those that have a moderate or long-term negative impact on the environment, including agriculture (not including erosion control), biotechnology, electricity generation and distribution, engineering, forestry, hydroelectric power, and mass-transportation projects.
- *Dirty Strictly Defined* projects may strip the environment of irreplaceable natural resources, as in the case of extractive industries (such as mining or logging), or those that severely pollute or degrade the environment, with immediate measurable negative impacts; examples include road and air transport as well as heavy industry (such as fertilizer, tire, and brick-making factories).

—from Roberts et al. 2009

---

scale; (3) performing monitoring and surveillance, and acting as watchdogs or whistleblowers when development is unsustainable; (4) bridging the chasm between science and management; (5) building capacity of local institutions to manage impacts on the coastal and marine environment; (6) channeling financial resources to institutions undertaking environmental protection and marine management; and (7) creating demonstration models of sustainable development in the marine realm (Agardy 2011).

One important role that NGOs have in changing the economic development paradigm from growth at any cost to growth that maintains, or even enhances, social and environmental benefits is in assessing and valuing ecosystem services, conducting trade-off analysis and scenarios, and structuring and launching sustainable financing. Concerning the latter, there has been a dramatic rise in payments for ecosystem services (PES), in which communities that have the ability to manage impacts on natural systems—and thereby maintain their delivery of ecosystem services—are paid for their trouble by industries or individuals who benefit from such services. PES schemes are most common in forest and freshwater ecosystems, but Forest Trends and other NGOs have been pushing the application of this sort of sustainable financing to estuarine, coastal, and even ocean environments.

Fundamental to PES and other innovative financing is a more sophisticated and robust understanding of the myriad ways nature benefits humans, and the translation of that knowledge into economic valuations that can draw attention to why it makes sense to protect natural capital. But there is ample evidence that valuations of ecosystem services often do not find their way into policy or decision making. The World Resources Institute (WRI), for instance, published a study showing that most ecosystem services assessments were not being used in the Caribbean (Burke, Ranganathan, and Winterbottom 2015). WRI's insightful and honest assessment of how economic valuation information has been used in marine and coastal policy decisions throughout the Caribbean hints that much information about ecosystem services remains stuck in the realm of science and conservation. This is not new, of course—the Millennium Ecosystem Assessment and the preceding Pilot Assessment of Global Ecosystems devoted significant effort to describing ecosystem services in ways that it was hoped would resonate with decision makers and the public. But neither succeeded to the degree the conservation community would have liked. Language remains an issue, as does scientific uncertainty about delivery of ecosystem services in changing environmental conditions. However, there are demonstrable ways to promote better uptake of information on ecosystem services, their worth to society, and the necessity of protecting our valued natural capital.

Valuations can raise awareness, inform planning, and generate the political will to take concrete steps to protect ecosystems and maintain delivery of ecosystem services. Yet suspicions remain about economic studies. When focused on a single ecosystem service (e.g., providing a particular commodity such as carbon, or a single regulating service such as protecting valuable coastal properties from storms), local communities can begin to fear that "their" ecosystems will be taken over by others profiting from the service. In the extreme, there are very real fears of asset or land grabs and privatization or other forms of exclusion that benefit the wealthy and powerful, while restricting access to local users. For this reason, economic valuations should be performed in the broadest possible way: across all ecosystem services and at the largest possible geographic scale. Furthermore, economic assessments should be complemented by valuations that also take nonmonetary values into account.

Rather than striving for absolute total values of the ecosystem services being generated from a site, it may be more effective to use the economic valuations to complement qualitative information on what matters to users. Valuations should be done in tandem, across all ecosystem services. This allows planners to identify relatively more valuable areas—information that can then be used in marine spatial planning, coastal planning, protected area siting and design, and trade-off analysis. Performing the broadest possible valuations and presenting the data in a way that can logically and easily be incorporated into planning and decision making will promote better uptake of ecosystem-services information.

Peering Toward the Future: The Dangerous Allure of Blue Growth

Despite advances in our understanding of what constitutes true sustainable development and advanced tools to secure all three pillars of green/blue growth, environmental and biodiversity considerations are still not mainstreamed into development policies or financing. This is especially true on the marine front, where a new push toward unlocking the potential of blue growth is often seen as a justification for wholesale resource plundering and also expanding large-scale commercial industries at the expense of the needs of coastal communities. Industrial fisheries have often proven to be largely unsustainable; yet international financial institutions and developed countries continue to overcapitalize industrial fisheries, to fund billions in government subsidies despite the vast profits businesses are making, and to resist the efforts of the UN Conference on Trade and Development (UNCTAD) and others to discuss perverse fisheries subsidies at the World Trade Organization (WTO). Continuing down this path preempts many small-scale, localized fisheries from becoming sustainable (Pauly 2018).

Development agencies would do well to invest their energy in trying to understand specific development needs and how certain marine management and conservation measures could resolve them. For instance, development agencies, alongside NGOs and academia, should further study what drives success in small-scale sustainable fisheries, in order to catalyze replication of carefully regulated (or self-regulated) fisheries alongside nature conservation. At the same time, development agencies should consider the broader context of governance and management when providing aid, for example, considering how development projects fit into marine spatial planning (MSP). MSP presents a dynamic system of rationalized use based on how people value the environment and can profit from its protection. When done well, MSP can draw in stakeholder groups in meaningful ways to co-create systems that will ensure that use today will not preempt use in the future. Thus, MSP and ocean zoning that has nature conservation at its core can bring other sectors into a carefully considered and participatory planning framework (Agardy 2010). It can thereby better assure that development projects will deliver intended outcomes.

Nonetheless, integrated marine and coastal planning, with the subsequent zoning and regulations on use that flow from it, is yet to be embraced as a key tool for steering coastal and marine development in a sustainable direction. This means that many countries are missing opportunities to use MSP to its full potential to promote sustainable use of ocean space and resources, while at the same time meeting social and conservation objectives. In the rush to promote blue growth, the focus in some places is on accommodating as many uses within the ocean space as possible. In such scenarios, MSP is used primarily to reduce conflict between big, industrial users. Effective MSP can do much more: it can sync with coastal planning to create truly effective ecosystem-based management, in which degradation of important ecosystems is prevented by focusing management on drivers of degradation (even if those drivers do not trace back to ocean use, but rather have their base in land and freshwater use). This sort of holistic planning also creates opportunities for transboundary collaborations to effectively manage shared marine resources. MSP and related ocean zoning can ensure that ecologically important areas are fully represented in a mosaic of use and protection. Finally, the planning process can ensure that the needs of local communities, and the safeguarding of values that extend beyond those captured by large maritime industries, are considered in decisions on how to allocate space and resources in an equitable way, while promoting economic growth.

As mentioned previously, the blue economy is getting much attention as ecosystem-services assessments emphasize the value of marine and coastal areas, and countries recognize that their marine resources are sometimes underutilized. Given the worldwide economic downturn, many coastal countries are now looking to "unlock the blue growth potential" in their maritime areas (e.g., Burgess et al. 2018) and using MSP to pack as many uses as possible into any given ocean space. Conservation is taking a back seat in many of these planning and policy initiatives; the consequence could well be both a lack of sustainability and a loss of traditional values.

The extent to which blue growth drives sustainable development varies around the world. In the Caribbean, MSP is used to defend traditional uses and to find ways to strengthen national and local economies, while still preserving traditional livelihoods and nonuse values. In southern Africa, the blue-growth agenda is just now unfolding, and conservationists have an opportunity to steer MSP in a more sustainable direction. In contrast, in the Mediterranean there is a clear tension between a European Union–led push to promote blue growth, on the one hand, and a regional push to practice ecosystem-based management, on the other hand, in which conservation is front and center and also traditional values are upheld. This calls into question whether MSP used for the purpose of blue growth should be supported, or whether the conservation and development communities need to take a more forceful stand about the role of conservation as the irrefutable base of all blue growth. In considering the competing discourses on the benefits of the blue economy, Voyer et al. (2018) suggests that careful contextualizing of blue growth, or marine development more generally, could prevent the privatization and neoliberalism that threaten community well-being in many parts of the globe.

To achieve long-term sustainable development using MSP and other tools, we need to get beyond the hubris of development experts who become infatuated with the next big thing. In the marine context, examples of this include throwing money at establishing coral nurseries to increase stock for transplantation onto damaged or degraded reefs, while the water quality remains so poor that transplanted corals cannot possibly survive; or declaring flashy, big marine protected areas that are made without consultation and then implemented without user buy-in. Better to invest in slowly but equitably designed marine spatial plans, such as the one that was developed in St. Kitts and Nevis, with the help of The Nature Conservancy and the financial support of aid agencies (Agostini et al. 2015).

Community engagement is necessary to ensure that sustainability limits are respected (Ayer et al. 2018), and to ensure that the benefits that flow from natural ocean capital—mostly from common-pool resources or commons-shared property—are shared equitably. However, communities that take on the burden of comanagement must be empowered to manage use of coastal and marine areas, with sufficient resources available to them for the long term. This is at odds with much development aid, which demands quick, positive results from investment in environmental protection. Thus we see a tendency, still, to invest development assistance in outputs, instead of in long-term outcomes. In a recent conversation we had on this subject, Marion Howard suggested that development agencies peddle "magic bullets" that too often in reality can just be putting old wine into new green- and blue-tinted bottles; that is, repackaging the economic growth model as blue growth or green growth that is still inequitable, externally driven, oblivious to power, not participatory across the range of stakeholders, and lacking in planning and evidence based on sound science and traditional knowledge.

Concluding Thoughts

Marine management regimes will undoubtedly be put to the test in the near future, given challenges peculiar to the ocean environment, including a lack of property rights, the difficulty and expense of monitoring and surveillance, and lingering ecological uncertainties. Against the backdrop of global climate change, and with the cumulative pressures from unregulated marine use and insufficient watershed management, new demands for ocean space and resources will push marine governance to its limits.

Against the inevitable push to expand the blue economy, the "low-value" uses of coastal and ocean space are ever more threatened. Whether it is sustainable small-scale fisheries or access to seascapes that provide communities with priceless spiritual and aesthetic values, large-scale, profit-generating industries are getting the upper hand. The environmental community has been working hard to enlighten decision makers and development agencies on the need to consider all values coming from the coastal environment and to steer economic development toward enhancing the capacities of government agencies and co-managing local institutions to protect critical ecosystem functioning.

Yet some of us have become somewhat disillusioned with the conservation community for pushing a nature-first ideology on coastal communities that are struggling with the overarching need to combat poverty and ensure food security in any way possible. These daily struggles are happening against the very backdrop of promises that blue growth will lift everyone out of poverty in equal measure, promises unlikely to be fulfilled. Even with such champions as Jackie Alder, senior fisheries industry officer at the UN's Food and Agricultural Organization (FAO), guiding blue growth in fisheries, I remain wary of the ever-popular push to "unlock the potential of the blue economy" and promote blue growth, as this could be wholly unsustainable and benefit only those in power and the wealthy corporations that support them. Rather than defending any of these ideologies, I'm convinced we need to demonstrate to the young folks about to inherit our mess that science and planning can be harnessed to benefit humans and nature simultaneously, and over the long term. The ecosystem-services idea is an obvious foundation for this view, but I think it is important not to become seduced by the quantification and valuation of these services (although both assessment and valuation can serve to highlight who benefits from nature and in what ways).

From my perspective, the key to being able to manage coastal/marine uses and keep ecosystems functioning healthily is to understand first how people can benefit from ocean ecosystems in a particular place, and then take the time to scope the problem to truly understand what is preventing people from realizing those benefits. I daresay those constraints are rarely that we don't know enough or that there are too few protected areas. Particularly in developing countries, it will be increasingly important to make sure the solutions we promote (and fund) are tailored to the circumstances of time and place. Many of our academic institutions in the industrialized world, along with the big environmental NGOs, are pushing solutions without understanding the problem or understanding what it is that will lead to lasting positive outcomes. Nonetheless, I'm convinced we can use coastal and marine spatial planning as a tool to: (1) effectively engage a much broader segment of society in co-creating solutions; (2) ensure that we devote sufficient management to areas that are ecologically critical for productivity and ecosystem function, so we don't kill the golden goose; and (3) identify comanagement opportunities that promote active, intergenerational stewardship for our global oceans. Development practitioners, social scientists, and educators may avoid focusing on the environment and may still forget about or marginalize environmental issues, whereas conservation scientists, natural resource managers, and environmental educators may need to be reminded that conservation that fails to consider poverty, hunger, and inequality isn't sustainable either. The opportunity is here to get across a holistic approach to scoping development problems and constraints; then identifying and implementing appropriate, workable solutions rooted in the local situation. Let's not waste it.

9

Reimagining Development Practice

Raymond Offenheiser

Let's work ourselves out of a job! What if that were the mission and vision of every international development funder, organization, and nonprofit? How would that change the way we go about our work? How would we reimagine our roles? How would we engage countries where we work? How would we spend our time and scarce resources?

I write this reflection shortly after stepping down as president of Oxfam America, a position I held from 1995 to 2017, and after more than twenty years of deep involvement in the changing role of a major international NGO confederation, Oxfam International. I have found it helpful to pose these questions to myself, my colleagues at Oxfam, and, at the right moment, to other professionals in our field. For me, it is a reminder that our work was inspired by noble intent—to help nations and people achieve a dignified way of life. It is a reminder that this should be a journey of accompaniment, not of control or domination, and that it is transitory. It is a reminder that we must be humble, respectful, and responsible in how we discharge this unique charge. Otherwise, we are likely to do more damage than good.

In truth, the intentions underlying international development, though noble on one level, were political and ideological on another. Shaped by historical facts of the Cold War era and the struggle between the United States and the Soviet Union to establish geopolitical presence in strategic locations across the globe, Western liberal democracy faced off against state-sponsored socialism in a battle for hearts and minds. International development was the soft-power side of this historic struggle. Underlying the idealism of President Kennedy's call to service that brought young people from the United States to this work and built the architecture of international development was a genuine realpolitik that was made manifest in Vietnam.

125

Geopolitics aside, multilateral and bilateral investments in international development made a difference in millions of lives. Never in world history was there a consciously driven effort to improve the welfare of nations on a global scale. And though paths to prosperity are never straight for any nation, there is evidence in nations across the globe of ways international assistance—through the professionals it educated or the institutions it built—improved the well-being, longevity, and livelihood opportunities of millions of individuals. Today, however, the field of international development is at a crossroads. In a globalized, multipolar world, the role of aid must change. Strong voices from North and South are challenging traditional mindsets and approaches. Governments, once willing to tolerate post-colonial models and burdensome obligations of bilateral donors from the United States and Europe, now are looking to China for major investments in infrastructure, resource extraction, and industry. They are less interested in governance, human rights, and political reform. The globalizing private sector has emerged as a major actor, moving beyond safe markets of industrialized countries and into more politically risky settings in search of raw materials and, where possible, new markets. Meanwhile, mass migration into the United States and Europe has given birth and legitimacy to nativist and hypernationalist movements, as some governments seek to block new immigrants and slash aid budgets.

The last several years have been marked by multiple responses to this new reality. Responding to growing critiques of aid practice, aid effectiveness summits produced the 2011 Busan Partnership for Effective Development Cooperation, which established principles for development practice that apply to all donor and recipient relations. This new vision rests on five core principles: (1) ownership, (2) alignment, (3) harmonization, (4) results, and (5) mutual accountability. The Busan Partnership set the stage for the approvals of the Sustainable Development Goals (SDGs) and the 2015 Paris Agreement on climate change. Both agreements were achieved with strong participation from developing countries and application of the goals to both developing and industrialized nations—setting standards for international summits, goal setting, and partnerships.

Finally, a sea change in development financing accompanied these processes. Donors made it clear during the SDG negotiation round in Addis Ababa in 2015 that they expected emerging economies to become real partners in achieving the SDGs. This would require building strong and transparent tax systems as the basis for mobilizing domestic resources needed for development. In 2016, the Chinese launched operations of the Asian Infrastructure Investment Bank, which will soon dwarf the World Bank as a global lender to developing economies. On taking office in 2017, the Trump administration took the notion of eventual graduation from aid and embedded it into US national security and foreign aid strategy documents.

Finally, other traditional donors that are struggling with weak growth, immigration, and rising nationalism are shifting funds to domestic refugee resettlement and signaling their intentions to focus future funding on refugee-sending nations and failed states. It is in this context that international donors, businesses, nonprofits, and Northern and Southern governments must rethink their roles, responsibilities, relationships, and goals.

What Is the Role of the Twenty-First-Century International NGO?

With so many changes in the air, established international nonprofit organizations are faced with staying ahead of this change or becoming irrelevant. Not surprisingly, they are asking themselves basic questions. What should their role be? How big should they be? Should they operate as highly integrated global federations, large complex confederations, loose but agile networks, or something else? Should their governance systems be dominated by Northern, often Anglo-Saxon, affiliates or should they become more global, and what does more global really mean?

Should they be playing the role of gap-filling service providers for states that are failing in their responsibility to provide basic services to their populations, or should they shift to being knowledge-based organizations working exclusively through local partners on strategy, research, and policy change? Should they be frontline advocates at the global, national, or local level or should they invest in building national leadership and institutions to assume this role at national and local levels? Should they operate large humanitarian operations that often supplant local civil society and government responses at the national level, or should they be empowering national actors to respond and lead in prevention and first response? Should they presume there is a need for them to continuously grow, or should they become smaller, smarter, adaptive, and more targeted in their programs and interventions?

These are but a few of the challenging questions being asked within the international nonprofit community. Beneath each one, however, is a deeper set of ethical and normative considerations. What legitimacy do INGOs have to pursue their missions beyond the boundaries of their home countries? How do the social and political values that accompany their funding and programs align with or disrupt countries that host them? Are they as organizations even aware of these disruptive outcomes? What responsibilities and liability should they have for social, political, or economic disruption their programs may cause?

What rights and responsibilities do they have before the countries that may host and receive them? What is the extent of their accountability to these nations and communities? What level and standards of transparency and accountability should they be held to by host countries and communities?

Does a sovereign nation have the right to determine the nature and role of international philanthropy within its borders?

The INGO community began to reflect upon these questions in the 1990s in a variety of informal forums. Subsequently, commentators, some from within these same organizations and some from without, justifiably began to pose a wide range of questions and challenges to the leaders of these organizations, prompted by the perception of their rapid growth in scale, resources, and influence through the late 1990s. These queries have generated important initiatives, mainly in the realm of humanitarian work such as the Sphere Project standards of 1997 and the Code of Humanitarian Service (CHS), that have challenged the INGO community to improve its performance, professionalism, accountability, and transparency before donors, host governments, and communities. Whereas the humanitarian community worked hard to establish clear performance criteria for its work, the development sector has been far less ambitious and coherent in establishing performance and practice standards for its work. Covering such a wide variety of sectors and interventions makes it virtually impossible to set comprehensive and uniform performance standards for them all.

Reimagining Oxfam in the 1990s

Seeking its response to such questions, in the mid-1990s, Oxfam began a process of self-evaluation and reform that shaped much of what the organization is today. In 1995, Oxfam was a loose network of eight organizations that agreed to affiliate under the banner of Oxfam International, a global confederation, constituted as a foundation under Dutch jurisdiction with a secretariat headquartered in the United Kingdom in Oxford. Through the act of confederation, the eight affiliates agreed to undertake an ambitious project of collective renewal. Central to that exercise were insights about the organization's origins, history, and impact that influenced the vision for change that emerged. Its leadership realized that its postcolonial origins continued to define its organizational structure and culture, that it had been overtaken by the process of globalization, that its grassroots empowerment strategy as practiced was simply not delivering meaningful impact at scale, and that increasingly, the poor were victims of global processes external to their social and political reality.

The work of Amartya Sen, Nobel Prize–winning economist, was highly influential to Oxfam as it reimagined itself, its mission, and its programs. His book *Development as Freedom* challenged the growth-obsessed development economists to lift their heads, look around, and ask whether growth was the real end of the development process. He posited instead that unless we offer humankind freedom of choice and the capabilities to grow to full potential, we have fallen short of the true goal of development. A nation may have a robust GNP and growth rate of 8 percent while 50 percent of that nation's population wallows in extreme poverty. Is this really development? Economists have been satisfied that if they see these kinds of numbers that in time the growth will absorb the mass of poor. Economic history has demonstrated that absent the ability of citizens to press for an equitable social contract, this rarely happens through sheer market momentum or invisible-hand logic. Sen argued instead that we should focus on the quality of growth and on investments that build capabilities to take agency in the form of collective social and political expression in pursuit of the common good.

Driven by these insights, Oxfam took several bold steps. Sen was honorary president of Oxfam for seven years in the late 1990s and early 2000s, and Oxfam decided to operationalize his ideas through all its program work. It rejected the basic needs approach to development dominant among international NGOs of that era in favor of a rights-based approach that defined poverty not as the absence of public goods but as social exclusion. Sen posited instead that unless we offer humankind freedom of choice and the capabilities to grow to full potential, we have fallen short of the true goal of development. Taking a rights-based approach meant seeing the linkages between a local injustice, a national policy, and an international institutional practice or failing. The result was a deliberate effort to explicitly link the local to the global in as much of its programming as possible.

For Oxfam, the rights-based approach, with its emphasis on social exclusion, drove a mind shift within the organization toward seeing every development issue in terms of power relations. Following Sen's vision, the core premise underlying this approach is that all citizens have rights to basic protections and services and that these rights should be guaranteed and protected by their government as the duty bearer of rights. If the poorest and most vulnerable citizens are to receive those protections and services, they must have the means and capacity to exercise voice and agency and to query their government as to why they are excluded from the benefits of those rights. The social contract becomes the basis for a civil conversation with government about its accountability to its citizens. This vision guides all of Oxfam's programming today.

This vision led Oxfam to join the Jubilee Campaign for Debt Relief in the late 1990s. Its contribution was to focus on an African girl child who was deprived of basic education owing to the policies of the World Bank and other international lending institutions that insisted that poor African governments repay loans incurred under military dictatorships no longer in power. Oxfam effectively told the story of how policies of these lending agencies were forcing African governments to close schools, potentially depriving multiple generations of African girls and boys access to education. Its work gave a human face to a highly abstract problem and mobilized faith communities and citizens of donor countries to demand solutions.

Lessons from this campaign were incorporated into a much more ambitious and multifaceted campaign focused on the World Trade Organization (WTO) in the aftermath of its disastrous trade meeting in Seattle in 1999. Oxfam released a very ambitious report on the injustices of the global trading system entitled *Rigged Rules*. This report took the then novel position that trade was not inherently bad for the poor but that the international trading system was rigged against poor countries. This unusual position from a pro-poor INGO confused advocates on both the left and right, and brought attacks from extremes of both camps. The strategic premise at the heart of this report was that the global trading system could be made to work for development but would require considerable reform. The report positioned Oxfam as a leading voice on trade throughout the Doha Development Round, held first in Qatar in 2001. The Doha Development Round was a series of conferences, sponsored by the WTO, aimed at lowering trade barriers and expanding trade. Negotiations broke down in 2008. Throughout this campaign, Oxfam brought the voices and presence of the most marginalized and affected populations to these meetings, where the most important decisions on these issues were being taken, giving agency and a voice the disadvantaged had never before experienced.

Oxfam: Getting Fit for the Twenty-First Century

At this point, well into the first decade of the twenty-first century, we paused again at Oxfam to take stock of our evolution and fitness for the challenges of the new century. There were important lessons to learn from the efforts to transform the organization over the previous decade. We learned that we had become good at global campaigning, but our global campaigning was disconnected from our field-based work. We learned that despite our rhetoric on our commitment to gender, it was not reflected in our practice and programs on the ground. We learned that we were uncomfortable working with government entities even when our goals aligned, and engaging in such collaboration might dramatically multiply our impact. We learned that much of our field-based programming was diffuse, disconnected, not strategic, and not scalable.

We learned that our partners did not think we were as good at partnership as we thought we were. We learned that the private sector was casting a large shadow over many countries where we work, and we were uncertain how to respond. We learned that our confederated model was costly, inefficient, anachronistic, and dominated by our wealthy Northern affiliates at a time when the world was becoming more global. We learned that though we were getting very good at insisting others be held accountable, we needed to demonstrate that we were accountable to multiple constituencies ourselves. We learned that while we were preaching an ownership agenda, in many areas we were still locked into relations with donors that reinforced traditional top-down operational behaviors. We learned that it was time for significant change in our positioning and approach.

Finally, and painfully, sexual misconduct was exposed in Oxfam Great Britain's humanitarian operations following disasters in Chad and Haiti.[1] We know that this egregious abuse of power contravenes the values for which Oxfam stands. We are reminded, as development practitioners, that we must be constantly aware of how power can be abused, especially in vulnerable situations and with already vulnerable people. We learn from Oxfam GB's situation and global investigations of other INGOs that the humanitarian and development world is not immune to abuses of power similar to those the #MeToo movement is exposing in the political, film, business, and other sectors. We have a responsibility to be alert to power imbalances, to uphold and model the high standards and ethical conduct that we envision for the world, to recognize problems, speak up, and be held accountable. Within our organizations, structural changes are needed to make abuse less likely and to ensure that any abuse that might occur will be dealt with transparently and promptly. To this end, we can all work to put in place policies and mechanisms that not only prevent abuse but also protect and support victims. Oxfam has now put in place safeguarding policies and a ten-point action plan, which is available on the Oxfam International website.

The Oxfam Response for the Twenty-First Century

Such epiphanies contributed to a major process of organizational renewal and change that is still underway as I write this in 2018. This renewal is driven by the belief that Oxfam must pursue three strategic outcomes while trying to address many of the questions raised in our internal reassessment of our role. It was agreed that Oxfam must seek, first, to become more global; second, to become more efficient; and, third, to achieve greater impact. With these goals in mind, Oxfam set about building a more global organization. Substantial investment has added a new generation of affiliates to its confederation from the Global South including India, South Africa, Mexico, Brazil, and China. Others are contemplated. The entrance of these Southern voices is rebalancing politics and priority setting within the global governance structure. It has also loosened the grip of Northern affiliate members on program direction by empowering each country program to be a freestanding country office that sets its own programmatic priorities at the country level, within the broad parameters of a global Oxfam International strategic plan. The long-range vision is that any country office can one day become a freestanding Oxfam affiliate if it meets standards of good governance and financial sustainability. This vision has been highly motivational for national staff, as it reinforces national ownership within each country program.

On its campaigning agenda, Oxfam has adopted what it refers to as a "Worldwide Influencing Network" (WIN) strategy, in which it hopes to put its considerable global and national campaigning capability at the service of social movements at the national level, where there are clear issues and grievances with real salience. This new model for campaigning presumes that Oxfam will launch and manage some campaigns at the global level, reframing global narratives to provide space for global and national action. Oxfam's current work on inequality is an example of such a campaign. In other cases, campaigns will originate at the national level, and Oxfam will provide technical and substantive support for those campaigns as needed and desired. In both cases, national programs can choose to opt into campaigns as they feel appropriate and feasible in their national context. Again, the critical point is that Oxfam wants country programs to have more ownership over campaign topics, tactics, and momentum so that the tone and approach to a campaign can be dialed up or down as the political environment requires or dictates.

On accountability, Oxfam has significantly increased investment in monitoring, evaluation, and learning, with the goal of being an industry leader. Its work, particularly on evaluation of advocacy, has been recognized as pacesetting. The organization has also made a commitment to ensure all program evaluations are available on its website to donors, partners, and the public. On leadership, Oxfam has created the global Oxfam Research Network that brings together all research assets of the organization into a virtual network, in which workloads can be delegated and shared across affiliates. Staff numbers in this global network probably exceed staffing levels of most national think tanks. On gender and diversity, with strong leadership from its secretariat and member affiliates, Oxfam made a major investment training staff in gender analysis and program design, giving much more emphasis to ensuring gender balance in both campaigning and field programs. In this new generation of gender-based programming, more attention is being given to intersectionality, and how it might be represented in program design.

A growing challenge of programming is the closing of civil society space. For varying reasons, governments are clamping down on the ability of civil society actors to press their governments for transparency and accountability. Freedom House reports that over ninety countries have passed laws that limit freedom of assembly and expression and use of popular social-media platforms for organizing meetings or for transmitting politically sensitive messaging. Many are following what is often referred to as the "Singapore practice," which limits advocacy in a country to organizations whose advocacy is financed from indigenous philanthropic sources. Few national philanthropies exist in poorer countries, ensuring that little advocacy will be financed or carried out. Governments across the globe are institutionalizing these practices at precisely the moment when there are more sophisticated and capable nonprofit organizations capable of engaging the state far more creatively.

On relations with the state, Oxfam has a long history of working in countries governed by authoritarian regimes and, as a consequence, many of its staff and affiliates developed over time a level of distrust and suspicion about working with state entities. Now, however, when Oxfam is championing a rights-based approach to development and the importance of taking leadership away from donors and transferring it to recipient partners, this cultural legacy is both paradoxical and at times paralyzing. Oxfam staff could get hung up on the merits of a dialogue with government officials in a variety of areas of mutual interest. Gradually, with time and experience, this cultural legacy is dissipating as dramatic breakthroughs have been achieved in working through some government agencies and programs, although skepticism is still merited in some contexts. In those areas where leveraging state resources and scale is possible, Oxfam is seeking through the example of innovative programming, policy advocacy, and participation in government-convened policy forums to engage state actors more proactively and aggressively with its policy agenda.

Relations with the private sector have suffered from a similar legacy hangover, based upon unsavory past interactions with major corporate actors around access to medicines or environmental catastrophes. Oxfam leadership has now built a strong team working on business and development issues through its field programs and campaigns. This involved considerable change in culture and required recognition of the growing scale of foreign direct investment in developing countries and the potentially disruptive impact of corporate supply chains on daily livelihoods and opportunity horizons of the poorest families. Again, major accomplishments through a careful inside-outside strategy of applying modest but smart external pressure, while seeking to work with internal allies, established Oxfam's reputation as a critical friend in the private sector space. It also helped persuade skeptical staff of the value of engaging the private sector as a critical but constructive stakeholder, without losing sight of core goals and values.

Taking a twentieth-century, global nonprofit working in ninety countries with over 10,000 staff and a budget of more than $1 billion that was designed in the early postcolonial period and turning it into an agile, truly global, efficient, and high-impact twenty-first-century organization is a Herculean task. It requires redesigning the entire architecture of the organization, from leadership to staffing, systems, culture, financing, and decision making at multiple levels. Oxfam has undertaken this journey with the best of intentions, but its complexity is daunting and its costs substantial. Changes must be tested before being fully embraced. It cannot be completed quickly.

So, Oxfam today is still a work in progress, sure of its direction but still imperfect in the execution of its change process, of its accountability, and of its oversight and remedy of some of its recent failures. Although it might like to be that twenty-first-century networked NGO that moves swiftly with the times and technological changes, it is a behemoth, constrained by history, back-donor requirements, outmoded and duplicative systems, culture and ideology, internal power imbalances, and inexperience in managing the equivalent of a twenty-company merger. Nonetheless, it aspires to embrace the best notions of development practice and concept of country ownership but is finding that the concept is far easier to espouse than to implement. Turning the traditional development agenda on its head with the goal of truly embedding the ownership agenda into every aspect of an organization's approach to its work has proven to be a tall order. However, there are areas where one can see how this model is likely to evolve and yield real impact. The following example illustrates what the future may hold.

Extractive Industries: A Twenty-First-Century Example

Extractive industries are often the first to enter politically risky environments in developing countries. They are attractive for the economic boost they can in theory bring to a sluggish developing economy. However, they are almost always highly disruptive socially and environmentally in the regions where they operate. They take over large geographic areas, often displacing rural communities; they require access to large amounts of water for processing, potentially undermining local agriculture; and they generate little local employment once operating. Most often, there is little effort by either central governments or the companies themselves to devote even a small portion of revenues generated to meeting local development needs, while billions of dollars of profit are secured offshore.

Oxfam began a very modest program looking at these issues in Peru in the 1990s. It was obvious that this sector was the financial engine driving Peru's extraordinary growth rates of 9 percent into the early 2000s, yet the INGO sector was paying no attention to its performance or social impact, apart from making small grants to assist companies working in the extractive industry in delivering small-scale social service programs. Oxfam funded the creation of a national coalition of communities affected by mining. Some thirty-four communities joined and elected leadership that began to press for enforcement of environmental regulations. One of its members held the first-of-its-kind community referendum on whether a community would accept the licensing of a mine that would jeopardize the local water supply for agriculture. The community voted down the mine proposal, and the government revoked the license to exploit. This made national and international news and contributed to launching the global debate on what has come to be known as "free, prior, and informed consent," or FPIC.

The experience in Peru led to other actions. An Oxfam-funded documentary film on a mercury spill in a highland Peruvian community led the World Bank to create a community ombudsman. Activism also accelerated in Africa. The film, *Blood Diamond* (2006), drew worldwide attention to some of the injustices related to extraction of minerals and expanded global awareness, while practical actions were taking place. Repeated reports of human-rights violations led the US State Department to support a multi-stakeholder initiative to create the Voluntary Principles on Security and Human Rights in 2000, which were the only human-rights guidelines designed specifically for extractive-sector companies. Oxfam, Global Witness, and other allies supported creation of the Kimberley diamond certification process, which was established in 2002, and the launch of the responsible sourcing process for a wider range of minerals. Campaigns targeting retailers for their sourcing policies forced both retailers and mining corporations to look more carefully at business practices at their mine sites. Growing public pressure on extractive industries led British prime minister Tony Blair to launch the idea of the Extractive Industries Transparency Initiative (EITI) in 2002 at the World Summit on Sustainable Development in Johannesburg. The EITI process continues today and sets standards that advance greater transparency within the industry on business practices, financing, profits, and contracts. By November 2017, fifty-one countries had agreed to implement the latest EITI global standard as revised in 2016.

Oxfam was a leader in this emerging field during this formative period and, along with other INGOs, contributed to these outcomes with a variety of others. Today, Oxfam is trying to adjust its program work in the extractive sector to embody many principles of reform outlined above. What does this mean? Within its new structure, Oxfam is presuming that its theory of change is driven by knowledge and campaigning and that its role within any country is to support the interests of local civil society to drive social change. Its role is to invest in building a new generation of civil society organizations with the political savvy and technical sophistication to lead the development process on behalf of their national populations.

To achieve this in the extractive sector, Oxfam established an extractive industries knowledge hub (EI Hub) within its new programmatic structure. The EI Hub is led by Oxfam America, which has invested in building an infrastructure of fifteen staff with key competencies to support its global work. Staff are based within affiliate HQs or confederation regional offices. Many are nationals from the regions. The EI Hub has reached out to country programs across the Oxfam programming architecture to solicit interest in securing support of the hub for work at the country level. Some thirty country programs have now self-identified as prioritizing EI work. In effect, country programs are taking ownership of this as a priority area for their country. For most of these countries, there is a burgeoning EI sector that is largely unregulated yet holding the promise of extracting significant value for that nation. In collaboration with the Oxfam's EI Hub, a country program develops a country strategy for its EI work that is suited to the stage of development in that country. Strong emphasis is given to mainstreaming gender analysis into these plans.

A good example of where this style of programming leads is Ghana, where the country program has supported development of a portfolio of partners that lead EI work. Unique in the Ghana case is an NGO called the African Center for Energy Policy (ACEP), a Ghanaian think tank staffed by graduates of the petroleum industry master's program at Scotland's Dundee University. ACEP has established strong links with the Ghanaian parliamentary committee charged with overseeing major new oil fields off Ghana's coast. It has also cultivated parliamentarians who are keen to work with ACEP in developing effective supervisory legislation for this new oil sector.

Around 2014, other national NGOs in Ghana organized a public interest campaign focusing on revenue and budgetary transparency called Oil for Agriculture. Oxfam's EI Hub assisted the national NGOs in designing their campaign, producing research reports, and developing a media and communications strategy to execute the campaign. The point of this campaign is to hold government officials accountable for how revenues from the oil industry are applied to the country's development needs and reported on. Their proposition was that 10 percent of oil revenues should be applied annually to investment in the agriculture sector. Working with members of parliament who championed the oil sector regulatory legislation along with ACEP, a coalition of Ghanaian NGOs and parliamentarians was successful in getting this bill through Ghana's congress. Now the coalition must turn its attention to seeing that the bill is properly implemented. Other partners closer to oil-field and mining areas are facilitating dialogues between companies and communities on displacement, compensation, environmental impacts, and the devastating effects of exploration and oil-rig construction on the artisanal fishing industry.

What we are seeing in Ghana in terms of investments in building an integrated program that works through indigenous civil society organizations at local and national levels is now being replicated in thirty countries where extractives play a major role in national development. In nearby Burkina Faso, a similar group of partners is implementing a campaign demanding that 1 percent of the revenue from gold extraction be devoted to agriculture. In Mozambique, the country program is focused on the development of offshore oil reserves. Throughout the country programs, women are in the forefront of leadership and negotiations with companies at national and local levels. Gender impacts of EI are embedded in program design. At the African Union, Oxfam has established representation to promote common standards across the continent for responsible mining policy and practice.

In addition to this important work that Oxfam EI Hub is doing to build the capacity of national partners and embed best-practice principles in national legislation and government policy, it also plays an important role at the global level. An allegation often leveled at extractive companies is their role in creating a culture of corruption wherever they operate. Bribing public officials, negotiating ridiculously low royalty payments, producing false invoices of annual production and profits, and evading their annual tax obligations are just a few commonly reported practices. The net effect is to rob poor countries of their nonrenewable resources and undermine their ability to finance their own development. When challenged, companies blame corrupt officials, and public officials blame corrupt companies. In the end, nothing is done, yet the implications of this behavior are enormous. The revenue that would otherwise be captured by poor governments would often dwarf foreign aid funding by several orders of magnitude.

Transparency of revenue obligations and flows is the key to addressing these problems. For the past decade, Oxfam focused on addressing this issue through legislation, among other strategies. An example illustrates the value of even minimal bipartisanship to achieve meaningful legislative outcomes. Working with US congressman Barney Frank, a Democrat, a proposal was developed in 2008 for legislation entitled the Extractive Industries Transparency Disclosure Act. For over five years, Oxfam staff worked to secure support in Congress to move this bill to a vote. It was unsuccessful in the House of Representatives. However, it secured the support of Senator Richard Lugar, a Republican, who was concerned about these issues of corruption in developing countries. Then a unique opportunity presented itself. The Wall Street Reform Act was moving through Congress with strong support from President Obama and the Democratic-controlled Senate. With Senator Lugar's support within the Foreign Relations Committee, Oxfam was able to secure support to quietly move this bill forward as an amendment to the Wall Street Reform Act. Democratic Senators John Kerry, Ben Cardin, and Chris Dodd played crucial roles in ensuring its inclusion in the final bill that was presented to both houses. The amendment was largely ignored in floor debates on this act. To the shock of the army of extractive-industry lobbyists, the bill with amendment was approved by both chambers in 2010.

Approval of this small amendment represented a revolutionary step forward in creating a legally binding obligation for companies to become more transparent in financial reporting at all levels. The law's premise was simple. Every company that was publicly traded on markets within the United States would be required to report to the US Security and Exchange Commission (SEC) all financial transactions with all governments in countries where they were active at the project level. The legislation would cover 95 percent of companies active globally in the extractive sector.

Industry lobbyists were shocked when they discovered the final bill contained this provision, and predictably, industry immediately began efforts to undermine it. It took two years for the SEC to write and release the relevant regulations to implement the bill, and immediately, industry sued to challenge the constitutionality of the legislation. The industry representatives won the first round and lost the second. The regulations were issued with support of the courts.

More important, once this legislation was passed within the US Congress, the Oxfam EI team immediately went to work to secure its passage in the United Kingdom and European Union. It was developed and passed relatively quickly in both jurisdictions. Thereafter, it was taken up and passed in Canada and Scandinavian countries. Throughout this process, Oxfam maintained a dialogue with companies, arguing that passage of this law would be good for them because, if they were properly paying taxes and royalties and not paying bribes or so-called service fees to governments or their officials, the legislation would focus attention on corruption of host governments and away from the companies. Several major mining companies accepted this argument and sided with civil society in supporting this legislation, whereas oil companies did not. Once the regulations began to be issued, companies organized their annual reporting to conform to its requirements. Because this reporting was required across multiple financial markets, companies assumed if it was required for one, they would provide it for all. It mattered little that Trump's first act as president was to strike down the provisions of this law. The requirements still exist for the rest of the world, so companies paid little attention to his move.

Let us for a moment reflect upon the various dimensions of this example from Oxfam's work with extractive industries and how it represents a different approach to international development. Oxfam takes a structural and systemic approach to the extractive-industry sector and its impact on development. Yet inspiration for the approach starts with poverty and the impact this industry has on poor populations. The work starts with a community grievance and traces its causes all the way up a technically complex supply chain to the boardrooms of some of the world's largest corporations. It is local and global simultaneously. It does not abandon community-based work but rather links it to explicit policy demands at national and global levels that are positioned within a human-rights framework. It requires state action to provide minimal protections against clear violations of personal security, as well as claims against threats to livelihoods and social welfare. It sets the stage for legal action, if necessary. It seeks to create local and national ownership through investment in building national partner organizations to take on leadership roles with legitimacy that a foreign organization would not possess. It takes a long-term perspective, recognizing that social change on a global or even national scale cannot be achieved overnight. It builds in gender analysis and considerations to ensure policy outcomes are not gender blind. It is founded on sound research on the industry it seeks to change, as well as on the reasonableness of proposals put forward. It operates as a learning unit within the larger organization, actively sharing learning across the thirty country programs and partner organizations that it seeks to serve. It focuses on simultaneously reshaping norms, policies, and practices. Rather than leading out front, it seeks to support from behind, responding to needs of national civil society organizations that it hopes will one day take over this work and allow Oxfam to work itself out of a job.

Final Thoughts

The field of international development will not disappear tomorrow. Governments will continue to include soft-power tools and minimal expression of public compassion in their foreign policy tool kits. Earthquakes, tsunamis, famines, and war will continue. The humanitarian imperative will continue to be relevant in the twenty-first century. What is, however, at an inflection point is the nature of investment in long-term human development. Rising China and India in the East, rising nationalism in the West, and emerging economies in the Global South are redefining geopolitics. The migration push prompted by climate change and an impatient, despairing youth population is likely to grow from a steady stream to a tidal wave. The security threat posed by fragile states will likely shift attention from states where success is probable to states in turmoil, rife with corruption and failed institutions. Pressure will grow, as seen with the Trump administration, to transition countries off aid and reduce aid budgets. Meanwhile, globalization will proceed, pushed by large corporations seeking new markets, secure commodity supply chains, and first-advantage market positions.

For international NGOs, this brave new world will require institutions well adapted to twenty-first-century realities. It will require organizations to use cutting-edge tools to translate patterns of local injustice into systemic global critiques. It will require modern information technology to streamline and simplify complex global business information and management challenges to drive cost savings and minimize brand risks in service of greater impact. INGOs cannot afford to run billion-dollar organizations on a global level with flimsy information infrastructure. Accountability challenges in today's world make that too great a risk. This new world will require rethinking staffing competencies, which may be less about on-the-ground implementation by altruistic expatriates and more about supporting emergent civil society institutions and leaders with knowledge, comparative experiences, and technical expertise. It will require a strong commitment to diversity, not only in hiring but also in rethinking governance structures to reflect a truly global identity. It will require educating the donor public to new visions for effectiveness in the use of their philanthropic dollars.

Many INGOs, old and new, have undertaken this journey. Efforts are underway among older, larger INGOs to reposition themselves more solidly and institutionally in the Global South, to drive diversity through their staffing (although not always their governance structures), to build more effective and responsive accountability infrastructure, and to transition from implementers to partners and investors in indigenous organizational capacity. These efforts are complex, time-consuming, and expensive. Those who have begun this journey are the first to admit they are far from perfect or complete. The journey is, in reality, a process and not a destination, and it must be seen that way.

Obstacles and impediments hinder achieving these changes. Many INGOs are tethered, in varying degrees, to donor demands, preferences, and accountability and compliance obligations. Although the obligations are understandable, given sourcing of funds from taxpayers who require account-ability from their legislators, they are onerous, complex, and constantly changing, and they lack consistency in principle among donors. Even though the Busan process calls for collaboration among donors to simplify reporting burdens for developing countries, little has been done to achieve this goal among donors. One excellent example would be to develop donor consortia at country levels chaired by planning ministries to establish principles of col-lective ownership. I sat on such a consortium in Bangladesh in the 1990s but have seen little comparable in other countries. Donors could also work together to develop unified proposal, application, and reporting procedures for governments that would lift burdens from countries while not sacrificing quality of reporting to donors. Similar work might be done among donors to simplify these procedures for INGOs and national NGOs.

Accountability is another major challenge. Donors want more and more accountability for impact but do not want to pay for it. INGOs are often criticized for having little evidence of their work's impact, but few donors include funding for evaluation in their contributions. And even fewer donors fund building institutional capability within INGOs to carry out this vital function. The philanthropic sector would benefit from a deeper discussion about what they are doing, or not doing, to enhance the field of impact assessment beyond current donor preferences for random control trials.

The Oxfam case is but one approach to what INGOs might do pro-grammatically as they evolve and contribute in a complex, fast-moving world. In the end, globalization is about creating a more interdependent world, in which the most effective institutions are moving people, ideas, money, images, and technology at ever-accelerating speed across a world with fewer and fewer boundaries. Private sector organizations do this successfully for profit. The INGO sector must reinvent itself to carry forth its mission for social justice. The state and market have an important role to play in preserving order and delivering goods to humanity at scale. In the end, the nonprofit sector will be judged internationally and domestically by how well it serves as the moral lever that ensures the state and market discharge their roles effectively, guided by concerns for equity, inclusion, transparency, and accountability to humankind's most vulnerable. Achieving this end is our task for the twenty-first century, as we truly endeavor to work ourselves out of a job.

Note
1. Editors' note: Although the author, Raymond Offenheiser, wrote this chapter after he left Oxfam America and before the news broke about sexual misconduct by Oxfam Great Britain humanitarian workers in Chad and Haiti, he chose to add a few words of reflection in response to that news. The editors are cognizant that the development industry is defined by power imbalances in the world and also that these imbalances can sometimes lead to abuse. This is an important theme of this book and is addressed in other chapters besides this one.

Notes

PART 2
Turning Development Around

10

Empathy: A Missing Link

Christian Velasquez Donaldson

Back in my country, Bolivia, I used to travel around hiking or biking for weeks into remote and rural areas, connecting with nature and listening to people's stories. Those many experiences were my main motivation for getting a degree in civil engineering with a specialization in road design and development. I believed that roads were the veins and arteries for development—the most important variable to catalyze development—not only for economic integration but also to promote social inclusion, connectivity, and opportunities to get out of poverty. Traveling and talking with people opened my view to different perspectives and concerns about our environment and how it is integrated with people's livelihoods and our society. It made me wonder whether it is possible to protect the environment without undermining local communities' development opportunities.

I remember that during those same years, there was an ongoing environmental debate in Bolivia. The first environmental law and the Ministry of Environment were created, and environmental impact assessments (EIAs) were becoming a formal subject in civil-engineering curricula as an important aspect of project design. It was years later, however, when I was in graduate school that I realized that the World Bank was, on the one hand, one of the most important actors not only in terms of promoting EIAs in the developing world but also in promoting the creation of ministries of environment, and later on, the creation of environmental units within different economic-sector ministries. On the other hand, the Bank had a reputation for attaching conditions to its financial aid, requiring major and controversial economic-policy reforms that imposed a development agenda on developing countries. And it was years after that, when I was already involved in watchdog and advocacy work to encourage change at the World Bank that

I realized that the late 1980s and 1990s were also the years when the World Bank was under heavy scrutiny and criticism for giving financial support to large-scale controversial infrastructure projects with significant social and environmental negative impacts.

Working for almost ten years on advocacy with other civil society organizations and movements to provoke systemic reforms at the World Bank, I realized that this apparent dichotomy of the World Bank—promoting environmental best practices, but also imposing controversial policies on countries—is merely a mirror of the complexities of development and the constant battles between diverse perspectives, visions, and theories of development practitioners, policymakers, and decision makers within an institutional environment that is also in constant internal competition with political-power dynamics and values. Even through the constant external criticism and internal diverse perspectives, since its formation in 1944 the World Bank has played, and continues to play, a very important role in the development field not only as a gatekeeper and broker for needed development finance but increasingly as a "knowledge bank," shaping the ideas and potential approaches to sustainable development.

From its origins until 2015, the World Bank's power of influence was intrinsically tied to its financial power. Most countries had very few potential sources for needed development finance to promote economic growth and to finance any extractive, energy, or infrastructure project—considered both then and now as the engines of growth. Countries had either to request a loan from commercial banks or private sources at very high interest rates and unfavorable contractual obligations, given the significant financial, economic, and social risks inherent to these sectors, or they could go to the World Bank and comply with specific policy conditionalities and requirements, but at lower or concessional interest rates. This was the reality for many countries. For decades, the World Bank was their only access to credit and development finance, and thus wielded significant influence over development issues.

Over the years, the World Bank went from offering only project loans to creating numerous credit and loan instruments tailored to different circumstances and conditions. In order to finance various aspects of government and institutional functions in need of resources, it created credit instruments to inject capital into entire sector programs, for example, Sector Wide Approach program loans or Multiphase Programmatic Approach loans. It also created general budget-support finance programs subject to policy and economic reforms and conditions through structural adjustment programs and Development Policy Loans. In order to prepare and justify specific requirements for these different credit tools, the Bank created technical-assistance programs, developed sector concept notes, and conducted research to identify constraints and opportunities within the client country's governance apparatus and development needs. Over time, and every time a country has a new government in office, the World Bank develops Country Partnership Frameworks, which identify development opportunities and lay out the amount of funding, type of credit instruments, areas, sectors, and projects to be financed by the World Bank Group over the next four to five years in each member country.

Since its creation in 1944, the World Bank has been continuously changing and adapting internally to new global contexts and conditions, as well as adjusting to internal and external pressures and criticism. In many respects, the changes have come as a result of direct pressure from communities affected by the shortcomings of its operations and investments. Change has also resulted from the Bank's need to maintain its own relevance and influence in the development field by getting access to an extensive and growing network of relationships with high-level government officials, government technocrats, multilateral forums, and private and financial sectors. In so doing, the World Bank has constantly positioned itself as facilitator of private-sector financial flows for development and as the trustee of global trust funds to finance climate action, infrastructure, and other basic services such as education and health. It went from financing and supporting mostly large-scale infrastructure projects such as transportation and energy infrastructure, for example, highways, large hydroelectric dams, and extractive industries led by government interventions, to promoting private-sector-led development in order to avoid political corruption and capture by in-country politicians. It moved from financial support being conditioned on macroeconomic structural changes via the Washington Consensus prescriptions to a more holistic approach that recognized the social and environmental dimensions of economic development.

In many aspects the changes and approaches to development the World Bank has undertaken over the years were the result of active civil-society advocacy work. Some of these gradual changes are attributable to its self-reflection; in part through the critical role of some individual staff with strategic political influence who positioned themselves as internal champions for progressive reforms within higher-level management. However, reform occurred mostly through a combination of factors. The most significant were external pressure, criticism, and demand for accountability and transparency from civil-society actors such as NGOs, indigenous people's movements, and labor unions, among others who were working on behalf of communities directly impacted by the World Bank's financial support of projects, programs, and policies in developing countries. Mounting evidence from academia also questioned the World Bank's development approach at different times. This, in turn, put significant pressure on its largest shareholders, such as the United States, which had the power to withhold authorizing legislation to grant any capital increase to the World Bank's coffers if reforms were not pushed forward.

Through my years working with civil society on World Bank reform and advocacy, when discussing the role of the World Bank in development with classmates, colleagues, and development undergraduate and graduate students, I have observed that the World Bank is seen as either "the" institution to work for if you want to be in the development field or as "the" institution with a hidden agenda of working for powerful interests. However, in both cases, the World Bank's institutional governance and political structure were very little understood. Either way, I am left wondering how the World Bank came to be this highly influential institution capable of unleashing such passions. Also, as development practitioners, what is to be learned from the World Bank's history, operations, and actions?

Since its creation to support the reconstruction of Europe after World War II, the International Bank for Reconstruction and Development (IBRD)—or the World Bank, as it is now most commonly known—has grown and evolved significantly from its origin as a single institution to a group of five distinct institutions: the original IBRD, the International Development Association (IDA), the International Finance Corporation (IFC), the Multilateral Investment Guarantee Agency (MIGA), and the International Centre for Settlement of Investment Disputes (ICSID). All together, these five institutions make up the World Bank Group that provides financial assistance, technical assistance, policy advice, and risk guarantees not only to governments in developing countries but also to the private and financial sectors both in industrialized and developing countries.

These five distinct institutions were created at different times to respond to different needs. The IBRD now provides medium-term loans (fifteen to twenty years) to middle-income countries with interest rates close to market levels to ensure profitability. Since 1948, the IBRD has earned a positive net income each year, ensuring its financial strength and the functioning of its daily operations and management, including its research arm, and allowing the World Bank Group to offer concessional credits to low-income countries. The IDA was established in 1960 to provide concessional loans (zero interest) and grants to low-income countries with a ten-year grace period and maturity terms of thirty-five to forty years. The IDA's funds are replenished every three years by contributions from donor-country members, with some additional funding coming from the IBRD's net income. The IDA replenishment responds to a significant political negotiation among donor countries. The IFC was established in 1956 to provide financing to the private and financial sectors at market rates without government guarantees. The IFC provides loans, equity, loan guarantees, risk-management products, and technical advice to a broad range of private clients, national and transnational corporations, commercial banks, private equity funds, and pension funds. The IFC, in many aspects, is the World Bank's income-generation institution and has made a profit every year since its creation. The MIGA, established in

1988, provides political and nonfinancial risk guarantees to private investors against losses caused by noncommercial risks such as expropriations, currency failures, war and civil conflict, breach of contracts, or changes in government actions that could disrupt investments. The ICSID, established in 1966, facilitates arbitration and conciliation of disputes between member countries and investors in member countries.

However, to make sense of the World Bank's dichotomy and different approaches to development—on the one hand, promoting best practices; on the other hand, imposing a development agenda—the most important aspect of the World Bank Group is its governance and political structure. The World Bank Group is owned by its "shareholders," who make up the board of governors and are its highest level of decision making. The members of the board of governors are the ministers of economy or finance of the Bank's 189 member countries. Each of the 189 member countries contributes funds by purchasing shares when they join the Bank. A small portion of the value of the shares each country purchases is "paid in" with actual money; the rest of the value is "on call" commitments in case the Bank suffers major losses and needs capital to repay its creditors. The Bank's daily operations are delegated to a board of executive directors, political appointees of their respective country's governor.

The World Bank currently has twenty-five executive directors responsible for day-to-day institutional decisions regarding its policies, operations, and loan approvals. Most of the executive directors' decisions are based on consensus or the absence of objection. However, their relative voting power is inevitably a leverage tool as it is determined by the number of shares held by the country the director represents.[1] The five largest shareholders, with about 35 percent of total share votes, are the United States, the United Kingdom, Japan, Germany, and France. Each of these countries appoints one executive director. The remaining 184 country members are grouped into twenty constituencies, each of which is represented by one executive director.[2] For instance, the more than fifty African countries are grouped into three constituencies, each one with only one executive director to represent their interests on the board. Thus, the largest shareholders, which happen to be the wealthiest nations, have far more influence and decision-making power than the developing countries.

The World Bank is not a monolithic institution; it is a dynamic and heterogeneous institution that experiences constant tension among political power dynamics, trade-offs, and values. To maintain its relevance and influence in development, it is constantly trying to adapt to new internal and external pressures, different ideas, interests, and political ideologies. From my experience working on advocacy to provoke systemic institutional reforms at the World Bank, observing its work from inside and outside, as well as working with civil-society watchdog organizations, I have come to the conclusion that one of the most challenging barriers to development is not ownership or skills or funding, but a lack of understanding of the implications of our own privilege as development practitioners, policymakers, and decision makers, and our limited (or lack of) empathy for the daily struggles of the people and communities supposed to be at the center of development projects such as those financed by the World Bank.

To be clear, I don't mean lack of exposure to fieldwork, good intentions, motivation, or passion for development, and I certainly don't mean lack of understanding of the technicalities and theories of development. To the contrary, most people I have interacted with are highly motivated, skilled, and passionate about development work. Rather, I am referring to empathy, to the ability to put oneself in the shoes of people for whom decisions are made, people who are affected by project and policy decisions made in places far removed from the day-to-day realities, needs, and wants of people on the ground who face the pain and suffering of the effects and unintended impacts of those decisions.

The point I want to make is that without a sense of empathy and without a clear awareness and understanding of our own privileges as development practitioners, policymakers, and decision makers—the advantages we have been afforded, our own bias in our views of development, our own perceptions of the trade-offs of short- and long-term development, and the time scale upon which benefits will be felt—we rationalize the development decisions we make with a comforting sense of aggregated benefits to society, what we call "the greater good," without considering the individual human faces, ownership, and equity implications of such interventions. Without empathy and awareness of our privilege, we tend to witness development from afar and can fail to see our own biases when making decisions about development trade-offs. Most likely, we take for granted the security created by our own cushion of assets, opportunities, education, networks, and social capital that the people submerged in poverty and vulnerable situations rarely have. People living with poverty and vulnerabilities may not be able to afford to hold out for long-term benefits that may accrue for society at large when their immediate situation is made worse. With emphasis only on the technical skills and theories of development effectiveness learned at development programs in major academies, somehow the development field has become a business distanced from the feelings, emotions, and daily struggles of people in poverty.

Through almost a decade of monitoring the World Bank, I've witnessed so many debates and discussions about its institutional polices, operations, investments, projects, and development decisions without ever meeting, or even consulting with, the supposed direct beneficiaries—real people miles away from Washington, DC, or the capital of any of the Bank's member countries. Take as an example one of the most traumatic negative impacts of development programs for communities: physical or economic resettlement and involuntary displacement of people to make room for a development project. Back in the 1980s and 1990s, one of the major criticisms of the World Bank was about the human-rights violations and suffering caused by resettlement programs of large infrastructure projects it financed that were meant to bring economic growth.

Examples are all too many. Projects such as Polonoroeste in Brazil aimed to establish agriculture in the Amazon basin but forced the displacement of thousands of indigenous peoples, causing a significant decline in their population and leaving many settlers in extreme poverty, which led to social and armed conflicts (Schwartzman 1986). The Sardar Sarovar Dam on India's Narmada River, the largest of over 100 dams planned for the river, which forcibly displaced thousands of people from their homes (Safi 2017). The Yacyreta hydroelectric dam in Argentina provoked the forced displacement of over 50,000 people without adequate relocation or compensation plans, caused irreversible disruption of fish biodiversity and fishery resources that were vital to the livelihood of the local population, and had huge fiscal implications for the country (World Bank 1997). To make room for the Chixoy Dam project in Guatemala, more than 4,000 Mayan people and 6,000 households in surrounding communities were forcibly removed at gunpoint (Johnston 2005). The impacts of these abuses are not static or isolated to one group or generation; rather, they are dynamic and cumulative, passed down through generations so that even now these communities are still struggling with the negative impacts caused by those projects undermining and limiting their opportunities, causing them to lose territory, patrimony, resources, and even identity, and forcing them and future generations to continue to be trapped in poverty.

As a result of these and other controversial projects and the growing pressure and opposition from impacted communities and international movements, the World Bank was forced to draft and approve its first environmental and social safeguard policies related to environmental assessment, involuntary resettlement, and indigenous peoples. The aim was to establish specific requirements to protect people and their environment during project design. For instance, EIAs identify risks and impacts, as do mitigation plans, while indigenous peoples' plans and resettlement plans ensure adequate protection to people and benefits. The approval of the first-ever safeguard policies by the World Bank had global implications because all multilateral development banks subsequently approved their own set of similar safeguards. Safeguard policies became mandatory requirements to access bank loans, and the Bank promoted them as social and environmental best practices, which led many countries to adopt environmental legislation and use EIAs modeled after World Bank safeguards.

As mentioned before, the introduction of social and environmental safeguards was happening when I was an undergraduate student in civil engineering in Bolivia. However, at that time, my classmates and I were not taught about this important history or the human and environmental costs that led to the development of these tools. For us, learning to use EIAs was just part of the curriculum. Years later, I came to realize that the inclusion of EIAs and mitigation plans as part of project design was the result of a painful global development failure and learning process, with significant costs to real people who saw their livelihood destroyed and were forced out of their homes and lives in the name of development. These human and environmental costs and the abuses and suffering that accompanied them must be taught to new development practitioners. Such knowledge is integral to understanding why safeguards are necessary, and why it is so important that we don't take them for granted or think of these tools only as instruments to comply with or boxes to check, as unfortunately happens too often.

Safeguard policies are not bureaucratic procedures but are critical tools to ensure that development projects do not cause harm to people and the environment, to ensure that not just some or the majority but all those affected have their livelihood restored and are better off than they were previous to project conditions, that all are treated fairly, and that impacted communities are not just statistics. But as is true with any tool, safeguards are only effective if the right incentives for their implementation are in place, if we are fully aware of the consequences of unintended impacts on real people and the environment, and if we use them with empathy for and awareness of the people that the project is supposed to benefit. I believe that project decisions would be different if we put ourselves in the shoes of those impacted when we make development decisions, if we asked ourselves whether we would accept the same arrangements if we were the ones to be displaced, if we had our source of livelihood diminished or lost, if we faced the possibility of our water being contaminated, or if we were forced to accept lower prices to compensate for our land and homes. If we could ask ourselves whether the project would be justifiable if we, and our loved ones, were going to be the ones to bear the consequences, intended or unintended, of making room for a project supposed to bring economic growth and development, then probably decisions would be different.

Given the lessons learned from all these past projects, one would think that project design, implementation, and decision making would be different now, especially after the creation of safeguard policies. In most cases this is true, but unfortunately we still have too many cases similar to the controversial projects of the 1980s and 1990s, in which countless people are left worse off than they were prior to the project, and for which governments and the World Bank justify their interventions in the name of economic growth. The International Consortium of Investigative Journalists' project "Evicted and Abandoned" found that from 2004 to 2013, projects funded by the World Bank in more than 100 countries have physically or economically displaced an estimated 3.4 million people and that the Bank failed to properly implement its own safeguard policies.[3] So the question remains, why is this happening despite the creation and implementation of safeguard policies aimed to avoid and prevent these types of situations?

The answer to this question is not simple because of the intricacies and, in many cases, contradictions of development. It is important to reflect upon the complex interactions between country power dynamics and politics often reflected in Bank leadership—the board of governors and directors—the political and career incentives within senior management, and the diversity of ideas and approaches among their highly trained development practitioners. These variables play a significant role in development decision making that should not be underestimated.

For instance, after the creation of the World Bank's safeguard policies, an interesting phenomenon unfolded. For years many countries submitted high-risk projects to the Bank for funding. But as a result of its safeguard policies, the cost of such projects increased significantly because of the risks, potential impacts, and required measures to mitigate and compensate for them. This situation led many countries to see safeguards as onerous and bureaucratic procedures. When loan disbursements were withheld by the World Bank because of noncompliance with its environmental and social safeguards, some countries argued that the Bank's safeguards were nothing but "conditionalities" forced on them. Consequently, many countries went looking for new credit options. As a result, the World Bank progressively had fewer and fewer high-risk infrastructure projects in its portfolio. However, this did not mean that the demand for high-risk projects decreased; on the contrary, the demand for new and fast sources of funding increased. With the global economy growing, oil and commodity prices at their highest levels, and emerging economies positioning themselves as new and influential actors, alternatives to the World Bank's approach for development finance started to emerge. The New Development Bank led by these emerging economies—the BRICS (Brazil, Russia, India, China, and South Africa)—was created with a rhetorical message of going beyond the conventional codes of multilateral banks and quickening the pace of loan disbursement without conditionalities.[4] China single-handedly created the Asian Infrastructure Investment Bank, distinguished by a commitment to less bureaucracy, fast disbursement of funds, and a callable capital larger than the World Bank's.[5]

Despite its efforts to promote safeguards, delays in loan disbursement because of safeguard compliance, along with pressure from countries to lend larger amounts with minimal conditionalities, created incentives to bypass safeguards and expedite loan approvals, leading the World Bank to undermine the integrity of its own safeguards. Moving loans out the door was seen as a career booster, whereas being a safeguards specialist was seen as a dead end. In conversations within the Bank's halls and elevators, many employees perceived safeguards as too costly, driving country clients away from the Bank, and felt the Bank needed to be more flexible. As the World Bank attempts to regain business, it is tending to make its policies more flexible, neglecting adequate monitoring of operations and compliance with social and environmental safeguards. As a result, at the onset of global discussions about the creation of the new institutions, the World Bank started several internal-investment lending reforms to increase its effectiveness in delivering development finance. It moved from reviewing its procurement, supervision, and country engagement policies to reviewing its decades-old safeguard policies.

Within this context, the World Bank undertook an extensive review of its safeguard policies from 2012 to 2016. Given its poor record of effectively including civil society in decision making and its controversial history with high-risk infrastructure projects, essential services, and other sectors, several civil society organizations and social movements were extremely active in the review process, pushing the Bank and its member countries to strengthen safeguards and uphold human-rights obligations as part of its investments. During this time, one of the most contentious debates within the World Bank was whether it should, or should not, hold country members to international human-rights obligations. Unfortunately, and to the disappointment of many, some member countries and bank management insisted that human rights are not an economic development issue, but a political one. As a result, the new policies refer to human rights only once in 121 pages.[6]

Despite the increased competition from new financial institutions, the World Bank's more than seventy years of experience, established management structure and governance, large and deep network of connections and relationships, and tested ability to adapt to new global contexts give it a significant and unprecedented advantage over its rivals. Despite all the rhetoric about better alternatives to the World Bank, the new institutions are modeled after it and are opting to co-finance projects with the World Bank, using its procedures until they are able to establish their own institutional and management procedures. Unlike during the twentieth century, the World Bank's power and influence are no longer in the delivery of development finance but reside instead in its capacity to leverage and mobilize development, commercial, and sovereign financing by giving its seal of approval, by coordinating donor involvement, and by influencing regional development banks and commercial banks. Its influence comes from offering technical and political advice on policy-reform measures via knowledge services, setting global standards for development, including social and environmental protections that influence governments and other development institutions, and positioning itself as the multilateral institution preferred by donor governments to manage global trust funds, for example, the Global Green Fund for climate finance, among others (Edwards 2017).

The current global-development agenda centers on the Sustainable Development Goals (SDGs) adopted in 2015 and the Paris Agreement on climate change that entered into force in 2016. One of the main constraints, however, is the huge financial gap in investments needed to achieve the SDGs and Paris commitments. According to some estimates, the world needs to invest an annual average of $3.3 trillion in infrastructure until 2030 (Woetzel et al. 2016). The UN Conference on Trade and Development estimates that achieving the SDGs alone will take $5 trillion to $7 trillion a year, with an investment gap of about $2.5 trillion a year in developing countries to support growth (UNCTAD 2014). In 2015, all major multilateral development banks, including the World Bank and the new institutions, came up with a joint commitment to mobilize development finance, "From Billions to Trillions: Transforming Development Finance," in which they agreed that the needed volume of development finance would have to come from private investors (African Development Bank et al. 2015). In 2017, the G-20 agreed on the Hamburg Action Plan, which sets out principles for multilateral development banks, including private sector finance for growth and sustainable development aimed to mobilize the required level of finance. This new approach of "maximizing finance for development" is actively promoted by the World Bank president, Jim Yong Kim, and is without doubt a huge step (Landon 2018). Certainly, private investment is crucial for the development process. However, a key question is how to balance the inherent for-profit interest of the private sector with development outcomes for the public that may have low financial returns (Eyler-Driscoll 2018). How can we ensure that gains are not privatized and losses socialized? The measure of success should not only be in terms of how much money institutions and governments can leverage from the private sector but, more important, should be considered in terms of positive development impact, outcomes, and benefits, especially for the most vulnerable and disadvantaged.

Having monitored the World Bank's operations for many years, I can confidently say that one of the most effective strategies to implement safeguard policies and achieve ownership and lasting change is to share the decision-making process with the communities and people impacted by any development intervention. It is critical to appreciate the value of listening and consulting, being transparent and disclosing all relevant information about development projects, and allowing for meaningful participation by sharing power and the decision-making process. If we are to learn something from the failures of past projects, it is that disclosure of information, consultation, and community participation have to be seen by practitioners as foundational elements of any safeguard policy and development intervention. These are the elements that help ensure ownership, equity in terms of benefits and opportunities, and avoid or minimize harm, particularly to those already in vulnerable and disadvantaged situations, be they indigenous peoples, women, those with disabilities, those subject to discrimination based on gender identity or sexual orientation, or others.

This is especially critical, given the increasing restrictions on civic-space participation that is happening in so many countries. According to the

International Center for Not-for-Profit Law (ICNL), more than 156 laws and other restrictions constraining freedoms of association and assembly were reported to have been passed in seventy-five countries since 2012. Meanwhile, Global Witness reports that 2016 was the worst year on record for murders of human-rights and environmental defenders—200 people were killed across twenty-four countries (Global Witness 2017). Development interventions should ensure participation processes that are safe from any intimidation, discrimination, or fear of reprisals from governments, the private sector, or any other interested party. This is especially critical now that the new 2030 Agenda for Sustainable Development gravitates around leveraging private-sector finance for development.

Billions of people continue to live in poverty. Our natural world is facing severe stresses. The world's remaining forested areas continue to decline significantly. As development institutions fund projects in the name of short-term economic growth, vulnerable populations often receive the short end of the stick. Development for whom is the question we need to ask ourselves every time we face decisions and trade-offs as development practitioners. Development should be about values, equity, people—the most vulnerable and disadvantaged—and their environment, and less about economic growth and financial feasibility. When we are aware of our own privilege and have the ability to empathize with the most disadvantaged and vulnerable, we are able to see the human side of development, to see that there is not greater good to society if we make conscious decisions to leave some behind. With constant awareness of our own privilege and a sense of empathy, we can start thinking about issues of equity, inclusion, human rights, and our connections to the environment as individuals and as members of a community rather than only as development practitioners.

Notes

1. More information on the World Bank's allocation of votes by organization and country can be found at: http://www.worldbank.org/en/about/leadership/votingpowers.

2. A list of the World Bank's executive directors and alternates can be found at http://siteresources.worldbank.org/BODINT/Resources/278027-1215526322295/BankExecutiveDirectors.pdf.

3. More information on the investigation and cases of "Evicted and Abandoned: The World Bank's Broken Promise to the Poor," by the International Consortium of Investigative Journalists, can be found at www.icij.org/investigations/world-bank.

4. More information on the New Development Bank can be found at https://www.ndb.int/about-us/essence/mission-values.

5. More information on the Asian Infrastructure Investment Bank can be found at https://www.aiib.org/en/index.html.

6. More information on the World Bank Environmental and Social Framework can be found at http://documents.worldbank.org/curated/en/383011492423734099/pdf/114278-WP-REVISED-PUBLIC-Environmental-and-Social-Framework.pdf.

11

Devolution: An Opportunity for Sustainable Development

Esther Kamau

Devolution has brought about the rights and interests of the marginalized groups. The Constitution gives power to the people so they can govern themselves and they can see their resources being used as they planned, and to be part of the planning process and to be involved in making those decisions.
—Kapelo Powon, chief of staff, West Pokot County, Kenya

Devolution—or the transfer of development authority, accountability, and resources to lower levels of government—is a subset of attempts to build good governance for development. The expectation is that devolution can enhance development, enable true participation, and give people more control over their futures. In Kenya, the 2010 constitutional reform devolved resources and authority from the national to the county level. In this chapter, I explore the potential of devolution to advance sustainable development by looking at the experiences in several of those counties.

Factors of Devolution in Kenya

Background

Regional social and economic inequality in Kenya resulted from postcolonial development policies that systematically overlooked economic investment in arid and semiarid lands, seen to have less potential than areas with richer terrain to promote economic growth. After Kenya got its independence in 1963, the government declared war on three "enemies" of the state: disease, illiteracy, and poverty. However, communities perceived to have a low potential for return on development investment were, in fact, marginalized by efforts to promote economic and social development. The "Sessional Paper Number 10 of 1965," which guided national planning and resource allocation for two decades in postcolonial Kenya, endorsed the allocation of scarce national resources to "high potential areas" for returns (Republic of Kenya 1965). The policy aimed to promote rapid economic growth, which would be redistributed to the entire country. However, the government did not put a mechanism for redistribution in place. Subsequent economic policies perpetuated the same ideology, leading to underinvestment and ensuing economic and social marginalization of the north over the years. Consequently, these areas have the lowest development indicators and highest incidence of poverty in the country. Such social injustices were believed to be the backdrop of Kenya's 2007 postelection violence. Social and economic inequalities were a key reason Kenyans voted for a new constitution in 2010, intending to institutionalize equitable distribution of national resources.

In a national referendum on August 4, 2010, Kenyans voted overwhelmingly to adopt the new constitution. The adoption of the Constitution of Kenya in 2010 marked a significant change in the way the country and its resources are governed. The new Constitution devolved political, administrative, and financial power and responsibilities to forty-seven counties. The main objectives of devolution were to enhance people's participation in governance, recognize the right of communities to self-manage, protect and promote the interests and rights of minority and marginalized communities, and ensure equitable distribution of national resources (Republic of Kenya 2010). Kenyans see devolution as an opportunity to level the playing field and resolve historical marginalization. Another major driving force of devolution was people's dissatisfaction with service delivery and socioeconomic development in rural areas.

The centralized government was bureaucratic and far removed from people's actual needs. People didn't have the opportunity to participate in how services were planned or delivered and didn't participate in activities related to development in their localities. Lack of people's participation led to missed opportunities, lack of accountability for resource use, and corruption at all levels of government. As a result, most services were not accessible to most people, and the few development projects that were undertaken were not sustainable. Devolution seeks to reverse this by bringing political, financial, and administrative authority to the local level. Devolution shifts power from appointed bureaucrats to elected leaders. It opens the political field for nontraditional, visionary, and committed Kenyans to seek county leadership positions. Further, it increases public participation for self-determination at the local level. By promoting public involvement, there is a higher chance of establishing inclusive service delivery, increasing accountability, building local ownership, and strengthening the sustainability of resultant development.

A New Brand of Leaders

Although devolution has created the structures needed to promote sustainable development, it is crucial to have effective leadership to catalyze and direct change. Devolution has created space for the entrance of visionary leaders who seek to accomplish collective goals rather than indulge individual ambitions. Most of these leaders left satisfying careers for public service. For example, the governor of Makueni County was an established law professor and activist for constitutional reform for most of his life. Similarly, the current director of public participation in Makueni County was an international development professor at an international university in Kenya. These leaders are well-educated, and most of them have advanced degrees in areas aligned to the sectors they lead. The county executive committee member for education (CEC education) holds a PhD in education, and the CEC health is a medical doctor. In a changing environment, these leaders are innovative, adaptive, and motivated by their vision and mission of achieving collective good rather than fighting to sustain themselves. They are focused not only on the current issues facing their society but also on future sustainability. For example, under the current leadership, Makueni County has been investing in climate change–related initiatives. The leaders embrace values-based rather than power-based leadership. Values include empowering the local people and a focus on human rights, justice, and sustainable development. The county leadership tends to work collaboratively as a network rather than being led by a single strongman.

Devolution has given people the power to choose their leaders, and county leaders are well aware of the cost of putting personal interests above those of the society, which includes people voting them out of office. They realize that for real change and sustainable development to occur, everyone's voice is essential. Rather than ruling through intimidation, they work to build trust and unity for a common goal. Toward this goal, Makueni trained all members of the executive branch in servant leadership, which requires them to put society's interest above their own and be of service to all. County teams focus on performance and accountability. For example, in West Pokot the executive team works under a two-year contract that the governor renews on merit. The new brand of leaders has redefined community leadership and the approach to solve chronic social, economic, and environmental problems. Their leadership style is bringing about economic, social, and environmental changes, leading to sustainable development in counties.

County Governments

Although sustainable development is often discussed at the international and national level, usually services and projects to address poverty are delivered and implemented at the local level. Three factors give county governments in Kenya an advantage in promoting sustainable development. First, because of their proximity and accessibility, county governments can be more responsive to people's needs than the national government. As one county leader stated, "National government is away from the people, who cares? When they come here with their airplanes, do they see our roads? . . . The governor is here with us. . . . He interacts and listens to the poor person; he has an opportunity to do so. . . . That cannot happen at the national level."[1] Local governments oversee services in many sectors, including provision of water, sanitation, health, education, planning, and waste management, areas that are a major part of sustainable development. If well governed, county government can promote inclusion and participation that leads to ownership of development and equitable service delivery within its jurisdiction.

Second, since devolution, there is a heightened public expectation of improved service delivery. Devolution gave people hope of good governance and inspired young, educated people to seek political leadership positions to serve their communities. Another reason that counties are poised to stimulate sustainable development is social standing. County leaders come from the local communities, and failure to deliver services and sustainable growth risks their losing face in societies where social standing is valued.

Third, it is understood by civil society that participation and inclusion, equity and nondiscrimination, accountability, and taking care of the environment are rudiments of sustainable development. In my professional experience, meaningful participation is a prerequisite to sustainable development. Without meaningful, inclusive public involvement, it would be hard to promote equity and accountability or to ensure inclusion and nondiscrimination.

Participation

The 2010 Constitution of Kenya makes citizen participation a central part of Kenya's governance system. Article 10 identifies participation as a national value and principle of governance. Article 174(c) states that the object of devolution is to "give powers of self-governance to the people and enhance the participation of the people in the exercise of the powers of the State and in making decisions affecting them." Article 196(1)(b) requires the county government to "facilitate public participation and involvement in the legislative and other business of the assembly and its committees."

Before the constitutional change, Kenyans expected citizen participation; however, very little participation occurred because there was no legal framework. The new Constitution of 2010 provides this legal framework, which is further expanded in the County Government Act of 2012, the County Government Financial Act, and rolled out in the County Public Participation Guidelines (2017). Two counties, Makueni and West Pokot, have been successful in establishing meaningful, inclusive citizen engagement to promote sustainable development. The two counties have demonstrated best practices in installing inclusive participation structures that give their residents real opportunities to participate in planning, budgeting, implementa-

tion, and monitoring. Other counties are learning from them. This innovation and diffusion would not have been possible with a centralized government. The following section explores how Makueni County has successfully supported economic and social development, democratic governance,
and environmental sustainability through a well-developed, devolved structure of public participation.

Devolution and Participation:
The Example of Makueni County

Makueni County is located in the arid and semiarid region of the former
Eastern Province of Kenya. It was one of the marginalized regions in
Kenya, with more than 61 percent of the population living below the
poverty level of $1 a day (Population Action International n.d.). The county
has six sub-counties that consist of thirty wards. Each ward has three sub-
wards. A sub-ward is the smallest unit recognized by the Constitution of
2010. To ensure that everyone has an opportunity to participate, the county
goes further down to the village level in its participation structure. Makueni
County leadership emphasizes that every person must be provided with the
opportunity to participate. To ensure this, the county presents information
in a manner that is accessible to all, and people are never expected to have
to leave their village to participate. Information is taken to them.

Before establishing structures for participation, the county government
hired a director of public participation, who trained leaders in the participation process. The county government then identified facilitators among
those trained, to train the public on citizen engagement and civic education.
Since the 2013–2014 development year, the county has allocated at least 30
percent of its annual development budget to public participation processes.
This composed 12 percent of its total budget. Allocating significant resources
to the public-participation process shows the county's commitment to public
engagement. Makueni County is the only county that has established the
position of participation director, whose role is to coordinate civic education
and public participation. Speaking about the role of leadership in making
public participation a reality, Makueni's County director of public participation explained, "We have an advantage that we have a governor who was into
civil rights. I think that's the biggest fortune that Makueni got. Getting some-
body to champion the foundations of devolution, who was the champion of
the Constitution. I think we attribute the success of devolution that you see to
that very fact."[2]

As a result, the county has been innovative in how it ensures everyone
has an opportunity to be engaged in county development. In most of the
counties, the participation structure starts at the ward level, which is far
removed from the common person in the village, making the participation

process susceptible to elite capture. However, in Makueni, participation is built from the most basic administrative unit: the village. The county has 3,455 villages. When developing the County Development Integrated Plan (CDIP), the county started the process of collecting interests. How this works in each village is as follows: A village headman convenes meetings for five days, during which members of the village bring ideas about what they want to do in their village. Each village elects an eleven-member committee to take village interests to the next level, which is a cluster of seven to fifteen villages, depending on population density and village size. After deliberating and reconciling the interests from their respective villages, they prioritize the projects, and each cluster elects an eleven-member delegation to represent their proposals to the sub-ward level. About 315 village clusters represent their constituents at the sub-ward level. At this level, about five clusters are grouped according to the commonality of their interests and geographical closeness; the village-cluster committees confirm that the projects presented are what they agreed to at the village-cluster level. To prevent elite capture, the committee cannot include a plan that did not come through the village forum, thus ensuring that the voice of the ordinary person is not lost. The committee discusses and prioritizes projects through consensus. Sub-wards elect a development committee of eleven members who present their priorities at the ward level. At this level, the committee selects a Ward Development Committee of eleven members to ensure that the proposals approved at the ward level are presented at the sub-county level, where about five wards meet to discuss and prioritize their development projects. The elected committee goes through the same process of deliberation, consensus, and prioritization at the sub-county level. The committees select a sub-county development committee of eleven members that takes their proposals to the county level. There are six sub-counties in Makueni, and each sub-county has an eleven-member development committee. These committees are part of 1,000 delegates in the County People's Forum that discusses and prioritizes the county's development projects. Other groups represented are special populations, including people with disabilities, marginalized groups, local organizations, development agencies, and nongovernmental organizations (NGOs).

During the planning meeting, the governor, cabinet, and county technical leaders listen to proposals. All the development committees attend, and they affirm that the plans presented are what they proposed. They also hear the ward representative, who may complain about projects that might have been dropped out or adopted inappropriately.

Before the development committee completes final prioritization, a technical committee at the county level aligns locally identified priorities with the national development plan, Vision 2030, and global goals such as the Sustainable Development Goals (SDGs). For example, if a local priority is to construct a health facility to reduce walking distance and improve access to health care, the technical committee would link this to SDG 3, Target 3.8. SDG 3 is to ensure healthy lives and promote well-being for all ages, while Target 3.8 relates to achieving universal health coverage.

At the county level, the governor's office and cabinet review proposals in the CDIP, before they submit to the county assembly. The county treasurer develops the budget and presents it to the county assembly and the public. The proposed budget and CDIP then follow the same path to the village level for the development committees to confirm what was agreed. Once the County Assembly approves the CDIP and budget, the participation structure monitors implementation and holds elected leaders and their office's accountable to deliver the plan. Budgets are available for review by local people, NGOs, and the media.

This transparent system undercuts corruption and misappropriation of public funds, as people are involved in monitoring the projects they proposed, which meet specific needs in their communities. The system has improved government performance.

Unlike a centralized government in which local people cannot hold bureaucrats who were appointed nationally by the president accountable, the county electorate now holds their elected leaders accountable when they fail to deliver. For example, in Makueni, all County Assembly members (MCA) elected in 2013 were voted out in 2017 because of unsatisfactory performance, infighting, and corruption. Currently, Makueni is considered one of the highest performing counties, despite its having been on the brink of dissolution in 2014 because of the problems just mentioned. The foundation of this performance, according to the governor and other county leaders, is public participation. Although there is public participation in many other counties, it lacks the depth and breadth of participation in Makueni and West Pokot. Many counties develop plans centrally and ask the public to give feedback. Most people do not understand the plans, so they have little influence on decision making, implementation, and monitoring. Elite capture and corruption in those counties have continued. Lack of meaningful participation has also led to unequal growth, leaving some populations behind.

Devolution and Economic Development

Poverty is a pressing issue for most of the population in Kenya. County governments have to wrestle with this problem. The question in the mind of the elected leaders who want to retain their position is (or should be) how to facilitate and speed up economic development to benefit their constituents. Traditionally, rural areas have experienced migration of their residents to cities and towns as people seek economic opportunities. With devolution, counties are looking for ways to retain their population by creating economic opportunities locally. This effort has led to counties looking inward to discover what they can do to stimulate economic development. I think this is a significant paradigm shift—that counties are looking at what they can do, rather than what they cannot do. They are identifying their strengths and resources.

Counties have natural endowments, depending on their weather patterns, geographical locations, and, to some extent, culture. Some counties share these endowments whereas the characteristics of others are unique. Traditionally, communities have created livelihoods out of their settings but have lacked support from the government in transforming the respective livelihoods into economic development. Climate-change-related factors and lack of access to markets have devastated communities' livelihoods. In the past, NGOs, particularly INGOs, linked people with markets and improved methods of production. Counties are now increasingly taking over this role, assuming economic development functions that were recently led by NGOs. This is an important shift, as it enhances targeting and strengthens sustainability. I highlight a few examples below.

In Makueni, the county government has supported the efforts of residents, especially youth, to create livelihoods for themselves. Like other arid and semiarid regions, Makueni has been categorized as a "low potential" region for a long time, despite the fact that the county has arable land that could be sustainably used for agricultural purposes. Furthermore, Makueni lies on the major Mombasa-Nairobi highway and railroad lines that are crucial for transportation of goods and products. Its weather and soil are conducive to growing fruits and other horticulture products that are in high demand nationally and internationally. After a series of citizen-engagement forums, residents realized that they "have been sitting on gold for a long time," as one of the leaders said. The county spearheaded building skills in different sectors to equip its residents to utilize these resources to stimulate economic development. After training, the county provided trainees interested in various areas with low-cost loans to initiate their livelihood activities. For example, the county trained young people in sustainable sand harvesting and marketing. In the past, people from other regions cheaply and unsustainably harvested the sand, leaving the land unusable and the local people deprived. In another program, the county partnered with SNV Netherlands to facilitate and improve farming vegetables and fruits, especially mangoes, which are plentiful in the region. Most of the fruits were growing wild and going to waste because market linkages and improved farming practices were lacking. The county and SNV trained residents in crop management and entrepreneurship, then linked them to markets. As drought is a major threat to farming, the county trained residents to dig water pans to harvest freshwater during the rainy season to irrigate their land in the dry season. To reduce post-harvest losses and stabilize mango prices to increase farmers' income, the county government constructed a fruit-processing plant in Makueni, which started operating in June 2017.

To offer a few examples in other counties, in Tharaka Nthi County, the county government collaborated with East Africa Breweries, Ltd., to farm high-quality sorghum, a local staple grain, for beer brewing. The region's hot climate makes it appropriate for sorghum and similar grains. Embu and Murag'a Counties capitalized on raising dairy cows to meet the growing demand for milk and other dairy products. Nyeri and Kiambu introduced fish farming to supply fish to nearby Nairobi. In Isiolo, a dry region, the county supported women to establish ventures in camel milk and processing dried meat.

Thus, like Makueni, other counties are becoming hubs for economic innovations through the use of local resources. They are in a position to develop local solutions to local problems by changing the way they use their environment and relate to their surrounding markets. It is important to mention that counties are required by the Constitution of 2010 and Vision 2030 to ensure equity as they improve old and seek new ways to create sustainable livelihoods. Participation of all population groups has been crucial in implementing equitable economic growth, especially in counties such as Makueni.

Devolution and Social Development

In addition to economic development, counties are finding ways to improve their residents' quality of life. The health, water, and waste management sectors especially have seen significant improvement through county efforts. In other areas that are not directly managed by the county, such as education, some counties are seeking ways to improve access to quality education for people who cannot afford it. As an example of social development efforts at the county level, I will focus on improved delivery of health care.

The new Constitution of 2010 guarantees everyone the highest attainable standard of health. Counties are mandated to ensure health care is accessible to all their constituents. Counties should ensure health-care services are geographically accessible to ordinary residents and are affordable, culturally acceptable, and of high quality. Makueni and Garissa Counties offer examples of innovations that make health services available to residents.

As reported by the *Kenya Free Press* on September 16, 2016, the governor of Makueni County vowed to ensure that his county would meet "provisions of Kenya's Constitution relating to health rights, and the United Nation's Sustainable Development Goals" when he launched the Makueni universal-health-care program. To make the right to health a reality, the county offered free health-care services to those over sixty-five and under five years old. After the county realized that it could guarantee free health care to its most vulnerable populations, it started Makueni Universal

Healthcare, an inexpensive program, to insure health care for the rest of the community. To register in the universal-health-care program, each family pays Kenya shillings 500 (about $5) a year, which gives members access to a range of in- and outpatient health services at no extra cost, including consultation, laboratory, prescription drugs, cancer screening, mental health, rehabilitation services, family planning, and ambulance referral services in all the health facilities in Makueni County. The governor of Makueni explained to the *Daily Nation* on September 16, 2016, that in 2014, among all the counties, Makueni allocated the highest percentage (48 percent) of its budget to health care (Maina, Akumu, and Muchiri 2016). This underlines the commitment of county leadership to take steps to realize the right to health of all residents. Makueni is Kenya's first county to provide universal health coverage, and other counties are learning from it.

In 2016, Garissa County won the Best Practices Award in service delivery for employing innovations to increase the number of mothers delivering in health facilities, aimed at reducing maternal mortality rates. The county had some of the highest maternal mortality rates for various reasons, including nomadic lifestyle, female genital cutting, and poverty. To solve this problem, the county health-management team visited Karamoja in Uganda, a community with similar characteristics, to learn best practices in maternal health. The county decided to work with traditional birth attendants (TBAs) to promote safer deliveries and reduce maternal mortality rates. Central government had opposed TBAs, even though local people considered TBAs to be a helpful resource. Government opposition failed to reduce maternal mortality rates; indeed, rates increased as the controversy drove TBAs to conduct deliveries in secret, unsafe places. With devolution, county government was able to examine the role of TBAs in the community and redefine it. It developed a system of awarding Kenya shillings 200 (about $2) to county health-extension workers and TBAs for every mother they brought to health facilities for delivery. The county also allowed TBAs to stay with the mothers for moral support. The county set up maternal shelters for mothers who traveled from remote areas. The county created an incentive program to provide mothers with free MAMA Kits[3] that they would typically have had to buy otherwise. The county health-management team used cell-phone texting to link mothers with health facilities. This innovation was credited for increasing the number of skilled deliveries by 48 percent between 2013 and 2015 (Ministry of Health 2016). The county also noted increased antenatal and postnatal care.

Devolution and Environmental Sustainability

As a crosscutting development issue, climate change has significantly affected populations across Kenya, mainly because livelihoods are primarily dependent on natural resources. Climate change adaptation and mitigation are, therefore, critical aspects of county planning. Kenya's devolved system opens the way for counties to be trailblazers for climate innovation. The law requires county governments to incorporate climate change action in all their functions and to have a county executive committee member dedicated to leading climate change efforts. They are also required to align their CDIP with Kenya's Climate Change Act of 2016 and the National Climate Change Action Plan.

Unlike those serving in national government, which is physically located elsewhere, county leaders experience the same effects of climate change as the local population, and citizens may also press county government to address climate-change issues that affect their livelihoods. Considering that counties are affected differently by climate change depending on their form of livelihood, counties have realized that there is no one-size-fits-all solution to the effects of climate change. Across the country, counties are employing various innovations to address climate change impacts. Counties most affected by climate change are in marginalized, arid regions. Some of them have realized that they need to allocate resources to find solutions to mitigate the impacts. Five of the most arid counties, led by Makueni, have enacted regulations to set up County Climate Change Funds (CCCFs) from their budgets to find appropriate solutions to alleviate effects of climate change on local populations. The counties partnering with Makueni are Garissa, Wajir, Kitui, and Isiolo.

Makueni was the first county in Africa to enact a law that mainstreams climate into its development plans. This initiative is consistent with the county's values of using citizen engagement and grassroots organizations to solve local problems. The county has elected committees organized at the ward level that identify climate-change-related impacts and solutions, and it has prioritized projects based on need and urgency, as outlined by the county's climate risk management. Some initiatives the county has undertaken are afforestation (establishing new forests), reforestation (recovering existing or recent forests), banning making charcoal in deforested regions, and supporting residents with alternative ways of creating income through agroforestry. The county has supported its residents in building sand dams and water harvesting to capture water during rainy seasons. Across the country, counties are implementing such projects and other practices to improve natural resource management and adapt to climate change.

Partners in Development

This chapter would be incomplete without exploring opportunities that devolution in Kenya has opened to change relationships among different stakeholders in development. As counties map their unique needs, establish resources previously not harnessed, and identify gaps between needs and resources, they look for development partners to accomplish mutual goals. For example, in Makueni County, after development committees have prioritized projects depending on their budgets, local communities take on the remaining projects, which they develop into community-action plans. They use local resources to implement projects in these plans. If there are funding gaps, communities find external partners to fill the gaps.

This practice is contrary to traditional development practice, in which donors initiate development projects in collaboration with communities. The shift gives communities power to be in charge of their development and changes the relationship from a donor-recipient relationship to partners in development. Counties are becoming community philanthropy centers where stakeholders who share common interests join to pursue a common goal or project. One example is in Makueni, where the county government brought in several INGOs, including World Vision, to build a dam. Rather than different actors doing small projects separately, in most cases duplicating resources, counties such as Makueni are bringing actors together to accomplish more significant projects.

As counties take back the roles of outside development agencies, one may wonder what the role of INGOs and donor agencies will be. I would argue that with the elected government moving closer to the people, there is a significant opportunity for organizations and donors to partner with counties to hasten the process of development—as pointed out above. An even more significant role, though, lies in civic education, building capacity for public participation, and enhancing accountability. As presented earlier, participation is central to creating sustainable change. Building the ability of communities to participate in planning, implementation, and monitoring development projects and programs requires enormous resources in money, time, and technical expertise, which counties alone cannot or may not want to supply. Motivated, committed leadership is needed to manage the process and overcome these hurdles.

Conclusion

Although devolution in Kenya is still in an early stage, some counties such as Makueni show that it presents an opportunity to redefine development. County governments are close to the people and, therefore, can understand specific problems residents experience. Democratically elected leaders at the county level are uniquely positioned to identify local development needs, including climate-change-related impacts, and to respond appropriately. Also, they have what can be considered multifaceted accountability. They are directly accountable to their electorate, which can remove them from office if they do not perform according to their mandate, and they are legally obligated to fulfill their duties according to the Constitution of 2010. Because the leaders come from the same community they are serving, they are motivated to maintain good social standing in their community.

Likewise, county government has provided an opportunity for local, transformational leaders to seek public office to contribute to the development of their communities. Counties have the potential, through meaningful participation, to eradicate corruption, strengthen accountability, and ensure broad-based, democratic ownership of development projects. Productive citizen engagement supports inclusive and equitable development. Counties play a crucial role linking local communities' priorities to national and international goals. They translate global agendas, such as the SDGs, into local actions. If well governed, they create a framework to define, implement, and monitor development goals through a bottom-up approach that ensures sustainability.

Counties are changing the traditional donor-recipient relationship by empowering communities so that they move from being just recipients to becoming partners, thereby shifting power dynamics. They are pooling resources from different actors to accomplish bigger goals. Although counties are assuming some roles recently performed by INGOs, this does not mean NGO and donor roles have diminished. Instead, the shift redefines donor roles as cooperating and collaborating with local communities to meet locally set priorities, especially in capacity building to plan, implement, and monitor development targets, as well as to hold their governments accountable.

Notes

1. Zipporah Wambua, Makueni County director of public participation, interviewed by the author, January 12, 2018.
2. Ibid.
3. A package used on the delivery table that contains a yard of cotton cloth (baby blanket), one bar of laundry soap, a pair of gloves, a piece of cotton wool, small gauze pads, cord ligature, and a yard of polyethylene sheeting.

12

Collective Action and Happy Accidents: Lessons from a Central Mexico Watershed

Agustin Madrigal Bulnes,
Andrea Savage Tejada, and Joshua Ellsworth

Agustin's cell phone rang as he patiently wrapped up a conversation with a partner from the Department of Ecology at a reforestation site in Santa Rosa in the Upper Laja River Watershed (river basin or catchment) in Central Mexico. Without looking at his phone, he guessed that it was either his longtime technician, Fernando, trying to reach him from one of the ongoing community soil restoration projects, or another collaborator from the municipal center of San Miguel de Allende, who wanted to talk before a meeting with several stakeholders near the Allende Reservoir. Agustin thanked his partner for his time and hopped back in his car to get to his next meeting, returning the missed call while he drove down from the high-altitude pine and oak forests to the drier mesquite tree and cactus-covered landscape surrounding the reservoir. He quickly glanced at the odometer, which was reading a frightfully large number—an issue for another day.

Agustin Madrigal Bulnes is the director of Salvemos al Rio Laja (Save the Laja River), which has been collaborating with a number of diverse actors for the last twenty years to improve environmental and human resilience in the face of the severely degraded Upper Laja River Watershed. The troubled state of the watershed has led to contaminated and dwindling water supplies and a struggle by rural communities to curb soil erosion that is jeopardizing their livelihoods. There are a number of initiatives to improve environmental conditions and protect people's livelihoods, but maintaining their momentum through time and across an expansive and complex landscape of ecosystems, actors, and financing is a critical challenge. Agustin, the Salvemos team, and their collaborators are working to overcome these challenges with a partnership program called Todos por el Agua (Everyone for Water). In this chapter, we reflect on strategies Agustin and his colleagues have found to help navigate, orient, and maintain their work on watershed restoration and rural livelihoods in Todos por el Agua and other programs. Each strategy has been seen to work over the long term within an unpredictable and complex context. We set the stage with background on the actors and location, then examine strategies focused on setting goals, catalyzing change at multiple levels, achieving dynamic sustainability, and building collective action.

Setting the Stage

The Actors: Todos por el Agua and Partners

When Agustin began working as director of Salvemos in 2007, he met Joshua Ellsworth, who was working with a US-based nongovernmental organization (NGO), Ecosystem Sciences Foundation (ESF), on a number of projects in partnership with the Municipal Department of Ecology in San Miguel de Allende. Along with Don Patterson, the department's director at the time, Agustin and Josh began meeting with communities, NGOs, researchers, and government agencies to explore ways in which rural communities could be incentivized to plant trees and improve grazing management and soil conservation. Over the next few years, Salvemos and Ecosystem Sciences Foundation formalized a partnership. In 2009, the partners started the program Todos por el Agua with funding from the Tinker, Overbrook, and Rio Arronte Foundations, and the Mexican Nature Conservation Fund (FMCN) as part of its Cities and Watersheds Program.

Starting in 2009, the Todos por el Agua program worked with six rural communities to help them identify and develop holistic rural development and environmental conservation plans. The program has linked individual and communal landowners with government and nongovernment programs that pay them to implement coordinated projects such as reforestation, soil conservation, and seed collection for nurseries. For example, communities have constructed thousands of soil conservation structures, such as terraces and water-capture pits, and have planted several hundred thousand trees and cacti on over 3,000 hectares, or about 7,400 acres. In the last three years, the work has been scaled-up to include eleven communities in five municipalities from the northeast and south of the Upper Laja River Watershed, with funding from the Guanajuato State Ecology Institute and the Institute for Assistance to Migrants and Their Families.

Todos por el Agua works primarily in impoverished, indigenous Otomí or mestizo communities. It works under two conditions: first, communities must invite the group to help them; second, the communities themselves must choose where environmental restoration will take place. Todos por el Agua does not direct communities, but rather the program offers them awareness, technical training, consultation, strengthening of their institutions, and sources of funding for environmental restoration. This allows the communities themselves to make informed decisions and empowers them by building their capacity to plan, access, and implement federally funded projects without the need for further nongovernmental support.

Todos por el Agua has worked steadily to engage an increasingly broad range of stakeholders within the watershed. In 2012, it helped form the Observatorio Ciudadano del Agua y Saneamiento de San Miguel de Allende (Citizens Water and Sanitation Council [OCAS]), which provides an independent (from government) review of water resources within the Municipality of San Miguel de Allende. The program also facilitates links with actors outside the region. In 2015, the Upper Laja River Watershed was selected as a "sister watershed" for a twinning project with the Willamette River Watershed in Oregon, funded by Australia's prestigious Theiss International Riverprize.

The Location: The Upper Laja River Watershed
Work at the watershed level tends to be challenging because of the complex economic, social, environmental, jurisdictional, and governance contexts within a given area. This means that many problems require sustained long-term interventions beyond the time frame a donor will typically fund. Agustin has regularly encountered such complexities in his almost thirty years of work in the watershed. Some of these complexities are summarized here.

Hydro-ecological conditions. The Upper Laja River Watershed is 7,000-square-kilometers (about 2,700 square miles), located in the highlands of Central Mexico in the state of Guanajuato. At one time this watershed helped replenish a deep underground water reserve called the Independencia Aquifer that provided the lifeblood for several great epochs in Mexico's history, such as Mexico's independence movement and the growth of a booming agriculture industry. The watershed covers ten municipalities and is the origin of the Laja River, one of the larger tributaries to the Lerma-Chapala river system, which is ranked as a globally outstanding freshwater ecoregion by the World Wildlife Fund (WWF) (Creel et al. 2000). This watershed is also the primary water source for Guadalajara, Mexico's second-largest city, and is recognized as a priority for river basin restoration and conservation.

Over the life of his decades of work in the watershed, Agustin has witnessed how continued mismanagement has had detrimental effects on the health of the watershed's residents, ecosystems, and economy. Years of deforestation, overgrazing, and legal and illegal gravel mining have reduced biodiversity and caused extreme soil erosion and compaction, which limit the soil's ability to retain water and recharge groundwater supplies (Sotelo

Nunez 2006). Contamination of surface water from municipal, industrial, household, and agricultural discharge has made the majority of surface-water resources unfit for domestic use. It is estimated that water for commercial agriculture makes up 85 percent of the water being pumped from the aquifer. Combined with other industrial and residential use (10 percent and 5 percent, respectively) roughly 700 million cubic meters of water are being extracted every year. This amount is three times greater than the aquifer's ability to be replenished (Mahlknecht et al. 2004). At the current rate of extraction, estimates reveal that on average the water in the aquifer will last fifteen to twenty more years, and probably less in some locations (Castellanos et al. 2002, Ortega-Guerrero et al. 2002).

Springs and wetlands that were once important habitats for migratory birds and endemic aquatic species have disappeared because of the falling water table. The effects of diminishing groundwater supplies on the rural communities Agustin has come to know so well are severe and more visible every year. Poorer communities that cannot buy bottled water are forced to pump water from wells contaminated by natural elements—such as fluoride, arsenic, and sodium—that have leached from volcanic rocks over thousands of years but are increasingly concentrated because of the dropping water table. Many wells have fluoride levels above the limits set by the Mexican federal government, and it is common to see severe dental deformation caused by fluoride poisoning (Ecosystem Sciences Foundation 2006).

Social, economic, and political conditions. Although there are a number of large irrigated farming operations that produce crops such as broccoli, spinach, and alfalfa for the domestic market and international export, most of the rural inhabitants are smallholder farmers who rely on the summer rains to produce staple crops for household use and village markets. Many men and some women from these communities have emigrated to the United States or urban areas within Mexico and send back remittances to support family members and cover capital expenses such as houses and wells. As a result, much of the agricultural work is performed by the women, children, and elderly who remained behind. The income from remittances is extremely important to their livelihoods, but emigration has led to a fracturing of family and community connections.

Many of these rural communities are underserved by the local, state, and federal agencies, including those agencies focused on rural development and environmental conservation. The enrollment of marginalized rural communities in Mexico's federal rural development and environmental conservation funding programs is hampered by factors such as insufficient outreach by federal agencies to remote, underserved communities; confusing eligibility requirements; application procedures that are inaccessible to underserved communities; limited local training in planning, writing up, and executing comprehensive conservation and development programs; and rural-to-urban migration resulting from limited economic opportunities, which has depleted traditional local knowledge about native ecosystems (Kosoy, Corbera, and Brown 2008, Cotler et al. 2013).

When these communities are able to access federal programs, the projects are often undertaken without the framework of a holistic, long-term approach. Therefore, projects tend to be isolated, lack sufficient funding for long-term impact, and can be rendered ineffective by other problems that go unaddressed. As an example, Agustin and Fernando love to recount how one community planted thousands of trees and cacti with funding from the forestry commission. The funding for the necessary fencing was coming from another agency. But the money for fencing was slow to arrive and, in the meantime, goats ate most of the new plants. The lack of coordination and follow-up is partly a result of the policies of Mexican federal agencies, as many of them require government-approved technicians to submit and sign proposals on behalf of communities and landowners. Also, these technicians are paid a percentage of the project's implementation cost as opposed to being held accountable for long-term results. Many of them are not from the communities, nor do they live nearby, and they often design and manage projects without tapping into local knowledge, request little if any input from locals, and merely assign tasks and do not build local capacity (Kosoy, Corbera, and Brown 2008).

Since the founding of Todos por el Agua in 2009, Agustin and Fernando have developed long-lasting relationships with a number of communities within the basin, including Tierra Blanca, Cruz del Palmar, El Salitre, San Antonio de la Joya, La Presa, and Agustin Gonzalez. Intermittent funding for restoration projects with these communities is still a challenge, but when money is available, the program provides community members with unique income opportunities closer to home and with work that can be accommodated around other household tasks (Stoltenborg 2011). This has often resulted in fewer men leaving for the United States. With participatory project management and ongoing continuity, watershed restoration provides an important solution to both environmental and socioeconomic problems.

Strategies for Maintaining Momentum

From their experiences and observations in the Upper Laja River Watershed, Agustin, Fernando, and their colleagues have found the following strategies to be especially useful for reducing interruptions in projects and continuing to make progress toward social, economic, and environmental goals. Each strategy has worked over the long term within an unpredictable and complex context. These strategies are: (1) setting achievable and measurable goals, in spite of inequality in resource use and hydrological complexity;

(2) catalyzing change at multiple levels to produce co-benefits and enhance impact; (3) cultivating dynamic sustainability to maintain momentum when funding ends; and (4) building collective action.

Strategy One: Setting Achievable and Measurable Goals

The longevity of interventions in the watershed is often limited by goals that are too expansive to achieve or too difficult to measure. It is especially difficult to define achievable, measurable goals in the face of hydrological complexity. One of the challenges to deciding on the type and location of restoration projects within a watershed is that once rain falls, the water does not stay in the same place. Some flows downhill to the sea, some is held in ponds or reservoirs, some evaporates, some seeps into the soil and is taken up by plants or stored for months, and some percolates through fissures in rock to the aquifer deep underground, which takes tens of thousands of years to accumulate. To make this even more complex, the proportion of water that goes to each location is highly dependent on weather, soil conditions, vegetation, and the permeability of the underlying geology. In the Laja Basin, all of these factors can vary greatly from season to season and place to place. As a result, if an intervention seeks to improve water resources, it must be carefully situated. This requires data about conditions and a deep knowledge of the eco-hydrologic system, but this is information that often is not available.

Equally difficult is setting proper goals within a context of inequality in resource use, access, and distribution. The context within which natural resources are shared is always complex and vulnerable to power dynamics, and water resources can be especially so, given their fluid nature. Groundwater is not limited by land ownership or political boundaries and is connected underground through geologic structures. This means that a well pumping water to irrigate a farm field growing broccoli for export to the United States might actually be pulling household water from a community many miles away, a community that has invested a lot in improving soil and forest conditions to recharge what people there thought was "their aquifer" for their use. It is also possible to extract water from multiple watersheds in situations where the aquifer underlies several river systems, and heavy withdrawal from one watershed impacts another watershed's groundwater levels. This open access is exacerbated by weak or nonexistent regulation and enforcement, corruption, and imbalances in power, so that actors with the capital, luck, and political sway get water through pumping or diversion, even if others have gone to great lengths to protect it. The open-access nature of water and the inability or unwillingness of governance systems to control or exclude use often results in farmers rushing to pump faster before their neighbor gets the water. This, often referred to as the "tragedy of the commons," is an everyday factor in the degradation of ecosystems, livelihoods, institutions, and trust among stakeholders.

Agustin, along with his collaborators, has observed how these inter-connected factors—the nature of water, the uncertainty of water systems, and the inequality in use and access—can limit the options for interventions to improve the health and resilience of human communities, ecosystems, and rural and urban economies in the Upper Laja River Watershed. It has been hard to get stakeholders who use water or other resources heavily to reduce consumption or participate in conservation efforts when they don't have incentives to come to the table.

Because of the well-founded public concern over the depletion and contamination of the groundwater in the municipality of San Miguel de Allende, Salvemos had originally included aquifer recharge as a primary goal for watershed restoration in the Todos por el Agua program. Agustin and his team received thoughtful pushback from a local expert, who pointed out that the program could not practically measure recharge and that the time horizon was way beyond any normal project cycle. They also realized that many of the capital-poor farmers with whom Todos por el Agua would be working to conserve soil and increase water capture might never have the deep wells to tap any recharge and would not benefit from the restoration efforts. This led them to revise Todos por el Agua's theory of change, so that the goal became improving land-management practices that, in turn, could increase quality and retention of surface water and shallow groundwater, as steps toward watershed restoration and resilience in an age of depleted groundwater. Although the team didn't lose sight of the greater problems affecting groundwater or disregard the persistent, unequal, and unsustainable use of groundwater, Agustin and his team realized that Todos por el Agua needed program goals that were achievable and likely to prepare communities to be more resilient in a resource-scarce future. They also saw the focus on water security and sovereignty as a way to educate the public, build a broader coalition for improving water resources, and rally support for changing the systems that allow a select few, such as industrial agriculture companies, to benefit from and exploit the open access to groundwater. This careful, collaborative framing of program goals has been important in guiding Todos por el Agua's actions and simultaneously enables the program to be linked to, and placed within, the context of other efforts by communities, civil society, and government agencies to address threats to water resources.

Strategy Two: Catalyzing Change at Multiple Levels
Although Todos por el Agua's primary goal is improving watershed health, livelihoods, and resilience through protection of surface water resources, Agustin and his team have adopted a strategy of looking for ways to simultaneously induce positive change on other levels within any given initiative. For example, a specific conservation project can be designed

and implemented to also change education, governance, and institutional capacity by catalyzing conservation-related activities that produce benefits on multiple levels. This strategy emerged from the team's collective professional experience—which taught them that one action can have multiple impacts, produce co-benefits, and work simultaneously on multiple levels—and also from the integrated set of programmatic goals of one of Todos por el Agua's primary funders, FMCN's Cities and Watersheds Program. Along with providing financial and technical support, the Cities and Watersheds Program created a national network of a number of watershed initiatives across Mexico. These initiatives all work to achieve four goals: (1) improve citizens' awareness of threats to, and opportunities for, water-resources conservation; (2) facilitate participation of local and national stakeholders in the protection of water and watershed resources; (3) innovate and test diverse financial, administrative, and technical strategies; and (4) implement projects that demonstrate participatory models of protection, management, and restoration of water resources and ecosystem services.

All initiatives receiving support from FMCN must work to achieve all four of these goals. In a few cases, Todos por el Agua has developed specific projects that narrowly address one or another goal, but more often multiple objectives are included in one project. For example, reforestation projects with the overarching goal of soil and biodiversity conservation will catalyze co-benefits by requiring that the community use local institutions to discuss and approve proposed actions, so that the project also strengthens institutions and civic involvement. The project might train a local bookkeeper to administer payments, so the project builds financial literacy, promotes local administrative capacity, and models transparency. Or the project will create forums where communities interact directly with representatives of state and federal conservation agencies, which gives marginalized communities more voice while also improving government responsiveness. Agustin and his team have found that any given project can incorporate such interconnected activities and methods that catalyze additional benefits, products, and outcomes. Because all projects require a major investment of time and resources, even if the main goal is simply to plant trees, consciously working at multiple levels maximizes positive impact for conservation and development and also adds value for money spent, improves the cost-benefit ratio, and opens pathways for dynamic sustainability.

Strategy Three: Cultivating Dynamic Sustainability

A constant challenge to achieving sustainability of development work across the board—whether in conservation, poverty alleviation, health, governance, and so on—is maintaining momentum when funding ends. In the case of Todos por el Agua, the key staff members implementing the program have been field technicians, such as Fernando, who work closely with the communities and funding agencies. Over the course of the program, levels of funding for Todos por el Agua have varied, with some periods of almost a year with no money to support the field technicians. Most funding from nongovernment sources is for limited time periods of a few months to several years, and these sources do not provide funding for long-term engagement. The length of government funding also varies, and changes in political conditions have led to funding being pulled before a project is completed. Many of the environmental, socioeconomic, and health problems within the watershed will require action over many years to resolve. Even discrete, time-bound actions such as constructing a rainwater harvesting system require ongoing support and building capacity to ensure system maintenance and proper use. Agustin and the team have observed, and have themselves used, successful dynamic approaches to continue a particular project in uncertain funding conditions or to sustain positive outcomes after a project has come to an end. They define these approaches as seeking happy accidents and trading project "ownership" for project multipliers.

Seeking happy accidents. Development practitioners often strive to design sustainability into the project with a clear idea of what benefits will continue to accrue, but even so, it is very hard to predict all the ways in which a project has had a positive effect. Even when a project falls short of achieving its stated purpose, there may be unforeseen positive impacts or co-benefits. Sometimes it's hard to notice such results if the project design didn't include plans or resources to monitor them. A major challenge and opportunity after any project ends is identifying and tracking what continues to happen in the target or neighboring communities, or within institutions working in the same focal or geographic area. Maintaining close communication, even if informal, with stakeholders is key to recognizing new opportunities that can build off previous interventions. The Todos por el Agua program invested resources in building capacity among the farmers themselves to try out and experiment with watershed and soil conservation strategies. The farmers adapted and innovated new approaches, which Agustin and his partners observed being replicated by their neighbors and in surrounding communities, in some cases even after government funding for the work ended. But monitoring such impacts in communities not in the original project has been difficult, as the sites, timing, and agents of adoption have been unpredictable.

Strategies for sustainability have also emerged ad hoc. During periods of low funding, the connection between the communities and Agustin's team could easily have been lost, but an unforeseen opportunity arose to shift the program's responsibility for fieldwork. When Todos por el Agua was nearly out of funds, Fernando realized that he could begin working as an independent technician certified by government agencies to help landowners and communities apply for their own funding. In order to do this, he needed to enroll in specific training courses. Todos por el Agua used funding it had left at that time to pay for his training. By investing in the future career of a former staffer, the program was able to build a new partnership that has kept work moving along in the target communities in line with its overall, original program goals. Now when Todos por el Agua has funds, it can enhance or help scale-up existing community-based projects in collaboration with Fernando and other former technicians. Fernando's work in the communities also enables him to keep an eye out for practices that are being replicated and improved by neighboring farmers but are difficult to monitor, as mentioned earlier.

Some of the most positive impacts were not a result of activities that were intentionally built into the program's original design and were only realized through interviews with participants after the program was up and running. Such unintended consequences became some of the program's happiest accidents. For example, in addition to the modest income residents received for planting trees and for using their terracing skills, Todos por el Agua discovered that community members valued working together on soil conservation and reforestation projects as a way to rebuild their familial and communal ties to the land and to each other after decades of fragmentation and estrangement caused by migration. Some of the important nonmonetary values that people see in the program were described in an interview with a young mother named Elisabeth Ramirez Ramirez:

> I used to work in a house in San Miguel de Allende, as a cleaning lady. However, they paid me about the same amount of money that I make in the restoration program, when you take into account the travel expenses back and forth. . . . I prefer working in the field, because I can bring my son along; I couldn't take him to my other job. In this way I get to spend more time with my son, while gaining an income as well. Also by taking him to the field I can teach him about our nature and make him understand that we have to take care of our land. (Stoltenborg 2011)

Recognition of the actual nonmonetary values that communities place on the program has helped Todos por el Agua adjust its goals and actions, so that now every reforestation and soil-conservation project consciously and thoughtfully includes components that promote community and family cohesion as co-benefits.

Trading project "ownership" for project multipliers. Agustin and his partners also found that organizations or people who were not leading or even involved in the original project can emerge as those best situated to expand and innovate the work going forward. In this way, an organic replication and scaling-up occurs. Effective actions, if recognized and picked up by other organizations and communities, can be adapted and multiplied many times over, allowing positive change to evolve, spread, and flourish. This works best when goals are shared and control is relinquished by the actors who originally felt they "owned" the project's innovations, methods, and results. Such coordination or collaboration is often not present, but it can be facilitated by collective action through formal or informal networks. One of the best and clearest examples of how project multiplication and a natural scaling-up happens predated the Todos por el Agua program but involved a number of the same communities and actors.

In 2005 and 2006, San Miguel de Allende's Municipal Department of Ecology (DMAE), the water utility, the University of San Luis Potosí, and Ecosystem Sciences Foundation partnered to study the quality of well water in San Miguel's urban and rural areas. The study found that well water in a number of communities was contaminated by naturally occurring fluoride. Because ingesting fluoride poses a severe health risk, DMAE and ESF began searching for strategies to provide clean water in schools in some of the most seriously affected communities. They developed a partnership with a Mexico City–based NGO, the International Institute for Renewable Resources (IRRI). These partners worked with a school health center and the community of Agustin Gonzalez to design and build two large rainwater-harvesting systems from which residents and schoolchildren could obtain fluoride-free water. Upon completion of this work, DMAE wound down building such systems, so IRRI began to partner on rainwater harvesting with the local Rotary Club that funded work in other communities. The Rotary Club then began a partnership with a rural development organization, the Center for Agricultural Development (CEDESA), which had been working on water access and quality issues for years. Together they expanded coverage and built hundreds of rainwater-harvesting systems in rural communities; some of which had no wells at all. During this time, a newer NGO, Caminos de Agua, began collaborating with many of these same organizations, along with new partners and communities, to expand well testing, develop low-cost water filters, experiment with new technologies, and construct hundreds of additional rainwater-harvesting systems. More recently, the State Institute of Migration supported a project in collaboration with Salvemos, community members, and the Municipality of San Luis de la Paz.

Taken together, these organizations, government agencies, and community members have increased knowledge of water contamination, innovated new technologies and approaches, and built systems to supply thousands of residents with clean water. Many of the actors have been working independently with little knowledge of what others had previously done. Some have felt that their work has received little credit because other programs progressed and were more widely recognized. Nevertheless, Agustin and his team believe that these impressive achievements in providing clean water resulted from each organization's willingness to partner with others, share their results and lessons, and give up their own organization's "ownership" to build a complex and diverse movement around a shared goal, successfully attaining true dynamic sustainability.

Strategy Four: Building Collective Action

After experiencing several interruptions in conservation efforts with rural communities when donor funding dried up, Todos por el Agua began purposefully and explicitly designing projects to build linkages between communities, NGOs, the private sector, and government agencies at multiple levels to broaden the base of potential supporters and carry out initiatives collectively. In the Upper Laja River Watershed, numerous NGO and community-based organizations (CBOs) are focused on improving environmental and livelihood conditions. Many of these organizations have specific capacities or programmatic and geographic foci that overlap. Despite this, working in the same area has often turned out to be complicated for a number of reasons. For one thing, staff simply do not have the time to communicate with people in other groups. Also organizations are forced to compete for the same funding resources and have very different guiding strategies and theories of change. For example, some seek partnerships with the government and NGO sector, whereas others openly confront the government through political and social action. Nonetheless, aligning goals for collective action among stakeholders has improved information sharing and allowed for more efficient use of resources across the watershed. It has helped incorporate sustainability by building it into actions, has improved the odds that organizations are carrying out actions that play to their strengths, and, in the case of Todos por el Agua, has helped diversify its partner base to include community and institutional partners that strengthen actions by offering other advantages.

Firsthand experience and observations have convinced the team that collective action is greatly enhanced when one or a few organizations are designated to facilitate and lead coalitions. Direct funding to support a facilitator makes it more likely that collaboration and coordination will happen. The FMCN supported Salvemos in recruiting members for, and initially convening, OCAS, in which individuals and representatives of NGOs work to bring attention to threats to water quality and quantity. Similarly, the Willamette–Rio Laja twinning program between the United States and Mexico has provided support to local NGOs to lead the Mexican-based network that interfaced with the coalition in Oregon's Willamette River Watershed.

Another factor that is crucial for collective action is a common understanding of problems and a plan specifying where to work. An integrated watershed-management plan for the Upper Laja River Watershed is currently being developed by a coalition of NGOs and university partners, with funding from the Rio Arronte Foundation. Even though the plan has not been finalized, the groups in the coalition are already coordinating the timing and location of their work. Besides recognizing the importance of formal collaboration, the willingness of actors within the Upper Laja River Watershed to work together informally or in anticipation of structured coordination has led to many interesting and successful initial actions. All too often, organizations wait until a plan is made final or all the funding comes in to start work. But often there are critical actions and innovations an organization can undertake with little funding that can set the stage for larger actions later on.

Conclusion

When Agustin jumped back in his car after the meeting by the Allende Reservoir, another call came in. Even though it was getting dark, he had to delay his return home to talk while he still had cell service. This time the call was from the State of Guanajuato's Institute of Migration asking about progress in a new phase of their rainwater-harvesting partnership project, now expanding action to a community in the northern reaches of the watershed. In the previous year, Salvemos had helped communities install hundreds of rainwater-harvesting systems. The organization was not involved directly in the initial expansion of the rainwater-harvesting systems in rural communities following the 2006 water quality study, so their current, very active, involved role was unforeseen even by Agustin. But the flexible ownership and informal experimentation and collaboration that have evolved since 2006 have now transformed into a network of organizations providing technical capacity to Salvemos, as it does its part to multiply and scale-up the number of community-built rainwater systems. In his work now, Agustin draws every day on the strong relationships he has built through years of collective action with diverse actors in partnership programs such as Todos por el Agua and others, relationships that maintain the momentum as they expand and spread the work. Eventually, after the formal back-and-forth of goodbyes that characterizes the conclusion of even the briefest of work calls in Mexico, Agustin jumped back in his car, turned on the headlights, and finally headed home.

13

African NGOs: Potential to Make Sustainable Change

Elkanah Odembo

African nongovernmental organizations (NGOs) and other types of civil society organizations (CSOs), such as local community-based organizations (CBOs), have played an important role in post-independence Africa. Over the years, the sector has grown in numbers, scope, and impact. However, it is a sector that has not always been appreciated, or even understood. Few would question that in a continent with unacceptable levels of poverty, where the basic needs of food, water, education, and health care are yet to be met, NGOs have made a difference in the lives of many, both African NGOs and international NGOs (INGOs), sometimes working together. They have contributed to the improvement of food and nutrition security through a range of agricultural and health programs. There are numerous communities across the continent where children have access to clean water and education because of the work of NGOs. The contribution of the sector has been not only in the social sphere, but also in the economic and political arenas. NGOs have introduced and facilitated projects that have made it possible for poor women to have access to credit, which has contributed to their economic empowerment. In a continent where elections are still violent and mostly not free and fair, NGOs have been active in civic education and other programs that have contributed to safeguarding human rights and the democratization process.

As used here, the term "NGO" refers to a not-for-profit organization set up for purposes of advancing the social and economic welfare of groups and communities that for various reasons have been denied their basic needs. NGOs have been established and developed by individuals, groups, welfare organizations, and even faith-based organizations. NGOs are generally considered to be a subset of CSOs, which are defined by the UN as non-state, not-for-profit, voluntary entities formed by people in the social sphere that are separate from the state and the market. CSOs represent a wide range of interests and ties. Within the context of international development, a CSO network or coalition is an umbrella of nonprofits that includes all types of civil society organizations and associations that may work with or independently of the development industry, meaning NGOs, local/indigenous CBOs, and others. But it does not include business or for-profit organizations or associations.

My focus here is African NGOs, at national and local levels, and I also explore the role of INGOs in Africa. The well-known and well-established INGOs have their origins in the North. Examples here would be Oxfam, ActionAid, Save the Children, Water Aid, World Vision, CARE, Plan International, Doctors Without Borders, Catholic Relief Services, International Planned Parenthood Federation (IPPF), Federation of Woman Lawyers (FIDA), Amnesty International, and many others. In Africa, these INGOs initially worked predominantly in rural communities, but with the increasing urbanization of the twenty-first century, many INGOs are now to be found working with the urban poor, most of whom live in the informal settlements of the numerous cities and towns around Africa. Of course, over the years a significant number of African NGOs have also played a key role in the development and evolution of the NGO sector. Third World Network, Afro-Barometer, the Integrated Social Development Centre (ISODEC) in Ghana and West Africa, the Kenya Water for Health Organization (KWAHO), the Kenya Energy and Environment Organization (KENGO), the Kenya Human Rights Commission (KHRC), the Institute for Economic Affairs, and SEND Ghana are examples.

The Potential

Many would agree that the African NGO sector can do much more to shape the development outcomes in Africa. But given the global trends of increased scrutiny of government and corporations, it is only fair that NGOs also demonstrate greater accountability and transparency. The sector, through its leadership, must make deliberate efforts to inform the public about the work, role, and value of NGOs in society. This includes disclosing the sources of NGO funding and also making public the financial reports of the organizations. Doing so would increase the credibility of the sector, which in turn would contribute to greater influence in national and subnational policymaking and programs. The potential of the sector is enormous, but it can only be realized through a critical, and honest, review of the sector's current strengths and weaknesses, and a strategic positioning of the sector in the current realities and trends.

For the African NGO sector to be effective, it needs resources. The NGO sector needs to better understand its resource needs—not just financial, but also human and intellectual. Further, the collective impact of the sector will depend on an effective structure and system of engagement with government and business, at both national and local levels. And given the reality of globalization, NGOs in Africa will need to step up their engagement with INGOs, acting in the global arena on the numerous global challenges such as climate change and gender equality. The Sustainable Development Goals (SDGs) provide an excellent opportunity for these global networks and alliances.

The Missing Leadership

Those familiar with the NGO scene in East and Southern Africa in the 1980s and 1990s will no doubt remember an extremely dynamic and innovative sector, a sector led by committed, idealistic, and, very important, passionate group of individuals. These were leaders with strong personalities and a vision for a just society—a society in which human rights and dignity were not compromised. These African NGOs were angered by the extreme poverty in rural communities and in the informal settlements in cities and towns. Although it is true that many organizations were preoccupied with service delivery, this work had an element of community empowerment and local leadership development, too. Community organizing was central, even to work that focused on ensuring the provision of basic social services.

There was also the group of African NGO leaders who asked difficult questions about the role and responsibility of both government and business. These leaders fully appreciated that government, if not checked and questioned, would fail to deliver on its obligations to citizens. It was important to ask government why essential services were not available or accessible to citizens. These African NGOs also reminded citizens in poor rural communities and urban slums to demand services, and they asserted that government should be responsive and accountable to citizens. These NGOs (and their leaders) often found themselves at loggerheads with government authorities who preferred to see and have NGOs in the service-delivery business only, and not questioning government. In Kenya, NGOs that sought to hold government accountable included the International Commission of Jurists (ICJ), the Kenya Human Rights Commission, Transparency International, Bunge La Wananchi, Ujamaa Centre, Kituo Cha Sheria, the Mars Group, and several CSO/NGO networks.

The 1980s were also the time when the power of business became apparent. Whereas the state and religion had dominated life in previous eras, business became the dominant force in society. Large multinational corporations owned and controlled enormous wealth, including land, and had incredible power to influence nations and citizens. The activists demanded that businesses share societal social responsibilities commensurate with their power and privilege. This caused some tensions between African NGOs and the business sector.

Ufadhili Trust, in its work to promote corporate social responsibility, regularly convened meetings with corporate leaders to challenge them to think not only of how they spent their profits but, very important, how they made the profits in the first place, and their responsibility to their various stakeholders. The East Africa Grantmakers Association (EAGA) has raised awareness among corporate foundations in East Africa about using their grant making to improve lives in the region.

It is apparent that the vision, passion, and commitment of Africa's NGO leaders of the 1980s and 1990s no longer exist today. This is not to suggest that the current NGO leadership does not have what it takes, but that there is need to build a critical mass of leadership that will ensure that NGOs across the continent are able to be effective agents of change in a fast-changing, technology-driven world. In terms of focus, the first big challenge that is facing Africa today has to be the question of how to equip the youth of Africa with the education and skills necessary for them to be productive citizens. Second is the question of how to ensure that communities in Africa contribute to, and benefit from, a global economy. No doubt, leaders will still need to ensure that NGOs are effective organizations, with well-managed resources, effective systems, and appropriate structures.

The Decentralization Opportunity

Since 2000, there has been a deliberate effort by many African governments to take services closer to the people. In many cases these efforts have resulted in some positive impact in the lives of communities. Devolution and decentralization have, in general, had some of the desired outcomes, including moving more resources and decision making to the local level and also improving provision of some of the essential services in education, health care, and agriculture. Decades of bad leadership and poor governance have been at the center of Africa's underdevelopment and underperformance, and they are a part of the reason for the introduction of decentralization/devolution laws and policies. Kenya and Rwanda in East Africa, Ghana and Nigeria in West Africa, and South Africa in the south are examples of countries that have adopted a decentralized/devolved system of government.

Some would argue that decentralization and/or devolution are today a prerequisite to any meaningful development and improved governance on the continent. The many years of experience and the expertise developed after working with communities at the grassroots level has to be of great value to decentralization and devolution. Resources meant for development, if better allocated and managed, can change lives. Health facilities can have staff and essential drugs. Schools can have classrooms, desks, books, and qualified teachers. Communities can have access to clean and safe water. Farmers can be assured of the necessary extension services and the right seeds and fertilizers in time for planting. In the northern region of Ghana, for example, the Pathways project managed by CARE International works closely with local government and CBOs to train community-based extension workers to ensure that farmers get the much-needed agriculture extension services.

In Ghana, in partnership with other NGOs and CBOs, CARE is demonstrating that strengthening accountability can result in better planning and budget allocation by district governments. Further, investments in infrastructure at the district level can benefit from community input in the planning and development of the project, as well as in the monitoring of value to citizens. These infrastructure projects are in a wide range of sectors, including health, water and sanitation, education, and facilities such as markets and roads. This project, the Ghana Strengthening Accountability Mechanism (GSAM), is a USAID-funded project that has influenced the auditor general's office in Ghana to go beyond auditing of finances, to measuring the use and impact of infrastructure projects and investment.

Significant changes in government systems raise critical questions for African NGOs. Do NGO leaders fully appreciate the implications of the shift from a highly centralized system of government to a system that moves resources, decisions, and accountability to local government? To what extent can NGOs organize themselves, form strong coalitions and platforms at the decentralized level, and be significant development actors in a decentralized/devolved government? How can NGOs contribute to the much-needed oversight in decentralized/devolved government, while at the same time ensuring that their work and resources are integrated into decentralized/devolved government? The effects of poor governance have been devastating to the poor. A large proportion of the population in sub-Saharan Africa survives on less than \$1.50 per day—which means a life not just of abject poverty but of great dehumanization. Does decentralization/devolution provide CSOs/NGOs with an opportunity to measure their impact on poverty, together with that of other stakeholders? What governance lessons have been learned to date, and how can these lessons inform future efforts and initiatives to enhance governance?

Strategic and visionary NGO leadership by Africans can make a significant contribution in the context of decentralization/devolution and, by so doing, influence the governance agenda on the continent. The starting point has to be a full appreciation of the laws, policies, principles, and programs of decentralization/devolution. Of course, an NGO's ability to influence local government will depend on the NGO and its leaders themselves being more transparent and accountable—transparent and accountable with their finances, their governance, and programs. Public trust must be earned. And for this to happen, as mentioned earlier, special commitment, skills, and professionalism will be required of NGO leadership. NGOs must practice what they preach. Failure to do so will result in loss of credibility and independence.

There have been previous efforts, some quite successful, to establish norms for transparency and accountability in the sector. The NGOs Code of Conduct in Kenya is one such example. This code was developed by NGOs in Kenya over a series of meetings and negotiations. NGOs in Kenya had advocated for self-regulation under the NGO Act of 1990. The law therefore made provision for such self-regulation. The NGOs in Kenya developed a set of core principles and values that reflected the aspirations of the sector. Members of the NGO Council were required to adopt the code. Another example is a code that was developed by CIVICUS, meant for the global civil society movement. CIVICUS is a global organization based in South Africa, which aims to strengthen civil society and civic action worldwide. This, too, was an effort toward self-regulation.

The Power of CSO/NGO Networks and Collaboration

Perhaps the best examples of the power of CSO/NGO networking and collaboration are at the global level. One example is the demonstrations at the World Trade Organization (WTO) meeting in Seattle in 1999. At this important global event, members of the WTO were confronted by protests by thousands of activists who argued that the WTO is a major contributor to the widening gap between the rich and poor, not just between countries but also within countries. Although the demonstrations were planned and meant to be peaceful, some demonstrators turned to violence. Nonetheless, the demonstrations in Seattle succeeded in shining a spotlight on the global trading system and its impact on the poor. Thus, CSOs and NGOs succeeded in starting a conversation about globalization and its impact.

About the same time as the WTO demonstrations in Seattle, the global campaign for debt relief for poor nations in the South was taking off. The campaign succeeded in raising awareness about the debt burden that African countries face. Poor countries were allocating from 30 to 40 percent of their revenues to servicing debts, leaving them with little for the basic services much needed by their populations. Debts, most of which were incurred by corrupt governments around the continent, rarely resulted in funding going to finance public goods at the community level. Governments were not held accountable for meeting the intended purposes of loans. This campaign succeeded in granting debt relief to some twenty-two countries in Africa, Latin America, and Asia.

International and national NGOs, working together, achieved other signal successes in policy change. The International Campaign to Ban Landmines (ICBL), which started in the 1990s, resulted in the UN 1997 Mine

Ban Treaty. This campaign brought together mostly Northern NGOs, but it had critical collaboration with local NGOs in Africa and Asia. In 1992, at the UN Conference on Environment and Development (UNCED), known as the Earth Summit, held in Rio de Janeiro, NGOs were able to influence the global agenda for protecting the environment and the sustainable management of the world's natural resources. That important meeting in Rio, held over twenty-five years ago, has shaped subsequent strategies, conversations, and decisions about sustainable development and the world's natural resources. The widespread level of global acceptance of the Millennium Development Goals (MDGs), the Sustainable Development Goals, and the Paris Agreement on climate change, all illustrated the power and value of organized civil society.

In Africa, though NGOs have been successful in raising awareness around a number of public policy issues, and even influencing some laws, much more needs to be (and can be) done. The few successful campaigns have depended on the vision and commitment of a handful of NGO leaders. Corruption, public debt, women's rights, and children's rights are but a few examples of areas where the collaboration of African NGOs could influence public policy and programs. Although NGOs are often eager to be a part of a network or coalition, few of the leaders have the full appreciation of the time, finances, and intellectual resources that are required to make networks effective vehicles for change. Too many NGOs are preoccupied with their projects in communities (which in most cases are what they receive funding for) and lose sight of the "bigger picture" and the context that needs to be influenced for long-term, sustainable change to occur. Visionary NGO leadership with critical, long-term, and strategic thinking is important. Leaders who will, for instance, appreciate the role of the private sector and understand how strategic partnerships among NGOs, government, and business can lead to successful outcomes. A good example is in agriculture, with the cooperative creation of value chains that can lift farmers out of poverty.

African NGOs need to be seen, heard, and felt at continental and global levels. The African Union (AU) in its Agenda 2063 had some input from national NGOs, but mostly from INGOs. Subsequent to the development of Agenda 2063, there was little engagement of African NGOs in shaping plans and programs for implementation. Do NGO leaders in Africa have what it takes to ensure meaningful engagement with the organs of the AU, or even those of regional blocs such as the Economic Community of West African States (ECOWAS), the East African Community (EAC), and the South Africa Development Community (SADC)? As recently as March 2018 in Kigali, Rwanda, the African Continental Free Trade Agreement (AfCFTA) was signed by African heads of state and government from forty-four of the fifty-five AU member states. Will NGOs play a role in AfCFTA? Do NGOs appreciate the possible opportunities (and risks) that may result from free trade on the continent? At the UN, where international and global agendas are crafted, African NGOs have little voice and presence. This needs to change. But African NGOs must realize that such spaces and stages require actors to be bold and organized. One does not get an invitation to these spaces. Organizations *demand* to be in these spaces.

Effective collaboration of NGOs is no doubt another critical determinant of NGOs' influence and impact. Therefore, such collaboration should be central to any NGO strategy for engagement at local, national, regional, continental, and global levels. African NGO leadership that can make this happen urgently needs to be developed. NGOs can achieve much more when working with one another, and cooperative efforts also generate greater leverage in their engagement with government and the private sector. Collaboration should therefore be a goal for all African NGOs that intend to have influence beyond the village boundary.

Who Pays the Piper?

NGOs need resources to do the work they do. For NGOs in Africa, these resources have mostly come from Northern partners and funders. INGOs that partner with local NGOs depend on their Northern constituencies or publics and also their respective governments. National NGOs and local CBOs in Africa are therefore dependent on funds from the North for their survival. This has caused many to question (and rightly so) the legitimacy and mandate of these organizations. In cases where African NGOs are strong in raising human-rights issues and challenging government policies and programs, governments are often quick to accuse national NGOs of being "agents of foreign powers."

If the work that national NGOs and local CBOs do is valuable to the societies they work in or with, then why is it that funding for their work does not come from local sources? These organizations find it easier to respond to calls for proposals from Northern INGOs, foundations, businesses, and governments. Granted, there are today local foundations and businesses that do provide resources to local NGOs. Some good examples exist in South Africa, Kenya, and Nigeria. There are even a few cases of African governments providing resources to NGOs. But these are the exceptions rather than the rule. Because of this dependence on external resources, the accountability of these organizations is mostly to the Northern funder. As mentioned, such dependence has led to some African governments questioning the legitimacy and accountability of national and local NGOs. It is therefore a matter of great importance, and urgency, that African NGOs develop a local funding base.

Local resource mobilization has been on the agenda for some time now in Africa. One may even suggest that it has resulted from the many training sessions conducted over the years by organizations such as the Resource Alliance and the East Africa Grantmakers Association that some successes in local resource mobilization have been achieved. But a change in attitude is needed. NGOs in Africa, just like their counterparts in the North (and even some countries in the South) need to look to their own publics for the resources to do their work. This will not only enhance legitimacy but will also ensure greater accountability locally. This local accountability will be central to the sustainability of these organizations in the very near future. But as already mentioned, new mindsets, visions, and skills will be required to achieve this.

Service Delivery Versus Advocacy

For a long time now, the debate has raged as to whether NGOs should be in the business of service delivery or should focus their energy and resources on advocacy. It really should not be an either-or matter. Those doing development work in the African continent know full well that the failure of many governments to deliver basic, essential services for the poor has contributed to unnecessary illnesses, and even deaths. There are numerous communities and populations in various countries on the continent whose very survival has depended on the work of NGOs, and this is the case not just in emergencies and humanitarian crises. There are communities where, if not for the intervention of NGOs, children would not have schools, health facilities, water sources, and even food.

Examples exist in Ghana, where partnerships between INGOs and some CSOs have brought about improvement in the quality of facilities and services provided by the decentralized (district) government. Focusing on capital projects, which consume on average 70 to 90 percent of local government development budgets, it has been demonstrated that citizens can participate in local government and even determine the quality of facilities and services meant for the communities. These projects include everything from schools to water and sanitation facilities. Enhanced accountability and performance of local governments in the planning and implementation of the projects has reduced the loopholes and opportunities for corruption. Civic participation in the development of scorecards to measure performance and impact has made it possible for citizens to do their own advocacy. Thus, service delivery has been improved, not so much by NGOs doing the service delivery, but rather by NGOs facilitating the capability of citizens to monitor, participate, and advocate. This change in NGO and civic roles demonstrates that advocacy can be about improved service delivery by government, and can take place within existing policies and programs. These are valuable lessons for the future work of NGOs in decentralized systems of government.

Pure service delivery by NGOs in the context of devolution and decentralization will be increasingly difficult to justify, given that the objective of decentralization/devolution is the effective and efficient delivery of services by government. Advocating for citizen participation, and building the capacity of citizens to advocate for improved facilities and services will be the value-added contribution of African NGOs. Innovative advocacy has been demonstrated in Ghana by the District League Table (DLT), which is an initiative of UNICEF and the Centre for Democratic Development (CDD). The DLT is a yearly ranking of districts that provides Ghana with a holistic overview and comparison of the level of development across its 216 districts. It provides information that can help policymakers, nonstate actors, and others see where progress and impact is being made. The table compares the districts by using a set of indicators in the sectors of education, sanitation, rural water, health, security, and governance. The DLT has thus become an important policy- and program-influencing tool that focuses attention on some essential services that government must provide for citizens.

The Founder Syndrome

Throughout this chapter, NGO leaders in Africa have been mentioned. It is therefore of some importance to discuss the individuals who start or lead these organizations. Leadership, as earlier suggested, has been critical in the development and evolution of the NGO sector. As noted, the visionary, committed, and passionate NGO leadership of the 1980s and 1990s contributed to the very vibrant NGO sector of the time. Unfortunately, this committed and passionate leadership did not invest as much passion and resources in developing the next generation of leadership. This has contributed to a general continentwide leadership gap in the sector. Moreover, these visionary and committed leaders did not invest much in establishing good, strong governing boards to provide the necessary oversight and facilitate the necessary leadership transitions and development.

In cases where NGOs did have boards, the board members were mostly friends and colleagues in the sector—people with similar worldviews and attitudes, therefore adding minimum value. The boards, when they did exist, were not clear about their roles and responsibilities. Board meetings were not regular, and when they did take place, the members often did not keep proper minutes and records. If recorded, the records were not properly signed and archived. Generally, the NGO executive directed the organization with minimal organized oversight by the board. The NGO executives for well-resourced, large NGOs became powerful and sometimes became corrupted by power. Some treated their organization like a personal entity and found it difficult to imagine life outside the NGO.

This personalization became known as the NGO "founder syndrome." The individual had invested a great deal of time and energy in the development of the organization and, after having stayed so long in the organization, started to believe that the organization could not survive without the founder. Any efforts to identify and develop new leadership were not welcome. Sometimes such efforts would be thwarted. Sadly, many of the organizations did not outlive their dynamic founders. Young men and women in these organizations were not supported to develop their full potential and leadership capacity. These future leaders did not have mentors and so moved on, and from one organization to another.

NGOs Today and Tomorrow

This chapter began on a positive note and will end that way, too. Africa still has a long way to go. The "Africa rising" narrative of 2000 to 2010 was about wealth and job creation and, most important, about economic growth, that is, gross domestic product (GDP). This rising was driven mostly by the higher commodity prices, private sector engagement, technology, and macroeconomic fundamentals. There was even some opening of the democratic space. The AU Agenda 2063 is indication that African leaders are starting to think long term about a future based on "inclusive growth and sustainable development." The NGO sector must define the role it wants to play in Africa's development over the next fifty years. The AU Agenda 2063 and the UN SDGs 2030, with their theme of leaving no one behind, provide a useful framework for African NGOs to step forward and provide some leadership. NGOs in Africa can, and must, develop a collective vision and strategy if the sector is to be an influential actor that impacts on development at local, national, regional, continental, and even global levels.

14

National Execution: China's Approach to Local Development

Lu Lei

Since 1978, China has opened its door to the outside world and welcomed foreign donors (e.g., international organizations/agencies, governments, nongovernmental organizations, the private sector, and so on) to participate in and support its economic and social development undertakings. Most of the development cooperation between China and foreign donors has taken the form of programs or projects. Since the 1980s, thousands of development programs or projects funded by foreign donors have been implemented in China and have achieved good results. For development programs or projects funded by foreign donors in China, different mechanisms have been adopted to coordinate and manage them, with the two most popular modes being national execution (NEX) and direct execution (DEX).

NEX refers to a management arrangement under which the host government or a national or local nongovernmental institution takes the lead in program/project development and/or implementation, while the foreign donor(s) or other international partner(s) concerned mainly plays the role of monitoring and technical support. Experiences in China show that NEX tends to be conducive to a better program/project performance in terms of aligning with the national development priorities, enhancing national or local ownership, strengthening national or local capacities, and sustaining and replicating the results.

DEX refers to a management arrangement under which a foreign donor or an international organization or agency, in close cooperation and

This chapter was prepared in collaboration with Arthur N. Holcombe, former United Nations resident coordinator in China and founder and president of The Poverty Alleviation Fund (TPAF).

consultation with the host government, takes the lead in program/project development and/or implementation, while the host government or a national or local nongovernmental institution mainly plays the role of supervision, support, and monitoring. Experiences in China show that DEX can complement NEX in such a way that international experiences and expertise are tapped in a more efficient manner. In some cases, DEX has proved to work well in terms of piloting and demonstrating new ideas or new methods regarding development and management of programs or projects, especially at grassroots levels.

In this chapter, we share some of our practical experiences in China with regard to execution and management of development programs or projects. Since the early 1980s, the Chinese government attached great importance to NEX with respect to development programs or projects funded by foreign donors in China. At the same time, the Chinese government also recognized that there were instances where Chinese governmental and nongovernmental institutions lacked the special expertise or capacities required to manage the foreign assistance that had an important role in helping to achieve national economic and social development objectives. In such situations, the Chinese government welcomed direct execution by foreign donors or international partners drawing on various resources worldwide. Such direct execution was generally undertaken in consultation with the government, often drawing on local government facilities and other resources (e.g., human, financial) where available.

Foreign donor development assistance to China has been important in several ways, especially in terms of the infusion of new ideas and best practices based on outside or local experiences that could improve the design and effectiveness of national programs in achieving their stated goals. Experiences in China with regard to NEX and DEX may have some useful reference values for other countries wishing to strengthen their national/local capacities in managing their economic and social development efforts.

Background

In 1978, China introduced new economic reforms and opening-up policies to the outside world as the basis for China's national economic and social development strategy. This involved reforms in three broad areas: its state-owned enterprises (SOEs), its financial system, and its administrative organizations. China's first experience with foreign aid as a source of technology, expertise, and best institutional practices commenced after 1978 with mutual "win-win" arrangements worked out with Japan. The aid arrangements involved comprehensive contractual trading agreements whereby China received financing for its priority national infrastructure modernization needs in return for oil and coal exports to Japan. Central to government thinking was that introducing and mastering improved technologies and best practices from Japan would enhance its ability to carry out additional programs of the sort on a self-reliant and sustainable basis. This early approach set the pattern for subsequent aid that China received from other donors.

During the 1980s and 1990s, China's new welcoming of foreign donors was on the basis of supplemental external support to priority development programs funded with national- and provincial-level financing. The foreign donors responding to the new opening-up policies included most Organisation for Economic Co-operation and Development (OECD) countries; multinational institutions such as the World Bank, the Asian Development Bank, and United Nations agencies; and international nongovernmental organizations (INGOs) such as the Ford Foundation and the Gates Foundation. Their assistance in China was conditioned on the willingness of the donors to accept Chinese national determination of assistance priorities and to agree to some form of Chinese government involvement in the implementation of the donor's assistance.

With time, Chinese civil society organizations (CSOs) expanded in number and capability and increasingly engaged in community-level development and relief programs. The CSOs generally had some association with a local government partner, but many also operated with considerable independence. In the mid-1990s, the top-down national poverty reduction programs encountered increasing challenges to achieving their poverty reduction objectives in more remote, often ethnic minority areas. As a result, the Chinese government gave increased priority to more participatory (bottom-up) activities focusing directly on the needs of poor households and village communities. Foreign donors found it possible to work directly with local CSOs in community-based activities intended to reduce poverty.

Forms of Aid Management and Implementation in China

Most foreign assistance in China is managed and carried out under a form of NEX, although some DEX takes place when the foreign funding agency is in the best position to manage the assistance itself and provide the expertise and other inputs needed to be accountable and achieve the intended results. In China, most foreign donor assistance has been managed and implemented using NEX. China's NEX system has generally proved to be an efficient and effective way to implement development activities and to coordinate them with the broader national development assistance it is supporting. Because of its size and complexity at the national, provincial, and local levels, government gives major attention to special arrangements to coordinate the implementation of development programs, including by the establishment of inter-ministerial leading groups, and by establishing systems to monitor, report, and evaluate implementation at the level of the intended program/project impact.

At the national level, the central government of China designates a government coordinating agency (GCA) for each foreign donor or source of funding. For example:

- the Ministry of Commerce (MOFCOM) has been the GCA for such foreign donors as the UN system and most bilateral donors;
- the Ministry of Finance (MOF) has been the GCA for such foreign donors as the World Bank and the Asian Development Bank; and
- the Ministry of Environmental Protection (MEP) has been GCA for such foreign donors as the Global Environment Facility (GEF), the Montreal Protocol, and some other foreign donors.

The GCAs are responsible for the overall coordination with foreign donors, making sure that the cooperation is in line with the national development strategies; for example, the Five-Year Economic and Social Development Programs or sectoral strategies in China.

For a specific program/project funded by a foreign donor, the particular GCA designates a qualified national or local institution (governmental or nongovernmental) to serve as the program/project executing agency (EA) for the identification and daily management of the program/project. The program/project executing agencies are responsible for formulating programs/projects, supporting the implementation of the programs/projects, and monitoring and reporting on the achievement of the intended results (outputs to outcomes).

For the implementation of the planned program/project activities, the program/project EA chooses one or more qualified national or local institution(s) (governmental or nongovernmental) as the program/project implementing agency(ies). The program/project implementing agencies are responsible for carrying out the planned program/project activities on a daily basis and for ensuring that the planned results (inputs to activities to outputs) are achieved on a timely and quality basis.

In recent years, INGOs wishing to work in China have generally established relationships with one or more local government counterpart departments that have helped to establish the necessary government clearances on the INGO's behalf. Since January 2017, INGOs have had to comply at the national level with a new law referred to as the Law of the People's Republic of China on Administration of Activities of Overseas Non-Governmental Organizations in the Mainland of China.

In China, the capacities of Chinese CSOs have improved significantly, particularly in the fields of health care, disaster relief, poverty reduction, and environmental protection at the community and household levels. The

Chinese government has welcomed such CSO involvement in national development and has increasingly cooperated and partnered directly with CSOs to help enhance their impact and effectiveness.

Government Execution in China

A major advantage of the government execution arrangement is that the donor-funded activity is generally supported by a departmental counterpart contribution in cash and in kind that can enhance the overall impact of the donor contribution. Local project managers often also use the donor contribution as an argument internally to leverage greater budgetary support within their own department or ministry.

The donor-assisted activities can be of any size and duration mutually agreed upon with the government. For example, in the early 1990s, the Chinese government, through the People's Bank of China (PBC) operating as the central bank of China, requested the United Nations Development Programme (UNDP) to help with the modernization of PBC activities by financing a study tour of PBC officials to France, Brazil, and the United States to learn about how foreign countries managed national monetary policy. The main objective of the Chinese government was to review the structure and functions of the US Federal Reserve Bank in Washington, DC, which it felt most relevant to conditions and needs in China. The PBC arranged the details of the study tour, including research for its implementation. After several weeks of detailed consultations and information gathering, the study-tour team returned to China and wrote a report recommending the inclusion in the PBC of new monetary policy responsibilities for the overall management of China's currency and for the oversight of China's banking system along the lines of the US Federal Reserve Bank's currency and banking policy controls. The team's report added "Chinese characteristics" to its recommendations, including one specifying that China should have a central bank and nine regional reserve banks instead of the twelve regional banks established in the United States. The recommendations of the study team were quickly approved by the top leadership of China at the time.

During the mid-1990s, UNDP was requested by the Chinese government to finance a series of national workshops for China Central Bank and Ministry of Finance officials on value-added taxes, taxation administration, foreign-exchange markets, and central bank legislation. Under the project, the International Monetary Fund (IMF) recruited highly experienced specialists from various countries' monetary authorities to share their experiences with China.

To help ensure maximum benefits from the assistance, the IMF consultants generally wrote papers on relevant experiences in their own countries. Those papers were then translated into Chinese by the IMF and submitted to the Chinese government prior to the workshops to help enhance learning from the foreign experiences. After the workshop discussions, it was up to the Chinese bank and finance officials to learn and adapt the foreign experiences to their own circumstances.

In the mid-1990s, the Chinese government requested UNDP assistance for four municipalities suffering from environmental pollution challenges. The assistance was intended to help the municipalities prepare detailed environment master plans that would help alleviate pollution and improve air quality. Local municipal government officials were responsible for preparing detailed master plans for reduction of polluting emissions in each case, but foreign environmental specialists with considerable experience with relevant emission pollution control in other countries were recruited to advise on the content of the master plans being prepared in each municipality. UN consultants were also brought in for short periods during the drafting process of the master plans to suggest ways in which the master plans might be strengthened. The experts also provided practical training to Chinese personnel who would later be responsible for implementing the master plans.

In another example of government execution, UNDP was requested to help reinforce the Chinese government's implementation of its 8-7 Poverty Alleviation Program, which was intended to reduce poverty in China by 80 million poor people over seven years (1994–2000). The government requested UNDP to help demonstrate ways to strengthen aspects of the overall 8-7 Program by directly targeting poor households in selected poorest counties in twenty western and southwestern provinces. The assistance in each province was intended to demonstrate how microloans could be provided responsibly to poor households in ways that could help them increase their income and food security. The provinces generally had not previously stressed use of microloans out of concern that they might not be repaid by the poorest households. The UNDP provided its funding through its national counterpart organization, with actual implementation being carried out by local poverty alleviation authorities at the county and township levels.

For example, UNDP financing for poverty reduction in China's Gansu Province illustrates how government execution was managed, as well as how the UNDP contribution complemented and reinforced the far larger efforts of the Chinese government. Gansu is a semiarid province in north-central China. Its poorest population was mainly located in isolated mountainous areas and was dependent on rain-fed agriculture. The far larger contributions of national, provincial, and county governments gave priority to investments in physical infrastructure (roads, irrigation, and communications), health care, and primary and vocational education. The UNDP was requested to provide assistance valued at $1 million over three years, targeting 10,000 poor families (50,000 people) in Gaolan and Wushan Counties. The government contributed an additional RMB 10 million ($1.6 million) in support of UNDP project activities in cash, and in kind for building materials, salaries of local project staff, office facilities, equipment, and revolving funds.

UNDP assistance in Gansu was intended to complement that of the government by focusing on specific needs of poor households in three main areas: (1) the establishment, operation, and management of a rural revolving fund in each county, providing small loans to each poor household; (2) social development activities, including maternal and child health care, adult functional literacy, and women's "sideline" income-generating activities; and (3) training local government officials in the promotion, and subsequent replication in other poor counties, of the project microloan activities found to be successful. The revolving funds were intended for productive investment in income-generating activities and were provided in each instance to the women of the targeted poor households to manage and repay. In each county, a project lead group was established to ensure coordination of efforts by the different technical bureaus; a project manager was appointed; and a project office was established to manage the operation of the revolving fund.

National Execution in China

During and after the 1980s, China saw a large and growing number of CSOs active in rural development and emergency relief activities. It is estimated that today there are more than 786,000 local CSOs active in China. Chinese CSOs and INGOs are generally registered and affiliated with specific government departments or institutions, which agree to take on responsibility for ensuring that their activities are consistent with national priorities. In recent years, an increasing number of Chinese CSOs have been provided with foreign and government funding to implement activities or provide services on their behalf.

In addition, there have been quite a number of government-organized NGOs (GONGOs) in China that perform certain functions entrusted to them by the government, especially in areas of technical support and service. An example of a GONGO is the China Foundation for Poverty Alleviation (CFPA), which was registered with the Ministry of Civil Affairs in 1989 and operates under the supervision of the Office of the State Council Leading Group for Poverty Alleviation and Development. CFPA has given priority to combating rural poverty in poor areas of China, with a focus on rural health care, rural education, improved rural livelihoods, and disaster relief. In 2005, it extended its work to include countries in Asia, Africa, and the Americas.

China has recently seen an increasing number of well-funded private foundations committed to carrying out a range of social development and emergency relief activities. One of the most famous is the One Foundation established in 2007 by Jet Li, a Chinese kung fu movie celebrity, to function as an independent charity in China. Its capitalization was drawn from five component foundations—the Jet Li One Foundation, the Lao Niu Foundation, the Tencent Foundation, the Vantone Foundation, and the Vanke Foundation.

An INGO working in China generally partners with one or more national or local institutions that are approved by the government. In most cases, this mechanism has proved to be effective. The Poverty Alleviation Fund (TPAF) was a not-for-profit organization, registered in the United States, which worked for many years in China, especially in promoting poverty alleviation in remote and ethnic minority areas of China.

TPAF held the view that China's 8-7 Poverty Alleviation Program provided important and concrete guidelines for poverty alleviation efforts. A key component of the guidelines was referred to as the "Five Ones" initiative, which included the following targets for improving food security and increasing income in areas where conditions permit: (1) one mu of farmland (1 mu is equal to 1/16 acre) per capita with stable and relatively high yields of basic food crops; (2) on average, one mu of orchard or other cash crops per household; (3) on average, one laborer per household securing off-farm employment in a township enterprise or a developed area; (4) on average, one line of business for income generation from livestock raising or other family sideline activities per household; and (5) on average, one enclosed meadow or "grass storehouse" per household in pastoral areas.

In many ways, TPAF's activities in China were designed and implemented following principles similar to those set forth in the UN Millennium Declaration (adopted in 2000) and China's 8-7 Poverty Alleviation Program (released in 1994). With regard to the management of activities in China, TPAF utilized both NEX and DEX, depending on the local situation. From 1998 to 2008, most of TPAF's activities in China were implemented in selected poor communities of the Tibet Autonomous Region (TAR). Those activities were identified in advance by the prefecture-level Poverty Alleviation Offices and fell within the priorities and guidelines of the national government for poverty reduction at the household level.

After 2011, TPAF extended its activities to Yunnan and Sichuan Provinces and partnered with China Philanthropy Research Institute (CPRI), a national CSO affiliated with the Beijing Normal University in Beijing, to continue its Tibetan village-based poverty reduction activities under NEX arrangements. TPAF provided funds to CPRI, which then worked through the county-level branches of the Ministry of Civil Affairs to implement a broad range of poverty reduction activities. Working closely with CPRI, TPAF was able to influence introduction of many of the types of community-based poverty alleviation activities that had earlier proved successful in the TAR. CPRI was also instrumental in finding a new project location in Litang County, in the Ganzi Tibetan Autonomous Prefecture of Sichuan Province. The personal intervention of a local, senior, living buddha greatly helped to ensure that necessary local cooperation and support was rendered to the planning and implementation of various poverty reduction activities in a timely manner.

Altogether, under the NEX arrangements, CPRI and the local governments successfully implemented an integrated program in three poor counties that included activities such as household greenhouses that enabled families to extend their high-altitude cold growing season from one crop to year-round food cropping; solar heaters enabling hot water for mixing warm livestock feed and for human cooking and hygiene purposes, while reducing the need for firewood gathering from distant degraded forest locations; additional livestock for domestic food and income needs; and training in maternal and child health care. These were activities that had been found helpful earlier in promoting income, food security, and more healthy family living in the TAR before 2008.

Direct Execution in China

In some cases, the Chinese government welcomes a greater involvement of foreign donors or partners in program/project development and implementation because of their special expertise and experiences that are lacking in China. In its support to local partners in the implementation of its activities, TPAF local program staff directly executed the village-level revolving microcredit that financed many of the household agricultural, livestock, and sideline activities. Microcredit loans of up to RMB 1,000 yuan were provided to women representing their families, as they were found most appreciative of the opportunity to receive credit that their family could not otherwise obtain. The women were organized in mutual support groups of five and proved able and willing to backstop each other in times of hardship to ensure the timely servicing of loans over a twelve-month period. When all group loans were repaid, the women qualified for a new round of loans that they enthusiastically welcomed. From 1998 to 2008, TPAF provided microloans to about 3,200 women, who subsequently achieved a 98 percent rate of payback.

TPAF also directly recruited local trainers from the private sector to train unemployed youth in a broad range of practical skills in areas such as motorcycle and farm-equipment maintenance and repair, housing and small-building construction, stonecutting, road construction equipment operation, and rural house electrical requirements. All training was conducted on the job at work sites, in order to provide trainees with practical experience and skills similar to those they would need in later employment. In connection with the motorcycle and farm-equipment maintenance and repair training, TPAF staff also provided further training in starting a small business, management, and accounting that enabled the most entrepreneurial trainees to go on to establish and operate small maintenance and repair workshops in their own townships.

Starting in 2003, TPAF directly implemented a project in China's TAR and Shangri-La in Yunnan Province, which was intended to help increase the income for poor Tibetan artisans. As part of the project, TPAF supported the establishment of two local social enterprises to promote training of local Tibetan artisans and marketing of their products. The project included the direct recruitment of two international artisan product-development specialists to help with the design, production, and sale of high-quality Tibetan artisan products believed most likely to sell well with international tourists in the Tibetan market and with interested buyers in the large US and European markets for artisan products. The international consultants initially assisted with the design of new artisan products they believed would appeal to the tastes of foreign tourists and overseas buyers. They then led many training workshops intended to help local Tibetan artisans master production of the new product designs. As part of their responsibilities, the foreign consultants also trained local Tibetan staff to carry on with the product design and training activities in the absence of the foreign consultants. Once operational, the two local social enterprises bought the improved products from Tibetan artisans and then managed their local and foreign sales. The project was highly valued by the local governments and Tibetan villagers. Later, the TAR government decided to provide funds to the social enterprise in TAR to help expand the numbers of Tibetan artisans trained and benefiting from the sales of their products.

Evaluation and Replication of Program/Project Results

Before the final conclusion of its program in China, TPAF commissioned a team of scholars from the Center for Integrated Agricultural Development (CIAD) of China Agricultural University based in Beijing to conduct two comprehensive evaluations of TPAF's activities in China, one covering the first phase (1998–2008) and the other covering the second phase (2009–2016). During the evaluations, the CIAD team visited a number of project sites in the Tibetan villages and interviewed local partners, program staff, and villagers. The reports of the evaluation team came to the general conclusion that TPAF made important contributions in terms of increasing income, enhancing food security, and improving the general health of the villagers in the project villages. It was estimated that over 100,000 poor Tibetan villagers benefited directly or indirectly from a broad range of community-based activities supported by TPAF. The reports also spoke highly of the participatory and household-based approach that TPAF took for activity planning and implementation at the village and household levels.

Based on the best practices and lessons learned from TPAF's and other donors' activities in China, the CIAD team developed several packages of training materials and undertook a series of training workshops in Tibetan regions of China for local government personnel engaged in poverty alleviation work. The training workshops covered such topics as planning, implementation, and evaluation of community-based poverty reduction activities. The workshops were intended to address the actual needs and challenges faced by the local poverty alleviation workers and to provide practical guidance in ways to improve the design and implementation of household-based poverty alleviation activities. During the workshops, best practices from TPAF's activities were welcomed by local officials who were looking for ways to help poor households boost their standard of living above the established poverty threshold, as required in China's Thirteenth Five-Year Poverty Alleviation Program (2016–2020).

Advantages and Disadvantages of National Execution

In China, NEX has been the most popular way of coordinating and managing development programs/projects with funding support from international donors. Past experiences have shown that this mechanism has been quite successful there, helping to build national/local capacities and achieving intended results. In the meantime, DEX has complemented NEX in important ways.

International donor assistance proved helpful in supplementing national resources, but the main benefit was in providing international expertise, experiences, technologies, and best practices not otherwise available. For this reason, the Chinese government consciously requested that foreign donor assistance include international dimensions that could be introduced, mastered, and replicated to the extent possible in local Chinese conditions. It is believed that the NEX methodology has several distinct advantages, such as the following. It could:

- help ensure closer foreign donor project linkage with the priority national development policies and programs being implemented by the government;
- help ensure greater governmental ownership and commitment to donor-program results in support of priority national programs;
- increase the opportunity for national and local personnel at the management and implementation levels to develop their operational capacities;
- strengthen the willingness of government to provide additional financial and human resources in support of foreign project implementation; and
- increase the likelihood that government would learn from donor best practices and results, then replicate them elsewhere in the country.

However, NEX could have certain disadvantages over more independent foreign donor execution arrangements, if not addressed. These might include:

- a more conservative traditional approach in terms of project design and innovation;
- less responsiveness to changing local situations or needs in a timely manner; and
- less effectiveness in capacity building at the community or household level.

UNDP and TPAF experiences in China show that once a solid and efficient partnership is established between foreign donors and the host government at various levels, the concerned national/local institutions, program/project performance, and effectiveness can be enhanced greatly. We believe that China's experiences with foreign donor assistance and national execution may offer some useful benefits for other developing countries as well. Of course, it would require adapting to the particular conditions and local needs of the countries concerned.

15

Global Frameworks: Using International Law and Civic Action

Fanny R. Howard and Rixcie Newball

In this chapter, we tell a story about how a community and a regional government agency—an agency we both work for—collaborated to advance sustainable development through the power of law. The heart of the case is about how our people—the Raizals, an ethnic group of the Colombian Caribbean—used international and national law to protect the environment that is essential to our livelihoods and identity. But before we get into the story, we need to say a little about international law. We're not legally trained, so this will be very simple. In many UN member countries, especially those considered "developing," national development and conservation policy stems from global conventions, protocols, declarations, and goals (such as the MDGs and SDGs) to which the country is a party. International law is often incorporated into a country's national law and policy. These laws and policies are then implemented (put into action) through local programs and projects. This means that the laws and policies that we need to achieve sustainable development and social and environmental justice are already in place in most countries, because they have signed on to international conventions and other norms. Nonetheless, these laws may not be implemented, enforced, or even regulated. But they are there and can be used to benefit the people—if they know how.

To give an example of how this works, Colombia is party to many international conventions, including those concerned with environment and human rights. One of the most significant is the Convention on Biological Diversity (CBD), which has been ratified by all UN member states except the United States. The CBD, a foundational document of sustainable development, requires countries to develop strategies to conserve and sustainably use biodiversity. The CBD was ratified by Colombia's congress in 1995 in Law 165.

Colombia's National Biodiversity Policy derives from this law. The Ministry of Environment sets policy for the nation, in accord with national and international law and priorities such as the SDGs. Then government bodies at all levels have the responsibility to support the law and policy by carrying out actions designed to achieve it throughout the country.

Understanding how this system works—combined with basic knowledge about a country's international, regional, and national legal and policy framework and commitments—gives us a powerful tool that can be used by local organizations and communities to advance their own development and protect their rights. Sometimes it helps to consult a lawyer or other legal professional, but not being legally trained doesn't mean you can't use law and policy to protect your rights and support your own development. The story told here of what happened in Colombia's San Andres Archipelago offers just one example of how law and civic action can be used to protect a community's environmental rights and livelihoods.

The story starts in June 2010, when Colombia's National Agency of Hydrocarbons (Agencia Nacional de Hidrocarburos [ANH]) auctioned off seventy-eight blocks in the Caribbean to international companies to explore for oil and natural gas. Two of these blocks were inside the Seaflower Marine Protected Area (MPA); the largest MPA in the Caribbean and part of the UN Educational, Scientific, and Cultural Organization (UNESCO) Seaflower Biosphere Reserve. The Seaflower Biosphere Reserve and MPA are managed by the Corporation for the Sustainable Development of the Archipelago of San Andres, Old Providence, and Santa Catalina (CORALINA), the government's sustainable development agency with jurisdiction over the archipelago's environment and natural resources. CORALINA, a regional autonomous public corporation established by congress in 1993, is part of Colombia's decentralized environment system (SINA) and is a government agency led and mostly staffed by Raizals. CORALINA set up the award-winning Seaflower Biosphere Reserve and MPA, declared respectively in 2000 by UNESCO, and in 2005 by the Minister of Environment, in collaboration with the community. We both worked on the projects to set up the Seaflower, which resulted from linking international and national laws with community-based initiatives.

To tell you a little about the San Andres Archipelago, it's a Colombian department (like a state) in the southwest Caribbean that includes three small inhabited islands, the largest open-ocean coral reefs and atolls in the Americas, and lots of ocean. There are two distinct population groups. The first descend from the original settlers. This group makes up about one-third of the population and is called "the Raizal people" (*pueblo Raizal*), categorized as a national ethnic minority by Colombia and recognized as indigenous internationally. We descend from English settlers who started arriving in 1630 on the *Seaflower* (sister ship of the *Mayflower*), Africans who were brought to San Andres as slaves or came as runaway slaves from other islands, a few settlers from northern Europe, and some Chinese migrants who found their way to San Andres, having been brought to Central America as laborers in the mid-nineteenth century in the infamous "coolie trade" that sprang up after slavery was outlawed. The archipelago's isolation, in combination with our ethnic differences, meant that the Raizal people stayed highly self-sufficient for over 300 years. We were mostly left alone until the middle of the twentieth century. Thus, we have a long socio-cultural and economic history unrelated to mainland Colombia, including a different language, religion, and customs. Today, the largest population group of San Andres (about two-thirds) is composed of migrants from the Colombian mainland and their descendants. These people are called "residents." They mostly arrived in the last decades of the twentieth century.

In 1953, Colombia declared San Andres a free port. After the free-port declaration, the island developed into an inexpensive tourism site run by mainland Colombians. The free-port status, combined with many neocolonialist policies, opened the door for mainland Colombians to take control of our land, natural resources, and economy. This led to a decline in quality of life that we have struggled to restore for fifty years. The Seaflower Biosphere Reserve is a major initiative chosen by our community to foster sustainable development. The Seaflower was designed to ensure long-term access to the natural resources all islanders need to sustain our livelihoods, heritage, and identity as a people through conservation and sustainable use.

Now, let us explain about the oil leases. Much to our surprise at CORALINA, we found out about them along with the rest of the Colombian public from a news story in the national media in December 2010. CORALINA's leadership, under the guidance of executive director Elizabeth Taylor-Jay, and our internal legal department, led by Rafael Medina-Whitaker, immediately went to work. SINA's decentralized structure and CORALINA's strong grounding in law and policy paved the way for action. Although CORALINA is a government agency with authority over a large region and substantial legitimate power, as a minority-led agency far from the capital city, exercising its power can be challenging. For a government agency to have power on paper, but not in reality, is not unusual in many countries; especially those with histories of centralized, opaque government like ours. Also CORALINA has little funding to carry out its mandate, which includes implementing international and national law and policy within its jurisdiction (the San Andres Archipelago). To ensure legitimacy and gain outside financial and technical support, CORALINA is careful to root all its projects and programs firmly in international law and policy, Colombia's National Constitution of 1991, and other national policies related to sustainable development, conservation, and civic participation.

In January 2011, CORALINA filed a Popular Action (*accion popular*) against the National Agency of Hydrocarbons to halt oil exploration in the

Seaflower Biosphere Reserve. A Popular Action is a constitutionally established legal mechanism similar to an injunction that allows a citizen's group to seek protection of collective rights and interests related to matters that impact citizens' homelands, environment, livelihoods, and other interests. The Popular Action submitted by CORALINA was soon joined by a local fishermen's cooperative and a native-rights group. The action claimed that the leases violated rights guaranteed to us in international environmental law, notably the CBD and Principle 15 of the Rio Declaration (1992). Known as the "precautionary principle," this principle reads: "In order to protect the environment, the precautionary approach shall be widely applied by States according to their capabilities. Where there are threats of serious or irreversible damage, lack of full scientific certainty shall not be used as a reason for postponing cost-effective measures to prevent environmental degradation." Colombia upholds the precautionary approach in its constitution and environmental framework law, Law 99 of 1993. CORALINA's legal team was careful to stress the precautionary principle as a preemptive move, because the team figured an argument from ANH would be that we couldn't prove in advance that oil exploration would cause damage to our environment or livelihoods. Also, CORALINA identified additional legal arguments to help the community plaintiffs strengthen their part of the Popular Action, if needed. For example, our rights as a community had been ignored because we hadn't been consulted as guaranteed in ILO Convention 169, the UN Declaration on the Rights of Indigenous Peoples, and the National Constitution of 1991.

The San Andres community—Raizals and residents—was united in opposition to oil exploration. A wealth of advocacy and protest actions, legal rights granted to Colombians in the Constitution of 1991, were carried out simultaneously with the court case. Public meetings and consultations were led by local institutions, including neighborhood organizations, churches, schools, cooperatives, and other private-sector groups. Well organized and publicized marches, demonstrations, and other avenues for civic protest echoed the widespread concern, including radio call-in shows and interview programs, newsletters, blogs and op-eds, and public interventions during visits of national officials. Allies on the mainland, especially in Bogota, carried out similar actions in their cities.

In response to the Popular Action, ANH temporarily suspended oil exploration. However, because ANH showed no intention of revoking the licenses, CORALINA and the civic groups did not withdraw the lawsuit. In July 2011, the case advanced to the highest regional court, the Superior Tribunal. The tribunal ruled in favor of the Popular Action, agreeing with its argument that the community's collective environmental rights had been violated. CORALINA didn't receive any legal or financial support for this case, but we would like to mention a strategy we used at the regional tribunal. Someone at CORALINA had a connection with a well-known lawyer from Bogota, discovered he agreed with our cause, and approached him. He volunteered to sit with our lawyers at the tribunal, appearing as if he were a member of the legal team. People who were in court that day report that the ANH lawyers were so shocked by the sight of this high-powered lawyer sitting at the opposition table that it threw them off, even though the entire legal argument was conceived, written, and argued by CORALINA's leadership and internal legal team, composed almost entirely of Raizals. We offer this small part of the story to show the power of using an "ally" from the ruling elite as a strategy, especially if you're fighting a case for and lodged by a vulnerable minority lacking power, an ethnic group not only underestimated by the opposition but not necessarily taken seriously or respected by the legal system. Just the physical presence of an ally offers a statement of support that can shift the balance of power. We would also like to point out that the cost to CORALINA in effort, time, and money was enormous. All of us were already overworked, and the long hours and months we had to spend on this case took time away from other projects and our day-to-day responsibilities of managing and protecting the environment and serving our community.

Meanwhile, at the end of September, the Office of the Comptroller General of Colombia (Controloria General de la Republica) issued a report stating that, in its opinion, the leases violated Colombia's responsibilities under international conventions, particularly the CBD. A few days later, the president of Colombia, Juan Manuel Santos, visited San Andres and announced that Colombia would not carry out oil exploration or production in the Seaflower Biosphere Reserve because of the high risk to the marine environment. He ordered the leases revoked.

But the case did not end there. ANH went on to appeal the Superior Tribunal's ruling to the Council of the State of Colombia in Bogota (Consejo de Estado de Colombia), which is one of Colombia's four supreme courts. On December 15, 2016, the high court found in favor of CORALINA and the civic groups, upholding the rights demanded by the Popular Action, citing the importance of the precautionary principle in Colombian jurisprudence, and ordering the permanent cessation of all hydrocarbon exploration in the Seaflower Biosphere Reserve. This was a true victory for the people and reinforced that international law can help communities solve large problems starting at the local level.

In Colombia today, more actions related to collective rights are being brought by vulnerable groups against the government or private corporations. The people and their courts are becoming more conscious of national and international environmental and human-rights legal frameworks. We call this "using the power of the Constitution."

16

From Local to Global: Four Microcases

Pallavi Gupta, Sarah Jane Holcombe,
Lu Lei, and Raymond Offenheiser

There are myriad examples of locally led innovations contributing to sustainable development. This chapter includes short studies of
four such cases. The first two cases are examples of how a good idea that
emerges from one creative, committed individual can move from local
innovation to scaling-up impact. The third case illustrates how the power of
national government policy and implementation, working in cooperation
with the local level, can achieve sustainable development. The fourth case
moves away from the local to illustrate how an international nongovernmental organization (INGO), as a civil-society actor, can legitimately hold
corporations accountable for their impacts on people and the environment.

Microcase One: Bringing Local Innovation to Scale
Through Bridging, *Pallavi Gupta*
Good ideas and practices are plentiful in communities around the developing world; however, scaling these ideas is increasingly beyond the capacity of
a single sector or organization. The resources, knowledge, and experience
needed for the purpose are dispersed across sectors and require multiple
stakeholders to work together. This is where intermediaries and bridging
organizations can play the crucial role of building trust and facilitating collaboration. This example of how bridging works comes from my work in
Uttar Pradesh (UP) in India as the founder and managing director of Fifth
Estate Trust. It starts with the story of a small organization, run by a concerned government employee named Anil Sengar, that set out to address the
plight of women who lack access to affordable sanitary napkins. Sengar had
a technical solution and found the means to overcome taboos and reach

215

women and families, but he lacked the resources to scale the organization in order to reach millions of adolescent girls and women facing the challenge.

Although the lack of access to affordable sanitary napkins is a prominent issue in poor states such as UP, the historic cultural view of menstruation as "impure" results in lack of awareness around the issue. Data show that a large number of girls in India drop out of school either because they lack access to sanitary napkins or because schools don't have toilets or running water. In many parts of India, including UP, women continue to use unsanitary means that include devising makeshift napkins from dirty rags of clothes or ashes from firewood used for cooking. This results in multiple health issues and urinary-tract infections, forcing girls to drop out of school. For girls in many parts of India, simply continuing education during puberty and talking about menstruation and related health issues are major hurdles.

The small organization that Sengar was running produced cheap, hygienic sanitary napkins for girls and women in his village. Although he figured out the production technology, as a man, he was not able to connect with women on these issues. He observed that even when an affordable product was available, women and girls continued to use older methods. There were two main reasons driving this behavior. First, the women believed that they did not need a "fancy" product, as the old ways had worked "just fine" for generations. Second, even though the product was cheap, purchasing it would require a difficult conversation on menstruation with their husbands or fathers in order to get the money.

To tackle these challenges, Sengar sought help from local women's self-help groups to organize workshops and discussion sessions under the banner of *chuppi todo aandolan* (literally translated as "movement to break the silence"). These women went around to different schools, speaking directly to girls and showing them what a sanitary napkin looks like and how they could use it. Slowly, they started organizing community meetings where both men and women gathered to see "what the fuss was all about." The men and women were initially hesitant to talk about such "unimportant" issues in the open. This is where the support from local administrative officials was crucial, as they encouraged families to participate. Gradually, men and women joined in. Women from self-help groups started discussing their experiences and challenged the taboo around the topic by carrying sanitary napkins and displaying them during the meetings in front of men— among giggles and sneers. Many progressive men from the village also began to join the movement, and the topic of menstruation and sanitary napkins ceased to be taboo. However, even after three years of work, the organization was able to deliver the message and reach out to only 1,500 women and girls in its village and neighboring villages in the district. Scaling the solution and the movement remained a challenge.

During our work as a bridging organization in UP, we came across Sengar's organization and facilitated its presentation in front of the state government's chief secretary (the head of state government), head of the health department, and head of the Panchayati Raj department that oversees local governance and development for the state. Although the organization was already supported by a local officer, bureaucratic hierarchies and other factors had prevented promotion and discussion of this innovation at higher administrative levels.

During this meeting, the chief secretary acknowledged the potential of the model as a much-needed service in the state and directed the two departments to create a plan to replicate it using government resources on the ground. After several facilitated presentations, the replication of the model was initiated in multiple districts in UP. In three years, through the partnership of state government, local administrators, civil society organizations, and self-help groups, fifty-two centers across the state were created using Sengar's model, reaching some 300,000 girls and women. Using a bridging organization to facilitate presentations, partnerships, and training meant that Sengar's innovative solution was made available to about 200 times more girls and women in the same three year time span.

Microcase Two: Leveraging Local Cultural Knowledge and Status, *Sarah Jane Holcombe*

Over more than four decades, Thailand's Mechai Viravaidya, activist and former politician, leveraged his indigenous social and political position and his cultural knowledge to catalyze change in public attitudes about family planning, condom use, and HIV/AIDS prevention. In a society traditionally reluctant to talk about sexuality, he successfully prodded government and the public to take action on contraception and HIV/AIDS prevention and, more recently, to galvanize corporate involvement in rural development. His signal achievements in the 1970s were to pilot and then scale access to community-based contraceptive services and to destigmatize and legitimize family planning. In the 1990s, he built public consensus on the need to address a growing HIV epidemic, using nonauthoritarian approaches to prevention. His nongovernmental organization, the Population and Community Development Association (PDA) provided direct services to clients in rural and urban areas, but Mechai's unique contributions were to shift the public attitudes and behaviors of ordinary Thais and, more influentially, of the elite public and policymakers.

Family Planning
In the early 1970s, first from government, then within the framework of NGOs, he set up and ran community-based contraceptive distribution strategies to

reach the country's rural population, still the majority at that time. Through the Community-Based Family Planning Services project (soon to become PDA), he piloted village distribution of condoms and pills by shopkeepers and other community leaders, eliminating unnecessary provider requirements. Mechai was a strategic disrupter. He embraced the role of "condom ambassador" with gusto, becoming known as Mr. Condom. Through PDA, he used creative strategies to popularize and normalize contraception, such as paying farmers to paint birth-control ads on the sides of their water buffalos, holding condom blowing-up contests, and providing free no-scalpel vasectomies every year on December 5—the birthday of Thailand's revered king. Whether talking with nursing students, first-year military recruits, prisoners, government officials, factory workers, or schoolchildren, Mechai and his team made condoms and humor an integral part of the approach. At almost every event at which he spoke, he would share condoms, whether as illustrative props during his talks, on tables at the entry to the event, or as favors to hand out. He used condoms as a symbol of the larger behavioral change he was promoting. These efforts resulted in his name becoming a slang term for condom. Mechai's operating strategy combined his cultural knowledge with his experience in radio and television and his early grasp of mass media power.

HIV/AIDS

In the late 1980s and early 1990s in Thailand, it seemed possible that some in government and the military would enact punitive measures to try to control HIV. Some felt that public prevention programs would only draw attention to the problem and threaten tourism revenue. Mechai, working first in government and then through PDA, launched a national publicity initiative to draw attention to the issue and build support for increased prevention efforts by government and the corporate sector. Mechai's comfort with promoting condoms stood him in good stead, as condoms were again an important defense, this time against HIV. Mechai made pointedly brash statements to reach government leaders, educated elites, and the general public. He was a master of public communications with a striking ability to seize opportunities and use them to communicate in short and catchy ways—in person and through radio. His blunt pronouncement that "dead men don't buy" was aimed at galvanizing business-sector engagement in HIV/AIDS prevention, as was an ongoing series of high-profile events with leadership and staff at major corporations. Mechai and PDA made the earliest efforts to promote corporate social responsibility in Thailand in family-planning services, HIV/AIDS prevention, and later in rural development. Their main contribution was to view corporations as having a responsibility to contribute to greater societal good, rather than just pursuing their own financial bottom line.

Strength from Inside and Outside

Mechai's flair for public communication and ability to capitalize on opportunities to share his message are central to his impact, but these are not common traits in Thailand. Born to a Thai father and a strong-minded Scottish mother, both of whom were physicians, he was educated in Thailand and Australia. Early exposure to multiple cultural contexts and approaches may well have given him the ability to identify and speak up about problems. He showed a comfort with experimentation and trying new options that might or might not work, not a typical approach in Thai culture. At the same time, many of Mechai's strengths and strategies stem from his roots in the Thai context.

Thailand was never colonized and has remained a nation with a strong social hierarchy and reverence for the monarchy. Mechai's connections to the royal family through his father and his wife, as well as his work both as a senior government official and as chair of his own NGO (which by 2007 had become the largest NGO in Thailand), gave him standing and opened doors. Connections allowed him to reach influential audiences and shielded him from attack. Mechai's motivations in part stemmed from his recognition of his advantaged position in society. Finally, Mechai's light and playful public-education strategies embodied the Thai cultural emphasis on *sanuk,* meaning "fun and play." Thais often use humor to disarm people and to desensitize issues, rather than being puritanical, judgmental, or threatening. Mechai was a blunt pragmatist who seized the spotlight and humorously encouraged change. He saw the importance of building larger social buy-in for the work. He focused on specific changes, not radical change of social institutions, such as traditional gender dynamics or Thailand's sex industry. During the 1990s, his most pointed criticisms of Thailand's commercial sex industry were directed at foreigners, evident in such statements as, "I find it disturbing that men who are products of highly developed economies come to a developing nation solely to exploit its women and children." He responded that way rather than criticizing Thai men, who make up the majority of the market. He sought to make the sex industry safer for clients and workers, rather than working to abolish it.

By leveraging his status and knowledge of how to operate within the social, cultural, and political context of Thailand, Mechai contributed to Thailand's lowered fertility and successful response to HIV/AIDS in ways that an outsider could not have done.

Microcase Three: Alleviating Poverty Through Targeted Measures, *Lu Lei*

At the end of 2014, 70.17 million people in rural China lived below the national poverty line, that is, per capita net income of farmers at RMB 2,300 per year (constant price of 2011, approximately $1 per day). The poor in rural China mainly populate 128,000 villages in the key 832 poorest counties in China.

In China's Thirteenth Five-Year Poverty Alleviation Program (2016–2020), the government set the target of lifting the remaining rural poor people out of poverty by the end of 2020 (under the current national poverty line). To achieve the above objective, the government has been making huge efforts, including implementing a much more targeted approach to poverty alleviation. The initial idea of alleviating poverty through more targeted measures, or *jingzhun fupin,* which literally translates as "precise poverty alleviation," was put forward by the Chinese president, Xi Jinping, during his inspection tour of Hunan Province in November 2013. Jingzhun fupin can be characterized by: (1) better identification of the poor (who and where they are and why they are poor); (2) more targeted measures to address the causes of poverty at the household level; and (3) stricter and more objective performance assessment vis-à-vis the intended results.

To achieve the objectives of jingzhun fupin, a lot of concrete mechanisms have been established at various levels. One of the key mechanisms is to send a resident-in-village work team known as a poverty alleviation task force (PATF) to each of the poor villages. In principle, each resident-in-village PATF is composed of at least three members who are responsible for helping poor farmers rise above poverty by the target dates. The resident-in-village PATF members come from the Communist Party of China (CPC) and government entities at various levels, peoples' groups (e.g., youth leagues, women's federations, and the like), other democratic parties, institutions of higher learning, state-owned enterprises, and public-service institutions (e.g., public hospitals, public libraries, public publishing agencies, and so on). In most cases, the original work units are responsible for covering costs incurred by resident-in-village PATF members. In principle, resident-in-village PATF members work at the village level for at least two years, and their performance is assessed according to a system of target accountability.

The targeted poor villages are encouraged to develop and revise their village-level plans to alleviate poverty with the help and support of the resident-in-village PATF. In the concerned poor villages, resident-in-village PATFs are specifically responsible for, but not limited to:

- identifying poor households and analyzing the causes of poverty;
- mapping out solutions and planning activities to address the causes of poverty (household-level work plans);
- assisting in mobilizing necessary resources (e.g., financial, technical);
- helping build capacities of poor households to generate income (e.g., production and marketing);
- guiding and monitoring implementation of planned activities;

- helping find channel(s) to get proper treatment (for poor households with very sick members);
- summing up best practices and lessons learned; and
- carrying out other activities that benefit the poor.

Normally, the resident-in-village PATF is accountable to the concerned county-level government (i.e., the county-level group leading poverty alleviation measures), which is responsible for the overall coordination and assessment of the work of resident-in-village PATFs. Government at township and village levels is responsible for supporting the work of resident-in-village PATFs on a daily basis. In many places, future promotion of staff members is connected to their performance in jingzhun fupin at the village level.

According to the Office of the State Council Leading Group for Poverty Alleviation and Development, 2.778 million people joined the resident-in-village PATFs from 2013 to 2017. By the end of 2017, there were more than 700,000 resident-in-village cadres focused on helping poor people in these villages in their arduous fight against poverty.

Data from the National Bureau of Statistics of China show that a total of 12.4 million poor people in rural China rose out of poverty in 2016, and the total number of poor people in rural China was further reduced by 12.89 million in 2017. By the end of 2017, the total number of poor people in rural China had decreased from over 70 million in 2014 to 30.46 million, with an overall poverty incidence of 3.1 percent.

Microcase Four: Changing How Global Companies Do Business, *Raymond Offenheiser*

For decades, the Oxfam brand was associated with hunger relief, as it had built its reputation responding to major emergencies, especially famines. Food production and nutritional security today remain central to its programs and identity, but its approach to dealing with these issues has evolved considerably. Today, it is still anchored on assuring basic livelihood and family food security but is more focused on resilience to climate shocks, systemic volatility, and impacts of foreign direct investment in national agricultural economies.

Emblematic of this new approach is Oxfam's campaign, Behind the Brands, which is directed at the ten largest global food and beverage companies. The inspiration for this campaign was recognizing the growing importance of foreign direct investment on the economies of poor nations. Today, foreign aid represents only 8 percent of overall foreign direct investment, a percentage that is declining. One of the most attractive, essential sectors for the global food and beverage industry is agriculture. From spice to tropical fruits to chocolate, tea, and coffee, hundreds of commodities that are served on the dinner tables of industrialized nations every day come from small producers in the developing world. Yet we are largely blind to the conditions of their production and the men and women who labor to produce them. Behind the Brands is an effort to lift the veil on this industry and challenge the global food and beverage companies on the policies at work in their supply chains that have a real impact on the lives of small-holders and landless laborers.

Oxfam determined that the most effective way for it to achieve this goal was to challenge the ten largest global food and beverage companies on the quality and strength of their sustainable development policies and practice. By 2010, many companies were publishing annual sustainability reports that touted their commitment to best practices across a range of areas. At the same time, many of these issues were being debated in multistakeholder global forums. Consensus evolved on gold standards for sustainable practice, and metrics were developed to track performance. Oxfam decided to take the agreed gold standards and challenge the ten top companies to a race to the top in terms of their performance against those global standards.

Each of the ten companies was contacted to inform it that Oxfam would be conducting this exercise. They were each told that their company was seen by Oxfam as an industry leader on sustainability, but we believed they could improve to varying degrees against these gold standards. Each was informed that Oxfam would be scoring them in seven basic sustainability policy areas: (1) land, (2) labor, (3) water, (4) women, (5) transparency, (6) carbon disclosure, and (7) small-farmer engagement. Each was offered the opportunity to help design the methodology for scoring to be used. They were also told that Oxfam would either score them on an external review of their policies in these respective areas or, if they were willing, on a deeper internal review of their policies in place as well as those under consideration. All ten companies accepted the invitation to work on the design of the methodology as well as on the deeper internal review of existing policy. Oxfam also explained to the companies that it would be conducting periodic campaign spikes to draw attention to areas where the companies were weak and could benefit from some external pressure. The scorecard was released at a media event at Bloomberg headquarters in New York City in 2013 by a panel of specialists on corporate accountability and portfolio valuation. Fifty percent of the companies sent representatives.

Over the next three years, Oxfam challenged chocolate producers Nestlé, Mars, and Mondalez on the treatment of women within their supply chains. Women are critical to the processing of cacao yet are often treated as ancillary labor. We challenged Coca-Cola and Pepsi on the handling of land claims filed against their sugar suppliers, providing graphic stories of massive, uncompensated displacement of communities from their lands from Cambodia to Brazil. And we challenged Kellogg and General Mills on their carbon-disclosure processes.

In each of these cases, the companies moved quickly to improve their policies. In each case, Oxfam worked internally with their sustainability teams to draft new policies and celebrated the release of these new policies with press releases. While the companies highlighted were responding to very specific critiques, other companies were quietly watching this process and taking action to improve their own policies as well. Oxfam updated the scorecard each quarter, recognizing the improvements made by each company. Companies changed their rankings throughout the three years of this program, improving their overall scores in the process. Now that the first phase of this campaign has been completed, Oxfam is organizing field visits to a randomly selected number of countries to investigate whether in fact companies have implemented their policies on the ground.

Although all of these companies were nervous about Oxfam's initial intentions and were not always happy to be exposed to public scrutiny through the use of campaigning tactics, they all maintained close contact with Oxfam throughout the campaign. Those that had the opportunity to work closely with Oxfam staff in the design of the scoring methodology, or in the drafting of new policy, came to value and appreciate the relationship. After Oxfam had established itself as a serious and credible critical friend, meetings with CEOs were secured, providing important senior executive support to corporate middle management charged with managing the operation side of the companywide sustainability strategy. The CEOs were impressed with Oxfam's willingness to engage them around risks to their supply chains and to offer sound advice for how those risks might be managed. As a result of the constructive relations that were established, Oxfam later had opportunities to engage with these same companies in other forums on climate, resilience, and related issues.

For Oxfam, this campaign marked a turning point for the organization. It demonstrated to staff who hold a strong anti-market ideology the power of the Oxfam brand and the organization's potential to engage some of the most powerful global corporations and foster positive change that will potentially affect billions of small producers across the world. The campaign proved to them that in a globalized world, the future livelihood of an African small farmer may be as much in the hands of a corporate board of directors in London or New York as in the hands of a local elite or village middleman. It showed that it is important to be present and alive to threats and opportunities that may arise within these contexts.

The campaign also taught us that focusing on supply chains can help make injustice and inequity visible in very concrete terms. That visibility enables us to give a name to that injustice, and then to challenge it with policy and propositions that will not necessarily require the elimination of the market opportunity but can humanize its effects and outcomes. Perhaps the most important achievement of the Behind the Brands campaign is that it reset the bar for sustainability for the global food and beverage industry. No company can now say that the policies put in place by the top ten are unachievable or unrealistic. A tipping-point effect has been achieved that should now set the standards of performance for other companies. Although we can all take some satisfaction from this victory, the road to true global sustainability is long, and many other challenges lie before us.

PART 3
Preparing Development Practitioners

17

Drawing Lessons from Reflection and Practice

Susan H. Holcombe and Marion Howard

In this book we have identified issues that hinder development and some of the many innovative solutions that development practitioners, especially Southerners, are demonstrating. These issues and ideas about how to approach their resolution emerge from the descriptions and reflections of a diverse group of contributors. They write about their varied experiences as Southern and Northern development practitioners from different development fields and a range of jobs that span geographic regions, cultures and stakeholders, political and social structures, and types of organizations (donors, recipients, government and UN, bilaterals and multilaterals, universities, and international, national, and local NGOs). The authors here describe specific examples of practical pathways and tools that worked, or show promise of working, and can be adapted across locations and cultures. The experience, knowledge, and stories presented in these chapters also lead us to comprehensive approaches that also provide solutions.

Most important, we argue in this book that development practice needs to be transformed, first by being turned right side up, and then by incorporating a truly sustainable approach. Communities and countries seeking development change—not donors or Northern development organizations—must decide on and implement change for themselves. The legitimacy for making sustainable change rests with communities and governments in the South. Development is about doers; it cannot be done to people. Northern practitioners have a different legitimacy and set of roles—those of listening to and supporting Southern-identified, -led, and -owned efforts; providing necessary but otherwise unavailable resources to achieve these efforts; and pressing for enabling, transparent global policy environments that permit these efforts to flourish. This includes the complex task of supporting the emergence of capable governments and communities in which disarray, conflict, and corruption can make sustainable change seem out of reach.

Upending the roles of Southern and Northern practitioners is a tall order—and some might dismiss our arguments as unrealistic, overly idealistic aspirations. Indeed, the power shift needed to reverse roles runs contrary to the political, military, or ideological motivations of much development assistance. The frequent conflation of development assistance with actual development has contributed to the creation of a development industry, discussed in Chapter 2 and elsewhere, that complicates reversing roles. The contributed essays in this book suggest that the time is ripe for upending assumptions, reversing roles, and building sustainability.

In drawing lessons from the observations presented here, we and our contributors, although diverse, do not represent all development practitioners or speak for all participants and organizations in the development effort. We also know that development aid as a tool of foreign or military policy will not cease. Nor will, or should, aid as charity cease. The noble human impulse to help those in need can be as strong as or stronger than self-interest. There are many possible charitable efforts, for example, donations of books or ambulances, or staging of cataract-surgery camps. Imagine the difference in an individual life if a person can once again see and read. Such admirable acts have untold value but remain charity, not development, unless they also contribute to building local capacities to sustain the changes started by outside resources. Humanitarian assistance will also remain necessary. Part of humanitarian assistance is about meeting the immediate and basic needs of people displaced or harmed by civil or natural disasters. Humanitarian assistance is not development, nor is it sustainable, but its practitioners can learn from development. This requires them to move beyond the immediate and necessary charity, and to see how to link their roles to long-term rehabilitation and build institutions that can prevent or mitigate natural, man-made, or conflict-induced disasters.

Our contributors—and many other observers—say that development practice is at an inflection point. It must change its approach, and indeed they note that development practice is already changing. Thomas Dichter tells us why: "We need to recognize that the nature of development as a business has in itself become an obstacle to country ownership and to intelligent long-term development, because structurally it favors 'us' and continues to put 'them' in a subordinate role." Raymond Offenheiser speaks of the imperative for change. The INGO sector will have to reinvent itself, he says, and "in the end, the nonprofit sector will be judged internationally and domestically by how well it serves as the moral lever that ensures that the state and market discharge their roles effectively, guided by concerns for equity, inclusion, transparency, and accountability to humankind's most vulnerable." Offenheiser notes that INGOs are already changing, through inclusive governance structures and increased emphasis on policy change. Tundi Agardy and Vinya

Ariyaratne focus on the shift to holistic approaches to development to achieve sustainability and socioeconomic change. And Laurence Simon and Patrick Awuah delve into building new models of education to train leaders to transform development practice.

Voices from the South describe how new leaders are making change. Esther Kamau tells us about educated, young Kenyans who, seeing opportunities created by governance devolution, have left successful careers elsewhere to play a leadership role in development change and encourage innovation at the subnational (county) level. Agustin Madrigal Bulnes, Andrea Savage Tejada, and Joshua Ellsworth look at the success of partnership efforts in Mexico led by diverse local actors. Awuah founded and has led the expanding Ashesi University in Ghana in the belief that "young Africans, educated at the university level in a way that nurtures ethics, innovation, and entrepreneurship, would become a force for change." There are a myriad of other examples of innovative Southern leaders independently making sustainable change. The Bangladesh Rural Advancement Committee and the Grameen Bank in Bangladesh are two famous examples of locally led organizational innovations that have reached a scale equaling or exceeding that of government. There are countless examples of sustainable innovations from the local to the national, from an agricultural university initiative of a cassava-processing innovation in Nigeria that increased incomes while lessening environmental waste to the conditional cash-transfer program initiated by the government of Brazil that reduced inequality and increased incomes.

In this book, we focus on voices and examples from the South. We recognize that development practitioners in the North are also exploring ways to turn practice right side up and create space for Southern decision making. INGOS have developed new governance structures that include Southern affiliates (though work still needs to be done to overcome the inequality inherent in dependence on Northern funding). Initiatives of the Millennium Challenge Corporation or USAID's direct budget support programs deserve examination, as do many other initiatives, including examples mentioned in prior chapters. But we intentionally avoid focusing on Northern examples. First, Northern voices have ample access to audiences where they can be heard. Second, as editors, we want to make a small contribution to upending Northern dominance and the inequality that exists when Southern development thinkers, scientists, and practitioners seek an audience. Third, as editors, our decades working with Southern organizations and teaching practitioners from all over the world have left us with no doubt that Southern practitioners and their communities can take the lead in development and can produce innovations that work effectively in their countries and beyond. Finally, we are aware that though we may be more industrialized and powerful in the North, we still have many problems. There is much we can learn from Southern practices, methods, and innovations that could help us solve our own development problems. But we can't learn from the South if we can't hear from the South.

We want to emphasize five major lessons that emerge from the authors' observations: returning to fundamentals, reversing roles, identifying pathways for change, upending barriers, and confronting ethical dilemmas. The importance of taking an integrated, sustainable development approach is woven through each lesson. Most of the authors refer directly to sustainable development as the way forward—Simon, Ariyaratne, Agardy, Velasquez Donaldson, Kamau, Odembo, F. Howard and Newball, Offenheiser, and the editors. The others, even if they do not refer directly to sustainable development as a model, examine development from the perspective of sustainability and offer examples of multifaceted initiatives.

Lesson One: Returning to Fundamentals

Turning development practice right side up begins with reflection on what sustainable development is and the values that animate it. Aid practice has lost sight of what development means. On the one hand, development as aid is smothered in project approaches and in the bureaucracy of the aid industry, which obfuscate the larger vision sustainable development practice seeks to achieve. On the other hand, though few remain who will say that development is only about economic growth, many continue to rely on gross domestic product (GDP) as the fallback measure of development. What we measure reflects both the values we bring to development and our failure to comprehend the holistic nature of development. GDP thrives as an indicator despite the considerable work done by UN Development Programme and country partners on an array of indicators in the Human Development Report (including Amartya Sen and Mahbub ul Haq's composite Human Development Index); the Oxford Poverty and Human Development Initiative (OPHI)'s multidimensional poverty index (based on the Alkire-Foster method); the environmental sustainability index led by Yale and Columbia Universities with global partners (that consolidates indicators in more than a dozen thematic areas); and others on measuring multidimensional aspects of human development, or the work on the reciprocating links between environmental health and human well-being.

Authors refer to the thinking of Sen, who defines development as freedom, the circumstance in which individuals and societies have the capabilities to act (be agents) in collectively and individually seeking to claim public goods from government or ethical practice from the private sector. This sense of agency and the legitimacy of one's claims must underpin the advocacy of civil societies, locally, nationally, and globally. Offenheiser reminds us that poverty is not the "absence of public goods but . . . social exclusion" and that we need to see "every development issue in terms of power relations." Development is not economic growth or charity that soothes but does not resolve poverty and injustice. Contributors stress the importance of looking at the structural causes of exclusion and inequality. Simon refers to the transformative work of Brazilian educator Paulo Freire, also quoted in Chapter 3, who addresses fundamental issues of power, oppression, and liberation. Simon also quotes Dom Helder Camara, the social-activist priest, who recognized the structural sources of poverty: "When I give food to the hungry, they call me a saint, but when I ask why they are hungry, they call me a communist." To ask "why" is indeed challenging. Contributors (F. Howard and Newball, S. J. Holcombe, Gupta, Agardy, and Madrigal Bulnes, among others) describe "bottom-up" initiatives that achieve local development objectives and also, sometimes indirectly, can impact the larger structures of power. Development practitioners need to challenge inequitable policies, laws, structures, and informal practices; for example, those that place the heaviest burdens of unsustainable resource extraction or climate change on poor people or excluded groups such as Africa's women farmers or the Dalits in South Asia. Northern practitioners may have more freedom and access, and thus responsibility, to tackle the structures and systems that perpetuate poverty and environmental harm, including overcoming a specialist-oriented worldview that can mask the complex, intertwined nature of development.

For Ariyaratne, it is fundamental that change starts at the individual and community level. He explains that the six-decade-old Sri Lankan movement known as Sarvodaya "always believed in the inherent capacity of even the most impoverished communities to surmount their plight if the barriers that prevent them from unleashing their potential are removed." The process that Sarvodaya evolved is based on Buddhist and Gandhian thinking and is known as "awakening"—starting with the individual and progressing to the family, the village, city, nation, and world. Awuah is eloquent about the capacity (and right) of Ghanaians and Africans to fashion innovation and change in their own societies. At the same time, some authors (Dichter, Offenheiser, Odembo, Agardy, Velasquez Donaldson, the editors, and others) emphasize the importance of individual and institutional reflection. Practitioners need to reflect on their own beliefs and biases. Biases may be so deeply embedded in our own culture and history that we cannot see that others have their own conceptual frameworks, which may be neither better nor worse than our own. Whether acknowledged or not, our values are reflected in how we practice development.

Lesson Two: From Values to Role Reversals to Southern Ownership of Development

The loudest message emerging from voices here is the recognition that we need to reverse the roles of practitioners from North and South. Author after author states explicitly or implicitly that leadership, decision making, and responsibility must rest in the South. Northern practitioners need to learn to take on new roles as supporting partners (rather than lead partners), mentors, and conduits for resources (funds, technologies, and contacts) unavailable in the South. The development industry must allow local people, their institutions, and their communities to lead development and control their own destinies, learning how to best support their work in ways defined by those affected. Given his years of experience with development projects, Christian Velasquez Donaldson states that one of the most effective strategies to create ownership and lasting change is to share power and decision making with the people affected by any development intervention, and if we cultivate empathy such strategies will become inevitable. Meaningful participation is a prerequisite for sustainable development, according to Kamau. To make this happen, leadership from the South needs "courage, confidence, and skill," as Awuah puts it. He describes this as the courage to speak up, to challenge, to ask questions, and to resist corruption. Part of the courage is the confidence of young leaders that they can make change based on their ethics and professional preparation. Simon, in orienting graduate students just entering a sustainable development program at Brandeis University, used an upside-down map of the world to challenge stereotypes. The Northern orientation of maps is, after all, a construct of Northern mapmakers. The reversal of which regions are "on top" can suggest the need for Northerners to practice humility, can cause students to question ingrained worldviews, and can reveal that our orientation has been defined by the powerful and accepted as reality. Simon implies that every step of an education program can emphasize that young professionals need to learn how to listen, respect their counterparts, and assist with implementation, not perform the implementation themselves.

Reversing practitioner roles is difficult because development is equated with aid—financial and technical aid needed by the South ("the receivers") that mostly comes from the North ("the givers")—and aid is likely to be a continuing feature of development. Disassociating development practice from the power inequalities built into aid practice and institutions will be difficult. Change can evolve from within development practice through changes in individual and collective practice; from courageous, confident, prepared leadership in the South; from empathy, attitudinal change, and a transformed skill set in the North; and from a commitment on both sides to grapple with the challenges of sharing power and mainstreaming values of sustainable development such as inclusion, local management, and participative decision making.

For transformative leaders and practitioners in the South, critical steps include knowing their development goals and deciding on their own (not the donor's) theory of how that change will occur. This leads to policies grounded in local commitment that can be implemented and sustained, not policies dictated by donors or the most powerful actors. This is not easy, but it leads to government policy and practice that make a difference. Some of the authors (F. Howard and Newball, Velasquez Donaldson, Odembo, Kamau, Agardy, and the editors, among others) point out that legal and policy frameworks for sustainable development and socioeconomic transformation are often already in place but still need to be implemented.

As mentioned in Chapter 2, our students sometimes admired top-down examples—the Chinese experience of rapid economic growth and massive poverty reduction, and the Cuban example of countrywide social transformation. Those achievements were the result of Chinese and Cuban national policies, not policies imposed or implemented by outsiders. Lu Lei describes the Chinese policy focus on poverty reduction and how China has attempted to erase deep and persistent poverty. Chinese policies are backed by government actions and accountability mechanisms that operate down to the local level. Getting national policies right is not easy, and that is not the only requirement. Ariyaratne talks about the challenge of remaining true to organizational vision and mission when negotiating with donors. The power inequality between donor and recipient stands in the way of true partnership and can hinder sustainable development, as emphasized in Chapter 3. Elkanah Odembo refers to the power of outside funding and how it creates a comfortable reliance of African NGOs on outside donors to support service-delivery projects, largely determined and designed by Northern donors. Odembo urges Southern NGOs to invest in raising funds within their own societies. Accepting aid from some donors can cloud the independence of Southern organizations and impede their ability to be effective advocates with their own private sectors and governments.

To counteract the dominating influence of aid and structural constraints of development aid as an industry, much is required of transformational leadership in the South. Getting goals and policies right is only the start. Making sustainable development change may mean questioning old ways and challenging existing power structures. That requires the confidence that the change can be made and the courage to take risks that lead to success, but it could also lead to failure. Awuah points out that for Ashesi to succeed, they had to learn from their mistakes—and they must keep learning. Embracing failure as an opportunity to learn and move forward is hard when both Southern and Northern organizations cover up failure rather than using it as an opportunity for learning, often because of the pressure to demonstrate success, measurable results, and cost effectiveness to donors and constituents.

The existence of Ashesi University is itself a statement that African institutions must take the lead in preparing African leadership and building a strong economy not constrained by corruption. Awuah's vision for Ashesi is grounded in a deep belief in the capacity of Africans to lead and innovate. The challenges of building courage, confidence, and skill may also be compounded in some developing countries by historical events, for example, a colonial heritage. Awuah noted the internal censoring of indigenous capabilities, which can be the legacy of a colonial past: "Some Ghanaian academics don't believe their students will ever become innovators. When we designed the Ashesi curriculum in computer science, we were quietly advised not to expect our students to advance much beyond workmanlike programming skills." Ariyaratne tells of establishing the Sarvodaya Institute of Higher Learning, which now is evolving into a university focused on building sustainable development, inclusive communities, and enlightened leaders—training Sri Lankans and welcoming students from the North as fellow learners.

Leadership is often locally and culturally grounded. Sarah Holcombe explains how Mechai Viryavaidan used his cultural knowledge of the Thai penchant for humor, and how he used humor to facilitate a culturally difficult conversation on commercial sex and the threats of HIV/AIDS. Viryavaidan is privileged and cosmopolitan, so he used his status and power to make change. Odembo also reflects this conviction that African leadership in civil society must and can play this change role. He tells us that civil society organizations in Africa must go beyond service delivery and take on policy-advocacy roles appropriate to their own political spaces. This also implies that Northern practitioners need to be conscious of the boundaries of their own political space, and in which areas they have legitimacy in supporting civil societies in the South.

Largely implicit in what some of the voices from the South have to say about making change is that it can be a lonely process. Clearly, it helps to be supported by allies. Kamau explains that the new leadership in Makueni County in Kenya had the benefit of working together as a cohort of young, educated leaders committed to implementing change and using the opportunity of devolution. At Ashesi, the effort to inculcate an ethical approach to entrepreneurship was a group effort, involving members of each class over the four years of their studies. Awuah recognizes that graduates going out into the world of practice may lose the reinforcing support of their classmates. Time spent in a university is a brief interlude, and practitioners need a community that will support them through the challenges of transforming development. The Sarvodaya model rests on building local leaders who work with village collectives to make sustainable change. Struggling to reverse roles will be lonely for Northern practitioners, too. Going against the industry, disrupting the status quo, and fighting for their own culture to change its norms, give up its power, and accept that it doesn't have the answers will require young Northerners also to have courage, confidence, and skill. The editors have observed that in acquiring the courage and confidence to make change, practitioners are embarking on a lifelong process.

Scarcely mentioned is the possibility that making change can be dangerous. Initiatives may threaten political power structures and even expose Southern change agents to imprisonment or assassination. Velasquez Donaldson refers to violence against human-rights advocates and the disturbing restrictions of civic participation and spaces now occurring in many countries. Again, this is a place where a supportive development community is vital, and where Northerners need to respect Southern voices and avoid pushing Southern leaders into actions that create risk; only Southerners can decide the risks that are worth confronting and that they are ready to confront.

Also evident from the experiences of our contributors is that spending time living and working in excluded communities, as well as studying or living in another country, opened doors and minds, introduced new ways of thinking, and built confidence. Velasquez Donaldson started his career in his home country of Bolivia and found that "traveling and talking with people opened my view to different perspectives and concerns about our environment." Simon observes that when students were confronted with new concepts, they struggled with deeply held convictions and assumptions. Dichter talks about the "heady experience" of building relationships with people different from ourselves. Ariyaratne points out that when Sarvodaya facilitated personal connections by having donors and recipient communities work together directly, the process transformed both sides of the development equation. Engaging with people who are different from us can nurture "cosmopolitanism," which is not simply being at home with different cultures but also being open to and provoked by new ideas and living in a place of mutual respect that comes from seeing all human beings as fellow citizens of the world.

Lesson Three: Pathways for Southern Leadership and New Paradigms

Turning development right side up might seem a fantasy to some. This is so if one focuses only on the pernicious effects of the aid industry or on the corruption of some governments and extractive industries operating in the South. But evidence from our contributors, and from many examples not included here, suggests that Southern leaders and organizations have found ways to upend practice.

Contributors look to government decentralization or devolution as a pathway for change. By the 1990s the World Bank and other donors were increasing investments in decentralization programs. The emphasis on aid effectiveness that started in about 2000 has intensified donor focus on government reform and devolution of responsibility, authority, and resources to the subnational level, with mixed success. The case of devolution in Kenya suggests that there are opportunities for shaping policy directions and implementation at the county level. Kamau demonstrates how devolution appears to be working in some counties, under the leadership of a team of educated, committed Kenyans and systems of social accountability and inclusion that emerged from a well-defined participatory process. Success in several counties may create a node from which spontaneous replication can occur in other counties.[1] It will be some time before we can know whether this is a devolution that assures sustainable development, but it is worth studying. Fanny Howard and Rixcie Newball tell the story of how a regional government agency (part of Colombia's devolved National Environment System), together with civil society, brought a legal case against the national government. The regional government agency won the case after taking it all the way to the country's highest court, illustrating the potential of devolution to change the status quo in traditionally centralized governments.

Southern NGOs and civil society can also transform development. Odembo reminds us that African NGOs can play a role in shaping the policy environment at local and national levels. It is easy for national NGOs to get lost in the weeds of day-to-day activities and for NGO leaders to lose sight of the bigger picture and the need for strategic thinking. The right processes and tools also offer pathways to introduce transformative goals and values more easily. Agardy describes how payments for ecosystem services (PES) and marine spatial planning (MSP) can serve as such tools locally, even if originally introduced by outside partners. MSP can be a "dynamic system of rationalized use based on how people value the environment and can profit from its protection. When done well, MSP can draw in stakeholder groups in meaningful ways to co-create systems that ensure that use today will not preempt use in the future." The use of tools such as these can promote adaptation to the realities of local place and time.

Collaboration with government and other local actors can leverage locally led change. One consequence of deeply held Northern biases is distrust of governments and of the private sector. This can result in the failure to build local capacities needed to sustain changes once donor money departs. Recognizing this, Madrigal Bulnes, Savage Tejada, and Ellsworth talk about the benefits their Mexican organization has received by collaborating with government agencies, local NGOs, and other NGOs and partners so that their individual resources work together to assure sustainability over time. Implementing sustainable change is complex, and the development industry processes seldom allow enough time. Project timelines and donor abandonment of projects once the funding is finished presuppose that development occurs in time-bound segments of a few years. Madrigal Bulnes and his colleagues decided to intentionally address this problem, using alliances with government agencies, NGOs, the private sector, and communities to build alternate flows of resources before projects ended.

Governments and the private sector are not devoid of people committed to human well-being and environmental stewardship. Blanket distrust of government or the private sector means forgoing opportunities to scale-up tested innovations or leverage needed resources. Pallavi Gupta talks about the function of a bridging organization that can bring together a small NGO with ideas and a government agency with the resources to expand the innovation.

Another pathway for change can be found in the many global instruments on environment or human rights that most governments have ratified; including economic, social, political, and environmental rights, and those of vulnerable peoples such as women, children, people with disabilities, and indigenous peoples. International agreements have periodic reporting requirements on progress made toward international goals, and governments have incentives to show progress. Civil society advocates can use these agreements as an acceptable way to increase pressures on governments to act. In F. Howard and Newball's story, international law served as a direct lever. In their example, a regional government agency, a local civil society organization, and a grassroots cooperative used international agreements and Colombian constitutional law to obtain a legal ruling that banned exploration and extraction of hydrocarbons in the territorial sea, thereby protecting the indigenous people from the consequences of oil leases on their marine ecosystems, local livelihoods, and culture. Practitioners in the South are generally aware of the importance of international law and policy as a tool of sustainable development, and they may already know how to use this tool effectively. As teachers, we editors found that most US students knew little about international law and basic protections for rights, indigenous peoples, or the environment, and they knew even less about how these might be used. As practitioners, we found the same to be true of many US-based NGOs.

Lesson Four: Upending Barriers to Role Reversals

Barriers to role reversals are both attitudinal and structural. Attitudinal barriers are difficult to disentangle from the knowledge and financial strength and structures of the North. For some, the economic and technical successes of the North support a bias of Northern superiority and suggest that Northerners have the answers that Southerners just need to adopt. Velasquez Donaldson, who is from Bolivia but has spent much of his professional career in the United States, writes about how difficult it is for Northerners to shed a sense of privilege. Lacking empathy, he says, "we rationalize the development decisions we make with a comforting sense of aggregated benefits to society, what we call the 'greater good,' without considering the individual human faces, ownership, and equity implications of such interventions." Economics without empathy cannot address poverty, inequality, or exclusion. As development practitioners become professionalized and focus on aggregate change, they can lose touch with the real purposes of development and with those who are excluded. Practitioners from the North (and elites from the South) need exposure to realities outside their communities of privilege. This is a part of global cosmopolitanism that can be overlooked. Although many Northern universities offer study and travel abroad, few of these opportunities actually expose students to the realities of poverty and social exclusion that could engender the kind of empathy Velasquez Donaldson describes.

Northern practitioners working in developing countries often live and work in a privileged environment that grants them a socioeconomic status far different from what they would experience at home. They may have access to housing, servants, and cars that are out of their reach at home and unattainable for most people in developing countries. And they can be perceived as the source of funding and opportunity for local colleagues or afforded unearned privilege, for example, because of nationality or skin color. This is not to say that Northern development practitioners need to live in deprivation or discomfort, but it does mean that they must be conscious of the potential for preferential treatment and also have the responsibility to assure that privilege does not translate into arrogance and abuse of power.

Structural barriers to reversing roles and addressing inherent power inequities may be less dramatic than extreme individual abuses of power, such as sexual misconduct, which is referred to in Chapters 2 and 9, but these impediments are nonetheless real. Structural factors and industrialization of aid, as Dichter notes, empower the North and keep the South subordinate. Assumed superiority of Northern approaches to development, along with power imbalances, are made nearly inevitable by institutionalized resource and funding roles. Perverse incentives, such as demanding measurable results in project time frames, referred to in Chapter 3 and by Madrigal Bulnes, Savage Tejada, and Ellsworth in Chapter 12, create formidable barriers to advancing sustainable development or upending the traditional practice of "donor knows best." Development funding, in spite of well-meaning pronouncements and agreements to the contrary, has remained largely top-down, with Northern agencies imposing a sequence of theories of one-size-fits-all solutions to problems. This also poses challenges to Northern practitioners. Northern practitioners do have access to more resources—particularly money, information, and technology. Sharing resources remains important in development, but Northerners need to cultivate more humility and less arrogance in doing so. They can, for example, share knowledge about multiple solutions to problems that have been tried elsewhere, but the choice of solution must rest with the country or affected community. Northern practitioners do have a legitimate responsibility and accountability for aid funds to taxpayers or donors. But Southern recipients are also responsible for proper use of resources, both to their communities and to their donors. We can see this accountability as reciprocal, in that taxpayers and donors in the North need to ask whether their resources are contributing to development that is sustainable or may actually be creating dependencies and doing harm.

Instead of imposing solutions, Northern agencies can introduce Southern partners to examples of how countries or communities around the world have solved problems similar to those they are struggling to overcome. Ashesi University offers an example. Leadership invited help in curriculum development from Northern partner universities but remained in control of curricular choices. As Lu Lei explains, China welcomed ideas and approaches but maintained the overall strategic direction of its development and poverty-reduction efforts. In Chapter 3, Marion Howard explains that the Colombian government agency she worked with regularly did this at the project level. First, the local community would identify the problem(s) its residents wanted to address. Then the project team would consult international experts and research solutions from around the world, share everything they learned with primary stakeholders (those most affected by the project), and the stakeholders would choose the solution. Some of the contributors here (Dichter, Offenheiser, Velasquez Donaldson, Agardy, and others) referred to the imposition of Northern theories or practices, such as neoliberal economics or unsustainable natural resource extraction, effectively making policy choices for the South; but the negative consequences of such policies were suffered by Southerners. Northern practitioners need to learn that despite wealth and technology, they do not have the answers for Southern communities. They need to learn to listen, ask how they can help, and provide useful resources and knowledge, as others work to solve their own problems.

Sustainable development, which includes building individual and institutional capacities, occurs over time and even intergenerationally, not in project time frames. Agardy describes this time dimension with respect to coastal communities that take on comanagement, noting that they "must be empowered to manage use of coastal and marine areas, with sufficient resources available to them for the long term. This is at odds with much development aid, which demands quick, positive results from investment in environmental protection." In Chapter 3, Marion Howard explains that sustainable development requires that communities participate actively and have access to the information and knowledge they need to make effective decisions. Besides taking time, these truly important aspects of sustainable development can be difficult to measure. If you measure only narrowly proscribed outputs, you may miss the bigger picture, for example, whether Southern governments and organizations are growing in capacity and whether communities are becoming empowered and managing their own change. Offenheiser notes that few donors will fund building capacities in governments and national and local NGOs to carry out evaluations that result in learning and enhanced organizational capacity: "The philanthropic sector would benefit from a deeper discussion about what they are doing, or not doing, to enhance the field of impact assessment beyond current donor preferences for random control trials." Ariyaratne points out that Sarvodaya found requirements of reporting to multiple donors a constraint, despite its commitment to learning from experience and being able to adapt practice to learning results. Time spent collecting data for Northern headquarters competes with the time and energy needed for local learning and adaptation. The editors have noted that donor organizations—whether bilaterals, multilaterals, INGOs, or foundations—often ask for data well beyond what is needed for learning and monitoring implementation.

Measurement of results has become a Northern mantra, even an obsession. But obsession with numbers may cause donors to overlook indigenous accountability systems. Southern practitioners also value accountability. National governments and NGOs may have their own systems that are less punitive and more effective than donor-imposed systems. For example, in Kenya, social norms may exact accountability. Kamau says, "County leaders come from the local communities, and failure to deliver services and sustainable growth risks their losing face in societies where social standing is valued." Lu Lei gives the example of China, where a strong government links annual performance evaluations to achieving priority goals. Taking advantage of indigenous methods can improve use of scarce project resources, simplify reporting, and reduce or even eliminate the likelihood that recipients will feel obliged to falsify results, as mentioned in Chapter 2. Existing systems of donor funding create perverse incentives for INGOs, national and local NGOs, and governments that see themselves as competitors for donor money and not as collaborators. There is a gap between the values espoused and what happens in practice, with few incentives for collaboration. For example, practitioners get rewarded for meeting donor deadlines and outputs; they less frequently get recognized for time invested in building management capacity, actively including stakeholders, and laying the foundations for sustainability.

Donors know the importance of leaders and of building allies for change, but they lament that there is little time for this. Madrigal Bulnes, Savage Tejada, and Ellsworth describe practical strategies to overcome competition and build coalitions across organizations and sectors. Kamau describes processes in Kenyan counties that have already reversed the model, moving from donor-led initiatives to bottom-up partnership projects brokered by communities. Offenheiser recognizes that change is already taking place among INGOs. Some have attempted to incorporate Southern NGOs as full members of international federations or confederations, with decisions on programming theoretically in the hands of the national affiliate. We do not know how such changes in governance structures will affect true and equal partnership with Southern affiliates and partners.

Despite changes in leadership and decision making, reliance on funding from the North will probably remain part of development. Some INGOs have moved away from being service-delivery or charity operations and toward new, legitimate roles, advocating for changes in global and rich-country policies that perpetuate inequalities among nations and people, such as some of the World Bank's policies, US agricultural subsidies, or practices of Northern- and Southern-based international extractive industries. As Velasquez Donaldson points out, now the World Bank and some other international financial institutions (IFIs) require implementation of social and environmental safeguards to promote sustainability, involve locals more actively, and reduce negative impacts and inequities of development projects. Practitioners need to be aware of such measures and insist they meet local needs.

Lesson Five: Confronting Ethical Dilemmas

Practitioners will encounter misalignment and even ethical dilemmas when their values conflict with the structures and systems within which they work. Our students and colleagues often talked about the frustrations they experienced as they tried to align the values they brought to development and the situations they faced in practice. Since the 1950s, the global community, including both donor and recipient governments, has created a series of universally recognized standards that should guide development practice. Sustainable development—with its three pillars and sustainability factors of inclusion, capacity, participation, partnerships, good governance, adaptive local management, and equitable distribution of power and benefits (see Figure 3.1)—provides a yardstick for individual, organizational, and global ethical practice. When in doubt, it should be possible, although not easy, to consider what behavior will best realize these factors and act accordingly. Standards include aspirations for development outcomes embedded in the globally endorsed 2030 Agenda for Sustainable Development and SDGs. The global legal and policy frameworks of development—starting from the Universal Declaration of Human Rights and the Declaration on the Right to Development, and extending through human-rights conventions and other instruments that protect vulnerable peoples, to Agenda 21 and environmental conventions—state clear principles rooted in values. The Paris Declaration on Aid Effectiveness and Accra Agenda for Action set out five globally agreed-upon principles for implementing aid designed to respect the choices, capacities, and interests of Southern partners. Going further, the humanitarian community developed standards for the behavior of humanitarian assistance workers in the 1997 Sphere Project. There is no similar set of standards for development practice, but there is ample global agreement on standards for development outcomes, development practice, and individual development-worker integrity.

Many authors mention ethics and ethical practice. The editors introduce issues of ethics in Chapters 1 and 2. In Chapter 3, Marion Howard gives examples of ethical dilemmas in a Southern government agency's struggle with Northern donors and partners. Dichter notes challenges for Northern practitioners working in the aid industry. Offenheiser reflects on ethical issues confronting INGOs. Simon offers tales from the field that raise ethical questions, and he discusses the importance of weaving ethics throughout graduate development studies. For other authors, values, which define ethical frameworks, are fundamental to their work. Ariyaratne stresses the principles on which Sarvodaya's work rests. Awuah describes Ashesi University's values and emphasis on ethical behavior. Velasquez Donaldson writes, "Development *for whom* is the question we need to ask ourselves every time we face decisions and trade-offs as development practitioners. Development should be about values, equity, people—the most vulnerable and disadvantaged—and their environment, and less about economic growth and financial feasibility." He points out that safeguards are a practical tool that can promote fair treatment and help ensure that development projects do not cause harm to people or the environment. In every chapter, the centrality of ethical practice is evident, whether explicit or implicit.

But in spite of strong values and clear objectives, defining ethical dilemmas is difficult; situations are often not clear-cut, but murky. Dilemmas exist at different levels of intensity and impact, and no definition fits all situations. A dilemma may involve trade-offs between the questionable and the good in order to achieve the possible. Many ethical dilemmas occur in small, incremental ways. A student working in Northern Ghana spoke of the INGO eliminating agreed-upon participatory approaches to implement a project because of time constraints; meeting deadlines in the project document was more important and the INGO could implement faster. The INGO and the local partner both needed to demonstrate their efficiency to the donor. Graduates have told us of the pressure to deliver results defined in the project document, even as the conditions on the ground suggested that the project approach was faulty and needed revision. Chapter 3 includes the example of a successful sustainable development project a Colombian regional government agency designed and implemented that was widely recognized for its innovative approach and won several international awards. When the project ended, one of the world's largest, most powerful environmental INGOs that had no relationship to the project (had not provided any funds or technical support or even had contact with the project during the project cycle) took credit for the project's successful design and implementation in its widely circulated annual report. The government agency found that nothing could be done to defend itself against the INGO. Perhaps worse, many international and even national organizations seemed inclined to believe the prominent INGO, even though no evidence supported its claim, rather than giving deserved credit to a Southern government agency staffed mainly by indigenous people.

Responding to ethical dilemmas requires being aware of the harm that can be done, particularly to vulnerable people, as well as to individual practitioners and their organizations. Development projects target some people and not others. Certain kinds of aid can create dependence. Sudden withdrawal of aid can leave communities in a precarious position, or distrustful of aid initiatives, or both. Governance projects pushing anticorruption interventions or civic participation can create security risks for local staff or participants. As mentioned in Chapter 2, inequitable treatment of local staff, as compared with international staff, within development organizations can set the stage for resentment and even corruption. Humanitarian assistance is an area where ethical dilemmas may be especially difficult to confront. A former student was working in the Eastern Congo with a major INGO delivering relief. He knew that some staff members were siphoning off relief supplies to sell in the market. He attempted to control this, but over time he learned, for example, that firing the staff responsible did not solve the problem. Local staff saw work with a relief organization as their time to take advantage and get "rich." New staff found ways to circumvent procedures and take their turn at getting rich. Still, some of the relief aid did reach intended recipients; visibly exposing the leakage of supplies could pose security risks, and perhaps create a public impression that INGOs were inefficient or corrupt. Another graduate, working in Haiti with a small NGO doing relief work following the 2010 earthquake, also encountered corruption among office staff. She was able to institute systems of greater financial control and remove staff responsible for diverting funds. In both cases, the individuals had the confidence to try to control corruption, but the process was psychologically wearing and led them to choose other paths in their careers. Nationals working in relief or development situations may have more limited options to confront corruption. International staff generally leave, but national staff stay and must continue working with colleagues behaving unethically. This is why the initiative of Ashesi University to create a cadre of graduates armed with the skills and practical tools to resist and fight corruption, such as bribery and other ethical dilemmas in the workplace, is so important.

Ethical dilemmas persist to some extent because the aid community has not always implemented agreed-upon standards. Post mortems of the relief efforts following the Rwandan genocide in 1994 revealed that refugee camps in the Congo sheltered those who had been responsible for the genocide and that their leaders commandeered humanitarian aid for Hutu fighters who had fled Rwanda. Recognizing this, in 1997 the humanitarian community started the Sphere Project to develop minimum standards of conduct of humanitarian assistance. Sphere standards in core areas are admirable, but implementation is uneven. In 2018, news broke about repeated sexual abuse of vulnerable peoples by INGO and UN staff. There is no dilemma in acknowledging that sexual exploitation is wrong. The dilemma occurs in how practitioners and their organizations respond. INGOs may avoid fully addressing incidents of sexual abuse by staff, arguing that public reporting tars the image of INGOs and threatens the reputation of their governments and funders. The dilemma is real, as many do look for evidence to discredit development and humanitarian work. Because aid is an industry and competition for funding is fierce, organizations want to avoid negative publicity. When leadership isn't transparent about its own staff's egregious violations of human rights and dignity, INGOs perpetuate unethical behavior and create cultures of impunity, particularly for the more powerful international staff.

We have no easy advice for practitioners facing ethical dilemmas. Awuah rightly calls for ethical courage, but one's capacity for courage may depend on the circumstances of one's financial and physical security, political influence, and type of government, and that will vary depending on what is happening in one's life at the time. Asking ourselves if we're adhering to the standards of sustainable development and the framework of global agreements, policies, and guidelines can help, but it is not always easy to interpret or do this without support. Self-reflection is an essential professional skill for development practitioners. Reflective practice can be learned and should be part of every development program and encouraged in every organization. Ashesi's students use methods such as brainstorming, dialogue, and skits to encourage self-reflection and come up with possible responses to ethical dilemmas.

One way to manage ethical dilemmas inherent in development work is through small, incremental steps that build the systems and culture that reduce the potential for abuse of power within organizations. As noted, we have a plethora of standards for behaviors appropriate to development practitioners and organizations, but organizations have failed to develop ways to implement standards. In an ideal world, we could reduce misconduct by establishing procedures that discourage abuse and support ethical behavior in the first place. For example, because of existing systems that require transparency and reporting, some public schools in the United States may have been spared the epidemic of sexual abuse that plagued New England's private schools, where serial abusers were often recycled through other private schools (similar to the Catholic Church moving priests from parish to parish). Similarly, ethical dilemmas may be easier to confront in government than in NGOs or private universities because rules and systems are already in place to deal with misconduct, if enforced. In other words, development practice should not wait until ethical misconduct occurs. Development organizations should develop procedures that demand transparency and accountability. Leaders can work to create an organizational culture that rewards ethical practice through example and positive incentives. Creating such an organizational culture is a leadership function, but leaders need support and engagement of their staff and outside stakeholders.

Conclusion: Change Is Possible

These lessons indicate that change is already taking place in development practice, that Southern innovators are leading change and Northern practitioners are finding new roles. Upending the roles of Southern and Northern practitioners may require transforming the practices and priorities of development organizations, but aiming to do so is not a pipe dream. And implementing globally agreed-upon standards of sustainable development will help make it happen.

Reversing attitudes, behaviors, power relationships, and practice will not come easily, but our authors point to some of the places where change can, and is, happening. If development practice is at an inflection point, change may be only slightly perceptible at first. Then, as small changes accumulate and begin to have mass, they can accelerate, producing a real turning point that transforms development practice.

Note

1. In 2018, a former student, Jacinta Odhiambo, chief executive officer in Kakamega County (a county not discussed by Kamau), led an event at Brandeis about taking advantage of devolution to use funding to engage participation and reliably deliver basic services.

18

Educating Development Practitioners for Positive Change

Marion Howard and
Susan H. Holcombe

We write in this book about the need to upend goals, values, and systems of development by reversing practitioner roles and implementing sustainable development. Development needs to be done *by* Southern institutions, communities, and people—not done *to* them by a Northern-controlled development industry—and needs to incorporate characteristics and values of sustainable development. But how do we do this? In Chapter 17, we identify lessons from the contributors that can help. In this chapter, we look at what this means for designing graduate development studies programs to educate and train professionals who want to transform the status quo. For aspiring development practitioners who seek to make a difference, graduate school is not just an academic exercise. For universities, it is not simply a matter of developing new curricula. It is much more. We do not learn only in classrooms, from assignments, or from books. We learn because we have an environment that encourages us to learn, question, and critique. We learn when we reflect on our own values, assumptions, and biases, and on those of our communities. We learn by doing. We learn if we're embedded in a learning community that challenges and supports us. We learn from interacting with and getting to know others. And we don't stop learning when we leave educational institutions, especially if we have a strong professional network.

Given the understanding that development should be done *by* Southern countries, their institutions, communities, and people, and not *to* them, we agree it is wise, as Dichter says in Chapter 6, to ask if universities should continue to prepare Northern students for development practice. We think that they should, especially for three reasons. First, in an upended development paradigm, there will still be a need for committed

247

Northern development practitioners, but practitioners who are trained to take on a very different role as supporters, as equal or subordinate partners, and as a resource to Southern-led development. Second, no country is fully developed, so what budding Northern development practitioners learn in development studies programs should also be applicable to addressing exclusion, poverty, overconsumption, environmental issues (climate change, extinctions, pollution, ecosystem degradation, loss of biodiversity, and so on), health and education concerns, and other development problems in their home countries, especially in the United States with its increasingly inequitable distribution of wealth, growing poverty, and problems with access to quality health care and education. Third, sustainable development needs development professionals from both North and South to upend existing paradigms and to work together in harmony and equality to achieve a united world and the shared vision and values of sustainable development in every country.

In this final chapter, we look at what development practitioners need to know to face the challenges of development in a rapidly evolving field. We start by laying out what we mean by a development studies program that aims to educate and train sustainable development practitioners; that is, professionals with a broad knowledge and set of skills about development. Next, we consider what development practitioners need to know that could be learned in a graduate program. We recount the ideas of graduates of Brandeis's sustainable international development program now practicing in the field to help answer this question. We consider what we learned from the experiences of our contributors, from our own experiences in practice, and from our teaching. Finally, based on all these ideas, we look at what could transform development studies to help upend development practice. We consider core competencies and educational strategies, and we provide a schema of how to structure a curriculum to prepare practitioners to upend development and advance the goals and values of sustainable development. We look at university culture and how to better harmonize development studies programs with the academy.

What Do We Mean by Education for Development Practice?

A development studies program that aims to professionally train practitioners needs to deliver concepts and skills required for all students to come to their own understanding of development within the general vision and consensus that sustainable development combines environmental, economic, and social priorities with fundamental principles of inclusion, equity, good governance, participative management, and so on (see Figure 3.1). Central to all practitioners is a sound grasp of one's own philosophy of development and the values one brings to development practice. Time spent as a student offers a rare opportunity to reflect on one's own values, biases, theories of change, strengths and weaknesses, and beliefs about how development happens. This requires knowledge of how to build an interdisciplinary, comprehensive framework to guide practice and keep moving toward intended goals.

Practitioners and Specialists

A sustainable development professional needs to have comprehensive, authoritative knowledge about sustainable development, along with the skills to put sustainable development into practice. As explained in Chapter 3 and discussed in many other chapters, sustainable development is an interdisciplinary field, so "specialists" in sustainable development (i.e., practitioners working in the development industry whose professional training and specific expertise are in the area of sustainable development) need to be "generalists" in a number of disciplines (i.e., have a basic, working knowledge of many subjects that pertain to sustainable development, such as economics, ecology, social policy, education, organizational management, human rights, ethics, and so on). On a practical level, development professionals need to be able to manage a range of specialist activities. On a strategic level, practitioners need to understand how different specialty interventions can intersect and work together to achieve sustainable, locally owned change.

Development practitioners need to know how to consult with and manage subject-area specialists when a specialist is needed to help advance a particular dimension or activity of development. This doesn't mean the practitioner has to be able to do the specialist's work; rather, the practitioner must be able to identify, recruit, work with, and supervise the subject-area specialist. It's important for development practitioners to know when they need to consult with specialists, how to work with them, and what support they can bring to a given project. This means knowing enough about a particular specialty to use and understand professional vocabulary and to be clear on what a specialist can deliver that the community needs, for example, in economics, public health, natural resource management, or international law. But development professionals are not usually specialists themselves, except in development.

At the same time, given the global consensus on the way forward, a development studies program that wants to be relevant and aims to train its students to upend the aid industry should be educating specialists in the field of sustainable development. Students who are already specialists in a related field such as economics, natural resource management, public health, or international law may come to a sustainable development program to learn more about how to apply their subject-area specialty in a strategic way within the changing development field and to build a related specialization in integrated, holistic development.

Leaders and Managers

It is important to distinguish between what the practitioner as manager needs to know and what the practitioner as leader needs to know. Practice-oriented development studies programs are preparing professionals to manage and to lead. In practice, the same person may fill both leadership and management functions because these functions overlap, but the distinctions are important. A practitioner needs to be able to recognize when and where leadership is required, and when and where management functions should dominate. Leaders play a change role—setting vision and grand strategy; initiating action at the organizational level; motivating organizations, staff, and stakeholders to implement the vision and strategy; and likely raising funds and leveraging support. The manager is in a stabilizing operational role—planning, budgeting, organizing, staffing the work, managing the team, and problem-solving to support the vision.

Some of the many skills needed for effective development management include planning, implementation, monitoring, problem-solving, managing organizations and finances, teamwork and team building, working with stakeholders, participatory methods, building partnerships, evaluation, statistical analysis, communications, and advocacy. The leader is not likely to be expert in all these skills but needs to know how important they are and how they contribute to the vision and strategy. The manager, too, may not be required to perform all these skills but needs to know how to supervise, delegate, and manage a team that collectively carries them out. And both leaders and managers should know when specialist studies are needed—such as an environmental-impact assessment, gender analysis, cost-benefit analysis, or GIS mapping. It is important to be able to identify the right specialists for the job, and to know how to define and apply their work. Getting the right balance of skills depends on the organization and particular intervention. Each project, program, partnership, and stakeholder structure will have different needs, requiring practitioners to be able to engage in a lifelong process of learning, remaining flexible, and adapting.

What Do Sustainable Development Practitioners Need to Know?

To transform development, a professional development studies program needs to take an integrated approach, in keeping with the global vision of sustainable development. To truly comprehend and be equipped to advance integrated, transformative development, a sustainable development practitioner needs to be grounded in a wide range of subjects such as the theory and history of development, development management, the basic principles of economics and ecology, governance, and aspects of exclusion and social development. Practical courses in development ethics, reflective practice, participatory methods, human rights, and international law and policy, among others, teach conceptual knowledge and skills that development practitioners need to transform how development is done, and such courses can stimulate important discussions and debates among diverse students. Knowledge of and sensitivity to the culture, history, religion, and language of the work site are also important.

Within the broad, interdisciplinary framework of sustainable development, each practitioner will work inside an organization that most likely focuses on a sub-area of sustainable development, for example, poverty alleviation, environmental conservation, urban development, agriculture, energy, health, migration, human rights, advocacy, or education, depending on the organization's mission or legal mandate. The depth of sectoral knowledge required will depend on the subfield of development in which the development practitioner is working. Still, the range of skills needed is so broad that no one practitioner can master them all, and no single program can cover all these subjects. A program training practitioners in sustainable development is likely to have to limit the number of sub-areas in which it can provide courses, taking into account resources and faculty expertise.

Learning About Development Practice: Thoughts from Alumni

As faculty concerned with curriculum, we periodically asked Sustainable International Development (SID) alumni working in a variety of development organizations around the world, what they need to know in their daily practices that they think could be learned in graduate school. We informally asked former students again when writing this book. They sent a variety of replies; most of their answers were repeated and could easily be clustered by theme. What they said is consolidated and summarized below, using mainly their own words.

In general. A graduate program should combine theory and practice but should focus on practice. Course content should be geared to sustainable development, which means an intersectional approach across a multidisciplinary curriculum. Knowing how to think and question development is important, as long as the emphasis is on teaching us how to be development professionals rather than development thinkers; that is, in our work we don't sit in the corner and think, we must be able to go out into the world and help communities develop themselves. It's important to learn to think critically and look deeply into structures and systems of oppression; this means learning how to use our privilege and power to support vulnerable people in becoming the agents of their own development. Practitioners need to analyze and learn why development isn't working and how to change the way things are done. We learned as much (sometimes more) from fellow students as from professors, so a graduate program is much stronger if the student body is very diverse and all the students have a few years of experience in development work before entering graduate school.

Course subjects and topics. For development to be sustainable, we need to learn how to incorporate the natural environment and climate change into all our work. It is essential to study governance, political systems, human rights, and international law and policies and to learn how to make and influence policy. Understanding adaptive management is very important, along with knowing how to share and manage knowledge in resource-limited contexts. We need to study the structural determinants of power, oppression, exclusion, vulnerability, privilege, and the like; this means learning how to use privilege and power to support vulnerable communities in becoming change agents.

Project and program management. Practitioners work with all phases of the project cycle, so we need tools for use at every stage (e.g., logframes and logic models, timelines, stakeholder analysis, SWOT analysis, needs analysis, and budgets). We need to analyze context, identify funding sources, and produce proposals. Monitoring and evaluation are equally important. Fundamental skills include understanding cost-benefit analysis, defining benchmarks and indicators, producing comprehensive progress reports, and knowing simple monitoring and evaluation methods that can be carried out in sites with limited capacity and resources.

Inclusion and empowerment. Practitioners have to work with communities, stakeholders, and partners, and they have to enable vulnerable groups to exercise power. Participatory methods and capacity assessment are useful. This includes knowing how to gather and include community opinions, engage and empower people, work from the bottom up, stand up/advocate for vulnerable cultures and beliefs (our own and others), carry out cross-cultural dialogue, and build bridges across cultures. Practitioners should be able to do gender analysis, mainstream gender, and develop gender action plans to enhance sustainability.

Navigating the field. Practitioners need to have knowledge about donors and how they operate and should have the skills to deal and negotiate with them. This means learning about alternative perspectives in order to work better with all the actors (donor, government, NGO, private sector, community). Practitioners must have a basic understanding of development institutions and their functions (e.g., UN, multilaterals and bilaterals, NGOs, foundations, global development policy, international law). This means learning as much as possible about how the development world functions, including about the growing involvement of newer actors such as the emerging power donors, the for-profit sector, and the military. It's very important that we know how to manage and work in diverse teams. Practitioners need to build and navigate partnerships and know how to shape and strengthen organizations and organizational culture.

Communications. Practitioners need strong communication skills; both to influence and advocate for policy choices and to explain sustainable development issues and actions (e.g., related to law and policy, economics, ecology, health, and so on) to communities in language they understand. Essential skills include written and spoken English (still the global development language), and the ability to ask and answer questions, to make a convincing case for a proposal or policy, to structure an argument, to present information and data in ways that are convincing, and to adhere to time limits. This calls for knowing how to prioritize and summarize information, structure data, and use visuals to better reach diverse audiences.

Basic methods of research, data collection, and analysis. Practitioners should have the skills to gather information, including designing surveys, conducting interviews, leading consultations, facilitating focus groups, and using participatory research methods. We need to be able to interpret data, understand statistics, and master statistical software.

Professionalism. Graduate school can help students learn to meet deadlines, handle electronic communications, and produce professional documents (terms of reference, letters of intent, consultant applications, curriculum vitae, technical offers). Networking is an important skill that can be honed by exposure to meetings, conferences, and other professional events while in school.

Basic computer skills. Practitioners need to have fundamental computer skills (e.g., Word, PowerPoint, and Excel), including the ability to present evidence using computer tools (tables, graphs, and charts) and be able to grasp new software as it evolves.

Experiential learning. In-depth field experience through a professional-level practicum, residency, or comparable experiential learning opportunities is a must, even for students who enter graduate school with several years of experience.

Learning About Development Practice: Thoughts from Contributors

There is also much to be learned from this book's contributors about how graduate education could be changed and restructured to help turn development right side up. Simon, Awuah, and Dichter explicitly write about education for development, challenging our thinking about how development is done and acquainting us with issues faced by development studies programs. If graduates aspire to change the present paradigm of Northern-defined and controlled development, they need academic programs that bridge the gap between what they need to know about the realities of development practice and what the development industry requires. To help students learn how to change the current paradigm, development studies programs need to invent new approaches. Most of the contributors are not talking directly about educating development practitioners, but what they have to say about working in the field is valuable for practice-oriented development studies programs. They offer examples that suggest new ways to approach development problems. Much of what our contributors say meshes with what the SID alumni practitioners said they need to know to do their jobs effectively and make change.

The alumni practitioners stressed the importance of learning about governance. Kamau and Lu Lei illustrate how governance, both devolved and centralized, can contribute to sustainable development. The alumni practitioners said they need to better understand the role of environment and conservation in sustainability. Agardy has a lot to say about this in her discussion of the connections between human well-being and sustainable oceans, and the differing viewpoints of development workers and conservationists. Madrigal Bulnes, Savage Tejada, and Ellsworth provide concrete, adaptable strategies to improve the incorporation of environment into development interventions. The alumni practitioners said over and over that they need to know as much as possible about development institutions, roles, and partnerships. Dichter puts us squarely in the middle of the development industry and the world of projects, contracts, consultants, and organizations. Offenheiser and Odembo teach us about international and national NGOs, and how NGOs shape development at different levels. We learn about the world of IFIs and global policy from Velasquez Donaldson, as he shares his knowledge of the World Bank and how it works. Madrigal Bulnes, Savage Tejada, and Ellsworth take us into the world of grassroots NGOs and multisectoral partnerships. Ariyaratne tells us a fascinating story about the growth and evolution of an effective grassroots social movement, at the same time introducing us to its world of donors, partners, and shifting institutional power. F. Howard and Newball broaden our understanding of how to apply international law and policy in practice, even to engaging the judicial sector through a court case. The microcases in Chapter 16 provide specific lessons on institutions, shifting power, and making change through bridging organizations, individual leadership, government approaches, and NGO oversight. Every chapter teaches us more about how development happens, about obstacles to making it happen, pointing out new pathways leading to sustainable development and the integrated approach that must be at the heart of development studies programs.

Learning About Development Practice: The Evolving Field

Contributors to this book describe their work within a context of multiple, often evolving approaches, again implicit if not explicitly defined. To change direction, practice-oriented development studies programs need to teach a variety of approaches that complement the integrated approach that underpins sustainability. Effective sustainable development can be rooted in any number of compatible approaches that help define program priorities, content, and implementation methods and achieve objectives. Approaches could be needs-based, rights-based, or based on capabilities, problem-solving, and liberation theory, to name a few. Learning multiple approaches and practicing them in experiential learning prepares students to question assumptions, apply what they've learned on the ground, build capacity to reflect on their experiences, and be flexible, keeping an open mind to new approaches throughout their careers. Practitioners should be prepared to reflect on their professional roles and approaches, on the roles and approaches of their institutions as outsiders or insiders in development, and to confront contradictions inherent in these roles and approaches.

Contributors point out that development is at a turning point; as elaborated in the policy framework that has evolved since 2005 or so (chapters refer to the Paris Declaration and Accra Agenda on aid effectiveness, 2030 Agenda for Sustainable Development, SDGs, and others) and in shifting institutions, players, and donors (chapters mention the BRICS, new cross-sectoral partnerships, changing institutional roles, and so forth). Practice-oriented development studies programs need to keep abreast of changes and remain at the cutting edge of practice as it evolves, which requires innovation and strategies to broaden the scope of academia. A few simple strategies are making space for practice faculty, expanding experiential learning, formalizing partnerships with other universities and development actors, and taking advantage of information technology.

Practice faculty. First, development studies programs need to engage active practitioners, not only academics, in creating curriculum, teaching, and advising and mentoring students. Not only does this ensure that students are engaged in a wealth of stories, examples, and challenges from the field, but it helps programs stay relevant as the field of practice changes. To attract practitioners with quality and experience, universities need to pave the way for them to benefit from the perks of academic life, to serve as active, well-paid faculty (not only as adjuncts), and to access opportunities for professional recognition and advancement.

Experiential learning. Second, experiential learning opportunities should be expanded. This can happen in any number of ways that combine community service/work and study, revolve around longer- and shorter-term professional field placements and practicums, involve students in active development projects, introduce more interactive learning activities into the classroom, incorporate field trips and longer group travel experiences into courses or extracurricular events, promote student voice and direct student involvement in program decision making, and provide opportunities for student-led events, working groups, and local advocacy. Experiential learning is critical to acquire practitioner skills. For example, for many of our students, working effectively in diverse teams was a challenge. Students often chafed under the requirement that assignments be executed and graded as group projects, especially students from individualistic societies, assertive social classes or cultures, or for whom English was their first language (versus colleagues working in a second or third language). Building an understanding of the benefits of team approaches along with the skills to navigate different working styles is essential but takes time and mentoring.

Partnerships. Third, setting up formal partnerships with universities around the world opens doors to a wealth of initiatives that include and go beyond opportunities for study abroad and multidirectional student exchanges (going both ways, as Ariyaratne says in Chapter 5). Interdisciplinary faculty exchanges, international visiting scholars, and collaborative teaching, research, public engagement, mentoring, recruitment, and fund-raising that involve students, faculty, and administrators are only a few such options. Partnerships can also be established with NGOs and other development organizations; allowing for professional training, practicum and resident placements, work-study, joint projects, student-practitioner exchanges and events, and other such practical experiences.

Information technology. Fourth, keeping up with the changing field requires keeping current with information technology. Among other innovations, development studies programs can implement a range of live web-based courses with partner universities and NGOs, bringing students from around the world together into a single classroom in real time for shared learning and dialogue.

How Can We Transform Development Studies?

To upend development, the shift in leadership, power, and privilege from North to South can start in graduate school. The diversity of the student body matters if universities want to change how and what they teach, including the range of differing voices in their own education and the breadth of their life and work experience. Effective learning to transform practice will emerge from diverse classrooms and graduate communities. This requires a student cohort from the South and North that is as diverse as possible across nationalities, cultures, religions, social class, ethnicities, gender, and other vulnerabilities. This is a difficult choice for a graduate program, if it means forgoing applicants from ruling elites in Southern and Northern countries whose families can pay the full cost of tuition and living expenses at high-priced Northern universities. There are formidable financial, social, and bureaucratic obstacles to increasing the ratio of Southern to Northern students, and it can mean devoting substantial energy to fund-raising. Simon and Awuah provide pointers on how to attract a diverse cohort of students and potential leaders. As universities make choices about diversity, it is important that they remember the underlying principle that Northerners, as well as Southerners, need to experience a shift in roles and power in their education.

Development Studies and Core Competencies

Core competencies—a concept that emerged from management theory for the private sector—are an important tool to guide design and set the boundaries of a practice-based, professional education program. A simple definition of a core competency is: fundamental knowledge, ability, or expertise in a subject area. Core competencies are of great value to education programs because they provide a frame of reference for developing academic courses and methods, for monitoring and evaluating learning and teaching, and for building a student's capacity as a professional who can translate knowledge into action. Therefore, a set of competencies for sustainable development practitioners looking to transform development practice would define an interdisciplinary package of knowledge, skills, and attitudes that would enable those who achieve them to sustainably solve development problems, transform institutions and structures, serve as agents of change, and train, empower, and support stakeholders and communities to shape and direct their own development.

Because sustainable development is multidisciplinary, no one course can, or should, cover all the core competencies; rather, the competencies are acquired from the curriculum as a whole. This means it is important to identify where competencies are taught within a curriculum and how courses connect. This process of mapping the competencies will uncover gaps in the curriculum, provide information to develop new courses and strengthen existing ones, and help create a living curriculum. An ongoing review process by students and by faculty will ensure that a curriculum (taken as a whole) meets established standards for practice. Box 18.1 offers an example of core competencies, in this case from Brandeis University's SID program (2008).

Development Studies and Values

Underlying the wide range of specific lessons we learn from each contributor are values and a unified, common perspective about the need for change, which helps us decipher how development studies programs can help upend the industry. Every chapter helps us see how values underlie sustainable development practice, even if values aren't mentioned explicitly.

Box 18.1 Core Competencies: An Example from Brandeis University's Sustainable International Development (SID) Program

SID's core competencies were approved in 2008 and guided the curriculum until a change of leadership at the Heller School and SID in 2014. Taken as a whole, the curriculum incorporated the general concepts and skills each student needed to master for a degree in sustainable development. In the first year, students acquired the competencies through academic study and community interaction. In the second year, they expanded their knowledge and skills through a six-month practicum, advanced study, or concentration that combined academic and experiential learning.

Explicit values of sustainability, human rights, inclusion, participation, capabilities, and a commitment to lifelong learning underpin the competencies. Courses, along with experiential and informal learning, encouraged reflection and analysis of values in talk and action. Much student learning came from dialogue and sharing experiences with peers. The diversity of the SID community was fundamental to building capacity; demanding that students learned to work effectively across national, ethnic, gender, cultural, religious, class, and experiential divides. Particular emphasis was given to community- and team-building exercises in courses and also in extracurricular activities.

In participatory evaluations, graduating students stressed that the critical factors in learning the competencies were the cross-sectoral, practice-oriented curriculum and the interaction with their peers. Therefore, during its first twenty years to ensure every student graduated with the core competencies, the SID program worked hard to attract an exceptionally diverse student body, and then to provide each student with a graduate experience rooted in multidisciplinary courses, experiential learning, and an array of complementary activities to build community and leadership such as workshops, guest lectures, professional seminars, team projects, field trips, group travel, and other special events on and off campus.

SID's competencies as approved in 2008 are summarized below, with each core principle in parentheses:

1. (Literacy) Basic literacy in the historical and current debates on the meaning and goals of sustainable development.
2. (Interdependence) Awareness of the interdependence of systems and of the mutuality of human and environmental conditions.

continues

Box 18.1 continued

3. (Systems, structures, and institutions) Understanding of the existing systems (status quo) and their relation to achieving the goals of sustainable development.
4. (Contextual analysis and application) Ability to analyze socioeconomic, political, institutional, and environmental contexts at the global and local levels and to use the analysis to support realistic sustainable change.
5. (Problem solving) Ability to use problem-solving methodologies in seeking innovative and effective sustainable development solutions.
6. (Evidence) Ability to use evidence to support the design, implementation, and evaluation of sustainable development policies, programs, and projects.
7. (Scarcity and distribution) Ability to understand concepts of scarcity and distribution and to make choices among alternative solutions in order to maximize change that fosters sustainable development.
8. (Relativity) Recognition of the function of time and of the need to make appropriate development decisions that suit differing time frames.
9. (Management) Ability to lead, manage, and support sustainable development organizations and interventions in order to maintain operational efficiency as well as to enable innovation and change.
10. (Communication) Communication skills necessary to lead and support organizations and interventions as well as to work with the range of stakeholders outside the organization.

Practice-oriented programs need to focus on values in order to turn development around—as well as offering an integrated, multidisciplinary curriculum; providing an innovative, challenging learning environment; and building a supportive, diverse community. So a graduate development studies program needs to be explicit about its values, while helping students identify their own values.

Students must also learn about the global principles and values that are already defined for sustainable development, on which their professional lives and work will be based. Practitioners need to understand the importance of values and come to terms with their own value preferences—for example, around the roles of the state, the private sector, and civil society, and in regard to such issues as equity, efficiency, conservation, power, human rights, gender, race, and class. They need to recognize how their value choices influence sustainable development strategies, methods, actions, and practices. Studying ethics will help students learn how to better base their work on values, how to grapple more effectively with dilemmas they will face in their careers, and how principles can help guide their decisions; studying ethics will help them develop ethical behaviors and even their own professional codes of conduct. Taken together, values and ethics help equip a student with a firm foundation for sustainable practice.

Development Studies and Curriculum

There is no single right way to design a graduate program for sustainable development or its curriculum. Ideals for an effective curriculum will always be tempered by factors outside our control; not the least of which are pragmatic concerns about access to financial resources, availability of faculty, and the size and nature of the student body. Furthermore, designing a curriculum is not a onetime, top-down process. A continuing responsibility of the leaders of a graduate development studies program is to facilitate participative curriculum review and redevelopment, assuring regular input from faculty, students, alumni, and other stakeholders to keep the curriculum fresh and relevant.

The backbone of a graduate-studies program is its curriculum. If a development studies program is committed to transforming development and upending how it's done, it helps to have a clear mission. For example, the mission of Brandeis University's SID program was "to build a new generation of development practitioners who could transform the conditions that give rise to persistent poverty and work towards a global society free of poverty, preventable disease, and environmental degradation." The idea was that students would be trained to become agents of transformation through the curriculum. For this book, we have designed an original framework of the curriculum for a graduate development studies program that aims to upend development practice and enhance sustainability, and that will prepare students to transform practice to achieve sustainable development and meet the needs of communities. It takes into account the voices of the SID alumni practitioners, knowledge from all the chapters, and our own experiences in the field and in teaching hundreds of graduate students in the SID program. It also covers all aspects of sustainable development, as outlined in our model in Chapter 3 (see Figure 3.1).

The curriculum schema (see Figure 18.1) calls for developing and providing courses in four focal areas. These are the three generally accepted dimensions of sustainable development—economic, social, and environmental—plus development management. Development manage-

Figure 18.1   Schema for a Sustainable Development Curriculum

<table>
<tr><td colspan="6" align="center">Transforming Development
Meeting the Needs of Practice: A Curriculum for Sustainable Development</td></tr>
<tr>
<td rowspan="2">C
O
R
E

C
O
M
P
E
T
E
N
C
I
E
S</td>
<td colspan="4">Multidisciplinary Areas: Examples of Required Courses
• The development industry: History, theories, and institutions
• Sociopolitical systems: Power, inclusion, and exclusion
• Integration of economic, social, and environmental theories
• Development ethics and reflective practice
• Development indicators and multidimensional systems of measurement</td>
<td rowspan="2">V
A
L
U
E
S</td>
</tr>
<tr>
<td colspan="4">MultidisciplinaryAreas: Examples of Electives
• International law, policy, and human rights
• Philosophical foundations of development theories and systems
• Corruption and development
• Climate change
• Conservation and development
• Vulnerability and resilience
• Demography, population, and migration
• Research methods and information management
• Geographic information systems</td>
</tr>
<tr><td></td><td colspan="5" align="center">Focal Areas</td></tr>
<tr><td></td><td>Economic
Dimension</td><td>Social
Dimension</td><td>Environmental
Dimension</td><td>Development
Management</td><td></td></tr>
<tr><td></td><td colspan="5" align="center">Focal Areas: Examples of Required Courses</td></tr>
<tr><td></td><td>• Development
economics</td><td>• Social policy and
justice
• Governance</td><td>• Ecology for
development
practitioners</td><td>• Adaptive
planning,
implementation,
and monitoring
• Evaluation
• Participatory
methods</td><td></td></tr>
<tr><td></td><td colspan="5" align="center">Focal Areas: Examples of Electives (all geared toward integrated development)</td></tr>
<tr><td></td><td>• Micro- and
macroeconomics
• Behavioral
economics
• Environmental
economics
• Household
economics
• Trade and labor
• Microfinance
• Cost benefit
analysis</td><td>• Education
• Public health
• Social movements
• Gender
• Disability
• Race and ethnicity
• Culture
• Religion
• Development and
the humanities
• Development and
the arts</td><td>• Environmental
impact
assessment
• Environmental
law and treaties
• Biodiversity and
extinctions
• Environmental
health
• Water and
sanitation
• Ecosystems
• Protected areas</td><td>• Fund-raising
• Organizational
management
• Working with
donors and
partners
• Financial
management
• Advocacy
• Communications
• Professional skills</td><td></td></tr>
<tr><td></td><td colspan="5" align="center">Practicum or in-depth field experience</td></tr>
</table>

ment expands the scope of traditional definitions of management. Definitions of management vary, but they generally include the mobilization of human and material resources within an organization to achieve specified goals. Specific functions of management may include planning, organizing, structuring, delegating, coordinating, reporting, and so on. Development adds transformative and enabling dimensions that change the status quo, including changing structures, systems, and paradigms. Development also entails a realignment of power, with deliberate effort to enhance capabilities and transfer power to those who have been marginalized or excluded.

In addition to the focal areas, the schema calls for the design of a newer kind of course within academia—a course that is multidisciplinary in accord with the integrated nature of sustainable development, which means cutting across all four focal areas. Implementing such courses can be very challenging, mainly because most professors are still trained in siloed specialties. Development studies programs therefore need to experiment with innovative forms of pedagogy and alternatives to traditional methods (team teaching, experiential and field-based learning, incorporating practice faculty, engaging guest speakers in-person or virtually, professional seminars, and so on). The focal areas and multidisciplinary offerings should have both required and elective courses to ensure that students can learn what they all need to learn and can also tailor their studies to their own professional goals and aspirations. Finally, the schema calls for an in-depth practicum or field-based experience, ideally of at least six months, so that students have the opportunity to apply and observe what they learned in the classroom in the real world of development.

Development Studies and Practice

Graduate students in development practice will themselves become the "outside experts," when they return to work in their own countries or even their home communities. In an upended world of practice, practitioners' roles include making new technologies and methods available, providing know-how, structuring inclusive processes, strengthening institutions, and sharing their power and knowledge with local organizations and communities. For example, development practitioners are no longer dictating solutions but are instead responsible for identifying and providing options of possible solutions, along with information that could be used to create original solutions. This will most likely include educating those who will make the choices and decisions, the communities that will be figuring out what will work best for themselves. This can also mean bringing in subject-area specialists who can work with, educate, and train the community in new technologies. As mentioned in Chapter 3, outside experts still have invaluable roles to play in upending development practice and advancing a new paradigm of sustainable development, rooted in principles of inclusion, local adaptive management, participation, and equitable sharing of power and benefits.

Chapter 3 emphasizes that we can't make proper choices if we don't know our options. In an upended model of development practice, practitioners need to know how to identify options through research, contacts, and prior experience; how to present them to stakeholders in understandable language; how to contact and bring in specialists, as needed; how to facilitate equitable, inclusive, legitimate decision-making processes; and how to advocate and ensure respect for decisions reached. To upend development practice and change the balance of power, students need to acquire a formidable arsenal of skills. These include knowing how to build capacity, empower vulnerable groups, strengthen institutions, identify stakeholders, and set up inclusive participatory frameworks. Practitioners must work with communities to plan, implement, and monitor projects; to connect stakeholders with resources needed for projects, including outside experts; to raise funds; and to share and communicate their knowledge so that stakeholders can understand and apply it. Conflicts will often surface in participatory processes, so practitioners can use training in how to resolve conflicts and differences. To be able to do all this requires new perspectives, knowledge, and skills that can be incorporated into the curriculum in development management courses, as well as in the three pillar focal areas and multidisciplinary offerings.

Finally, in this curriculum schema, all aspects of the sustainable development curriculum are framed by core competencies and values to ensure that students are educated and empowered to become agents of change and leaders who envision a new world society. This framework explicitly requires courses that enable students to identify theories and principles to guide their professional work, help them learn to challenge and question the values they bring to graduate school and to their future practice, and build not only the practical skills they need but also the "courage and confidence" to struggle to transform the status quo, development industry, and their own organizations.

Some of the challenges faced by formal education programs stem from differences in learning style, which can be greatly exacerbated in international programs with their diverse cohort of students from around the world. For most people, learning is iterative. We can envision this as a widening spiral. At the first stage, what is learned is limited and narrow but expands in successive iterations. A multidisciplinary approach requires that concepts be repeated, reinforced, and reintroduced in new ways in courses across disciplines. Programs need to know if, where, and how the iteration needed for multidisciplinary learning is happening. It is easier to take a multidisciplinary approach when core competencies are defined, mapped across the curriculum, and monitored for where and how they are being learned. Proper sequencing of courses also deepens learning, particularly if students need to be able to use concepts and skills taught in a few key courses in subsequent courses.

It's especially important for students to be able to connect concepts and tools that they learn in graduate school to on-the-ground development issues that are real to them, that they've experienced or seen themselves. Case studies, stories from experience, and experiential learning help students make these connections. This content can be student generated as well as professor generated, especially from professors of practice. The microcases in this book offer examples of development case studies that can support classroom learning and stimulate discussion.

Development Studies and University Culture

Professional graduate training and university cultures are sometimes an odd fit. Much of the university is devoted to scholarly research and teaching, not to applied learning. To some extent, exceptions can be found in professional schools—medicine, law, and social work come to mind, and perhaps in business schools that combine research with competency in practical skills. These professional schools are often well-established, financed, and normally lack the social-change mission required for a graduate program in sustainable development. This creates particular problems for practice-oriented development studies programs. To be effective, a development studies program first needs a highly diverse student cohort and then needs to create a positive learning environment. Today many US universities are struggling with the challenges of managing diversity in education. In truth, universities are inadequately structured and poorly prepared to manage diversity in a positive learning environment. Our contributors and our own experiences suggest several conditions that are necessary to build such a learning environment, if development studies programs are committed to educating a diverse student body and not just elites who can pay the high costs of education. These conditions can be very challenging to achieve.

First, there needs to be financial security for all members of a diverse learning community. This calls for fund-raising by program leaders and for effective financial management. It involves time and energy on budget management and negotiation with university officials about budget expenditures that are not necessary for a homogeneous, domestic student group. This includes funds for orientation, professional-skills support (for example, language, writing, computer skills, and communications), community building, and counseling that do not fit a traditional academic mold. It requires time nurturing links with institutional funders and individual philanthropists who may fund scholarships and endow fellowships for students or pay for special activities such as bringing in visiting practitioner-scholars and facilitating student exchanges or group travel. Program leaders and supportive faculty will struggle with the tension between their expected academic roles of research, publishing, and teaching and the demands of program management, outreach, and immersion in the needs of the community and community building. They will be forced to balance the opportunity costs of raising financial and technical support and building a diverse community with their own aspirations for academic advancement.

Second, students entering an environment of diversity need security (financial, intellectual, and emotional) and the opportunity to develop cultural competence and confidence. The shock can be great for students from the Global South arriving in the United States. They may struggle with how to adjust to and navigate a consumer society when they have limited means (sometimes severely limited). They may struggle with language, cultural cues, challenges of writing academic papers, unfamiliar standards regarding academic integrity and plagiarism, and different social norms with respect to relationships between the sexes or to distinctions of gender and sexual orientation. They may have left behind family or have come from situations of conflict and violence. US students are familiar with US academic life and social norms but, if the program is truly diverse, they too may feel out of place, uncomfortable, and dislocated. They may experience being a minority for the first time. Indeed, many of our domestic students expressed discomfort, and chafed at finding themselves in the minority. Northern students are likely to find that they know less about the field of development practice than their Southern counterparts, have fewer answers, and need to lower their voices.

Third, within this context, creating a secure, supportive environment in which students can effectively learn requires dedicated, experienced program staff, in addition to faculty. Universities can be very hierarchical institutions where authority and status are reserved for high-level administrators and faculty and where delegation to nonacademic staff is unusual. But committed staff can be incorporated into the mission of a program and significantly contribute to creating a learning community. At SID, for example, from organizing winter-coat drives, to lending an ear to a student who was lonely or having difficulty keeping up with work, to providing support to student-organized cultural evenings, to linking students to local "host" families, staff enabled students to adjust and feel at home and supported so they could make the most of their academic opportunity. Staff were rewarded with enriching relationships that lasted long after students graduated. To be sustainable, development studies programs need to invest in their staff as well as their faculty, not only financially (although a fair, equitable wage is essential) but also with incentives, inclusion in critical activities and decision making, creative ways to recognize and acknowledge a job well done, and opportunities for learning, enrichment, and professional advancement.

A Leadership Role for Universities

Educating development practitioners for transformative development practice is a legitimate role for universities today. Educating sustainable development professionals should not be confused with the current interest in workforce development. In this book we are stressing that we need practitioners who have not just the skills to perform jobs but also the values, critical thinking, and adaptability to use these skills to make a difference in human well-being and to transform societies, their structures, and the very nature of the industry within which they work.

Universities have traditionally had a mission of knowledge generation through teaching, research, and publication. They have also had the mission of facilitating educators and preparing learners to put that knowledge to work in the service of humanity and to solve difficult social, economic, environmental, and ethical problems in local and global societies. Increasingly, universities are called upon to resolve age-old problems of exclusion and racism. Providing a home for practice-oriented development studies programs that embody global, not parochial, perspectives and that embrace diversity and sustainability will advance that mission. Engaging with sustainable development practice is part of bridging the divide between knowledge generation and social action.

Universities have a critical role to play in upending development practice and in fostering global sustainable development. At their purest, universities are a neutral meeting place for people and ideas. Development studies programs can create an environment for learning and a living laboratory for problem-solving, innovation, and advancing global well-being that is sustainable, inclusive, and equitable. But to do this, universities have to change too—going beyond siloed disciplines and specialties, embracing new kinds of students and student-centered education, building new paradigms for learning and creating leaders, experimenting with new forms of excellence, and moving beyond business as usual. Perhaps the "ivory tower" needs to turn, too—not upside down or right-side up, but on its side, so it can reorient itself into a more horizontal, adaptable, less hierarchical structure with many doorways, one that can more easily be embedded in and accessible to the community, country, and globe, and that can open its expanding doors to a more inclusive system of education.

In keeping with the sustainable development agenda, the UN Decade of Education for Sustainable Development 2005–2015, which was led by UNESCO, had the goal of instilling in every human being the knowledge, skills, attitudes, and values necessary to shape a sustainable future. To do this and to achieve sustainable development requires leaders who are educated to develop and implement policy and programs to advance the transformative vision of sustainable development, that includes eradicating poverty, improving human well-being, and restoring the earth's balance. Graduate education in sustainable development has the power to bring about a sea change in how we live, in how we think, in our values and approaches, and in the ways we work with each other and with our planet.

References

Adelman, Irma. 2001. "Fallacies in Development Theory and Their Implications for Policy." In *Frontiers of Development Economics: The Future in Perspective,* edited by Gerald M. Meier and Joseph E. Stiglitz. New York, NY: Oxford University Press.

African Development Bank, Asian Development Bank, European Bank for Reconstruction and Development, European Investment Bank, Inter-American Development Bank, International Monetary Fund, and World Bank Group. 2015. "From Billions to Trillions: Transforming Development Finance, Post-2015 Financing for Development: Multilateral Development Finance." Development Committee.

Agardy, Tundi. 2010. *Ocean Zoning: Making Marine Management More Effective.* London, England: Earthscan Books.

———. 2011. "Civil Society and Ecosystem-Based Fisheries Management: Traditional Roles and Future Opportunities." In *Ecosystem-Based Fisheries Management,* edited by Andrea Belgrano and Charles W. Fowler. Cambridge, England: Cambridge University Press.

———. 2017. "The Five-Node Resource Nexus at Sea." In *Routledge Handbook of the Resource Nexus,* edited by Raimond Bleischwitz, Holger Hoff, Catalina Spataru, Ester van der Voet, and Stacy D. VanDeveer. London, England: Routledge.

Agardy, Tundi, and Jacqueline Alder. 2005. "Coastal Systems." In *Millennium Ecosystem Assessment: Strengthening Capacity to Manage Ecosystems Sustainably for Human Well Being,* Vol. 1, Current State and Trends Assessment. Washington, DC: Island Press.

Agardy, Tundi, John Davis, Kristen Sherwood, and Ole Vestergaard. 2011. *Taking Steps Toward Marine and Coastal Ecosystem-Based Management: An Introductory Guide.* UNEP Regional Seas Reports and Studies No. 189. Nairobi, Kenya: UNEP.

Agostini, Vera N., Shawn M. Margles, John K. Knowles, Steven R. Schill, Robbie J. Bovino, and Ruth J. Blyther. 2015. "Marine Zoning in Saint Kitts and Nevis: A Design for Sustainable Management in the Caribbean." *Ocean and Coastal Management* 104 (February): 1–10.

Alvaredo, Facundo, Lucas Chancel, Thomas Piketty, Emmanuel Saez, and Gabriel Zucman, eds. 2018. *World Inequality Report 2018.* World Inequality Lab. https://wir2018.wid.world.

Atwood, J. Brian. 1993. "Statement of Principles on Participatory Development, November 16, 1993." Washington, DC: US Agency for International Development.

Ayer, Austin, Stuart Fulton, Jacobo A. Caamal-Madrigal, and Alejandro Espinoza-Tenorio. 2018. "Halfway to Sustainability: Management Lessons from Community-Based, Marine No-Take Zones in the Mexican Caribbean." *Marine Policy* 93 (July): 22–30.

Ayittey, George. 2009. "George Ayittey on Dead Aid." TED Blog, April 9, 2009. https://blog.ted.com/ayittey_on_dead_aid.

Bain, Katherine, David Booth, and Leni Wild. 2016. *Doing Development Differently at the World Bank: Updating the Plumbing to Fit the Architecture.* London, England: ODI.

Balatsky, Alexander V., Galina I. Balatsky, and Stanislav S. Borysov. 2015. "Resource Demand Growth and Sustainability Due to Increased World Consumption." *Sustainability* 7 (3): 3430–3440.

Bauer, P. T. 1974. "Foreign Aid, Forever? Critical Reflections on a Myth of Our Time." *Encounter* (March): 15–28.

Benjaminsen, Tor A., and Ian Bryceson. 2012. "Conservation, Green/Blue Grabbing and Accumulation by Dispossession in Tanzania." *Journal of Peasant Studies* 39 (2): 335–355.

Block, Fred, and Margaret Somers. 1984. "Beyond the Economic Fallacy: The Holistic Social Science of Karl Polanyi." In *Vision and Method in Historical Sociology,* edited by Theda Skocpol. Cambridge, England: Cambridge University Press.

Bowles, Ian, and Cyril Kormos. 1995. "Environmental Reform at the World Bank: The Role of the US Congress." *Virginia Journal of International Law* 35: 777–839.

———. 1999. "The American Campaign for Environmental Reforms at the World Bank." *Fletcher Forum of World Affairs* 23 (1): 211–225.

Brinkerhoff, Jennifer. 2008. *Diasporas and Development.* Boulder, CO: Lynne Rienner.

British Council and IPSOS. 2014. *Mobilising the Humanities: The Development Perspective.* Washington, DC: British Council.

Bruckner, Pascal. 1986. *Tears of the White Man: Compassion as Contempt.* Translated by William R. Beer. New York, NY: Free Press.

Burgess, Matthew G., Michaela Clemence, Grant R. McDermott, Christopher Costello, and Steven D. Gaines. 2018. "Five Rules for Pragmatic Blue Growth." *Marine Policy* 87 (January): 331–339.

Burke, Lauretta, Janet Ranganathan, and Robert Winterbottom, eds. 2015. *Revaluing Ecosystems: Pathways for Scaling Up the Inclusion of Ecosystem Value in Decision Making.* World Resources Institute, issue brief, April 2015. Washington, DC: World Resources Institute.

Castellanos, Javier Z., M. Adrian Ortega-Guerrero, A. Grajeda, Antonio Vazquez-Alarcon, J. J. Villalobos, B. Munoz-Ramos, J. G. Zamudio, B. Martinez, P. Hurtado, Carlos Vargas, and S. A. Enriquez. 2002. "Changes in the Quality of Groundwater for Agricultural Use in Guanajuato." *Terra* 20: 161–170.

Cooley, Larry, and Richard Kohl. 2012. *Scaling Up—From Vision to Large Scale Change.* 2nd ed. Washington, DC: Management Sciences International.

Cotler, Helena, Silke Cram, Sergio Martinez-Trinidad, and Eduardo Quintanar. 2013. "Forest Soil Conservation in Central Mexico: An Interdisciplinary Assessment." *Catena* 104: 280–287.

Creel, Juan E. Bezaury, Robert Waller, Leonardo Sotomayor, Xiaojun Li, Susan Anderson, Roger Sayre, and Brian Houseal. 2000. *Conservation of Biodiversity in Mexico: Ecoregions, Sites and Conservation Targets; Synthesis of Identifications and Priority Setting Exercises (Draft)*. Washington, DC: The Nature Conservancy.

Creel, Liz. 2003. *Ripple Effects: Population and Coastal Regions*. Washington, DC: Population Reference Bureau.

Dollar, David, and Lant Pritchett. 1998. *Assessing Aid: What Works, What Doesn't, and Why*. World Bank Policy Research Report. Oxford, England: Oxford University Press.

Easterly, William. 2001. *The Elusive Quest for Growth*. Cambridge, MA: MIT Press.

———. 2006. *The White Man's Burden*. New York, NY: Penguin Books.

Ecosystem Sciences Foundation. 2006. *Calidad del Agua de los Pozos en San Miguel de Allende. Fase 1: Resultados y Conclusiones*. Boise, ID: Ecosystem Sciences Foundation.

Edwards, Sophie. 2017. "World Bank President Kim Calls for a 'Different and Difficult Conversation About Development Finance.'" *Devex*, April 12.

———. 2018. "Aid Sector 'Sluggish and Delusional' in Responding to Sexual Abuse, MPs Find." *Devex*, July 31.

Eyben, Rosalind. 2013. "Uncovering the Politics of 'Evidence' and 'Results': A Framing Paper for Development Practice." Paper prepared for The Politics of Evidence. http://bigpushforward.net/resources.

Eyler-Driscoll, Samantha. 2018. "The Other World Bank Scandal: A New Study Documents How Corporate Collusion Hurts the Bank's Credibility—and Harms Sustainable Development." *ProMarket*, January 23.

FAO, IFAD, UNICEF, WFP, and WHO. 2017. *The State of Food Security and Nutrition in the World 2017: Building Resilience for Peace and Food Security*. Rome, Italy: FAO.

Frank, Leonard. 1986. "The Development Game." *Granta Magazine* 20: 229–243.

Freire, Paulo. 1970. *Pedagogy of the Oppressed*. New York, NY: Continuum.

Gelpke, Nikolaus, and Martin Visbeck, eds. 2015. *Sustainable Use of Our Oceans— Making Ideas Work*. World Ocean Review 4. Hamburg, Germany: Maribus.

Gismondi, Mike. 1990. "Denis Goulet, New Ethics of Development." *Aurora Online*, Issue 1990. http://aurora.icaap.org/index.php/aurora/article/view/51/64.

Global Witness. 2017. "Defenders of the Earth: Global Killings of Land and Environmental Defenders in 2016." https://www.globalwitness.org/en/campaigns/environmental-activists/defenders-earth.

Gutierrez, Gustavo. 1983. *The Power of the Poor in History*. Maryknoll, NY: Orbis Books.

Hancock, Graham. 1989. *Lords of Poverty*. New York, NY: Atlantic Monthly Press.

Holcombe, Susan. 1995. *Managing to Empower*. London, England: Zed Books.

———. 2012. *Lessons from Practice: Assessing Scalability*. Washington, DC: World Bank.

Howard, Brian Clark. 2018. "Blue Growth: Stakeholder Perspectives." *Marine Policy* 87 (January): 375–377.

IEG. 2015. *Learning and Results in World Bank Operations: Toward a New Learning Strategy Evaluation 2*. Washington, DC: World Bank Group.

International Development Committee. 2018. "Sexual Abuse and Exploitation in the Aid Sector." Parliamentary report, July 31.

Johnston, Barbara Rose. 2005. "Chixoy Dam Legacy Issues: Overview." *International Rivers*, March 17.

Katona, Steven, Johanna Polsenberg, Julia Lowndes, Benjamin Halpern, Erich Pacheco, Lindsay Mosher, Anna Kilponen, Katherine Papacostas, Ana Guzman-Mora,

Ginny Farmer, Luca Mori, Olive Andrews, Sue Taei, and Sarah Carr. 2017. "Navigating the Seascape of Ocean Management: Waypoints on the Voyage Toward Sustainable Use." *Report of Open Channels: Forum for Ocean Planning and Management.* Woodinville, WA: OCTO.

Kosoy, Nicholas, Esteve Corbera, and Kate Brown. 2008. "Participation in Payments for Ecosystem Services: Case Studies from the Lancandon Rainforest, Mexico." *Geoforum* 39 (6): 2073–2083.

Landon Jr., Thomas. 2018. "The World Bank Is Remaking Itself as a Creature of Wall Street." *New York Times,* January 25.

Laski, Sarah. 2016. "Making Sustainable Development Work: A Case Study of Partners in Health." Master's thesis. The Heller School for Social Policy and Management, Brandeis University, Waltham, MA.

Lawson, Max. 2018. *Reward Work, Not Wealth.* Oxfam Briefing Paper, January. Oxford, England: Oxfam GB.

Mahlknecht, Jurgen, Jean F. Schneider, Broder J. Merkel, Ignacio Navarro de Leon, and Stefano M. Bernasconi. 2004. "Groundwater Recharge in a Sedimentary Basin in Semi-Arid Mexico." *Hydrogeology Journal* 12 (5): 511–530.

Maina, Thomas, Angela Akumu, and Stephen Muchiri. 2016. *Kenya County Health Accounts: Summary of Findings from Twelve Pilot Counties.* Washington, DC: Futures Group, Health Policy Project.

Maren, Michael. 1997. *The Road to Hell: The Ravaging Effects of Foreign Aid and International Charity.* New York, NY: The Free Press.

Miguel, Edward, and Michael Kremer. 2004. "Worms: Identifying Impacts on Education and Health in the Presence of Treatment Externalities." *Econometrica* 72 (1): 159–217.

Millennium Ecosystem Assessment. 2005. *Ecosystems and Human Well Being: General Synthesis.* Washington, DC: Island Press.

Ministry of Health. 2016. *The Best Practices in Health Sector: Open the Door to Innovative Practices.* Report for 2014–2015. Nairobi, Kenya: Health Sector Monitoring and Evaluation Unit. http://www.health.go.ke/wp-content/uploads/2017/06/REPORT-BEST-PRACTICES_fin-as-of-20170531.pdf.

Morris, Timothy. 1991. *The Despairing Developer: Diary of an Aid Worker in the Middle East.* London: I. B. Tauris.

Moyo, Dambisa. 2009. *Dead Aid: Why Aid Is Not Working and How There Is a Better Way for Africa.* New York, NY: Farrar, Straus, and Giroux.

Munk, Nina. 2013. *The Idealist: Jeffrey Sachs and the Quest to End Poverty.* New York, NY: Doubleday.

NPR (National Public Radio). 2018. *Living on Earth.* Broadcast, March 24.

OECD-DAC (Organisation for Economic Development and Co-operation, Development Assistance Committee). 2017. "Development Aid Rises Again." Paris, France: OECD.

Ortega-Guerrero, Adrian, Javier Castellanos, Ramon Aguilar-Garcia, Antonio Vazquez-Alarcon, Eduardo Alanis, Carlos Vargas, and Francisco Urrutia. 2002. "A Conceptual Model for Increases of Sodium, SAR, Alkalinity and pH at the Independence Aquifer in Guanajuato." *Terra* 20: 199–207.

Panday, Devendra Raj. 1989. "Administrative Development in a Semi-Dependency: The Experience of Nepal." *Public Administration and Development* 9: 315–329.

———. 2011. *Looking at Development and Donors.* Kathmandu, Nepal: Martin Chautari.

Pauly, Daniel. 2018. "A Vision for Marine Fisheries in a Global Blue Economy." *Marine Policy* 87 (January): 371–374.

Perera, Jehan. 1995. "In Unequal Dialogue with Donors: The Experience of the Sarvodaya Shramadana Movement." *Journal of International Development* 7 (6): 869–878.

Population Action International. N.d. *Population Dynamics, Environment, and Sustainable Development in Makueni County.* Washington, DC: Population Action International. https://pai.org/wp-content/uploads/2014/07/PAI_Makueni.pdf.

Republic of Kenya. 1965. *African Socialism and Its Application to Planning in Kenya.* Nairobi, Kenya: Government Printers.

———. 2010. *The Constitution of Kenya, 2010.* The National Council of Law Reporting. http://www.icla.up.ac.za/images/constitutions/kenya_constitution.pdf.

Roberts, J. Timmons, Bradley C. Parks, Michael J. Tierney, and Robert L. Hicks. 2009. "Has Foreign Aid Been Greened?" *Environment: Science and Policy for Sustainable Development* 5 (1): 8–21.

Rodrik, Dani. 2002. "After Neoliberalism, What?" In *After Neoliberalism: Economic Policies That Work for the Poor.* Collection of papers presented at the conference "Alternatives to Neoliberalism." Washington, DC: The New Rules for Global Finance Coalition.

Saenbut, Nittaya. 2014. "The Rhetoric of Participation and Ownership and the Reality of Development Practice: A Case Study of a Ghanaian NGO and the Innovative Community Benefits Health (CBH) Project Design." Master's thesis. The Heller School for Social Policy and Management, Brandeis University, Waltham, MA.

Safi, Michael. 2017. "Indian PM Inaugurates Sardar Sarovar Dam in Face of Activist Anger." *Guardian,* September 12.

Schwartzman, Stephen. 1986. "World Bank Holds Funds for Development Project in Brazil." *Cultural Survival Quarterly Magazine* (March).

Sen, Amartya. 1999. *Development as Freedom.* New York, NY: Alfred A. Knopf.

Shreeve, James. 2006. "The Greatest Journey." *National Geographic Magazine* (March): 61–69.

Silver, Jennifer J., Noel J. Gray, Lisa M. Campbell, Luke W. Fairbanks, and Rebecca L. Gruby. 2015. "Blue Economy and Competing Discourses in International Oceans Governance." *Journal of Environment and Development* 24 (2): 135–160.

Sotelo Nunez, Esthela Irene. 2006. "Recomendaciones Tecnicas del INE por Subcuenca." In *Atlas de la Cuenca Lerma-Chapala: Construyendo una Vision Conjunta,* edited by Helena Cotler Avalos, Marisa Mazari Hiriart, and Jose de Anda Sanchez. Mexico City, Mexico: Instituto Nacional de Ecologia (INE-SEMARNAT).

Stoltenborg, Didi. 2011. *Farmers' Perception on the Payment for Environmental Services Programs in the Watershed of Rio Laja, Mexico.* Wageningen, the Netherlands: Wageningen University.

Taylor, Elizabeth, Mark Baine, Annette Killmer, and Marion Howard. 2013. "Seaflower Marine Protected Area: Governance for Sustainable Development." *Marine Policy* 41 (September): 57–64.

UNCTAD. 2014. *World Investment Report 2014: Investing in the SDGs; An Action Plan.* Geneva: United Nations Publications.

UNDESA and UNDP. 2012. *Sustainable Development in the Twenty-First Century: Implementation of Agenda 21 and the Rio Principles.* New York, NY: Department of Economic and Social Affairs.

van Bochove, Jan-Willem, Emma Sullivan, and T. Nakamura, eds. 2014. *The Importance of Mangroves to People: A Call to Action.* Cambridge, England: United Nations Environment Program and World Conservation Monitoring Center.

van der Bliek, Julie, Peter McCormick, and James Clarke, eds. 2014. *On Target for People and Planet: Setting and Achieving Water-Related Sustainable Development Goals*. Colombo, Sri Lanka: International Water Management Institute (IWMI).

Voyer, Michelle, Genevieve Quirk, Alaistair McIlgorm, and Kamal Azmi. 2018. "Shades of Blue: What Do Competing Interpretations of the Blue Economy Mean for Oceans Governance?" *Journal of Environmental Policy and Planning* 20 (5): 595–616.

Willmann, Rolf, Kiernan Kelleher, and Ragnar Arnason. 2009. *The Sunken Billions: The Economic Justification for Fisheries Reform*. Agriculture and Rural Development Series, World Bank and FAO. Washington, DC: World Bank.

Woetzel, Jonathan, Nickolas Garemo, Jan Mischke, Martin Hjerpe, and Robert Palter. 2016. *Bridging Global Infrastructure Gaps*. New York, NY: McKinsey Global Institute.

World Bank. 1997. *Argentina and Paraguay—Yacyreta Hydroelectric Project: Review of Problems and Assessment of Action Plans (English)*. Washington, DC: World Bank.

World Bank. 2017a. *The Sunken Billions Revisited: Progress and Challenges in Global Marine Fisheries*. Environment and Development Series. Washington, DC: World Bank.

———. 2017b. *World Development Indicators 2017*. Washington, DC: World Bank.

World Commission on Environment and Development. 1987. *Our Common Future*. Oxford, England: Oxford University Press.

The Contributors

Tundi Agardy is a marine conservationist with extensive field and policy experience in Africa, Asia, the Caribbean, the Mediterranean, North America, and the Pacific.

Vinya Ariyaratne is general secretary of the Sarvodaya Shramadana Movement, Sri Lanka's largest grassroots NGO, with extensive experience in community development.

Patrick Awuah founded Ashesi University in Ghana in 2002 and serves as its president; Ashesi graduates are known for their integrity, initiative, and skills.

Thomas Dichter has over fifty years of international development experience working in more than sixty developing countries on four continents and with major donors.

Joshua Ellsworth is a practitioner with decades of experience in sustainable development, environmental education, and ecological restoration; he lectures at Tufts University.

Pallavi Gupta focuses on bridging mechanisms. As founder of Fifth Estate, she has worked on projects linking technology, business consulting, and social development.

Sarah Jane Holcombe began her career with the Population and Community Development Association in Thailand and now focuses on reproductive health and rights.

Susan H. Holcombe, professor emerita of the practice at Brandeis University, capped development practice in the field and headquarters with teaching development.

Fanny R. Howard is an educator and educational psychologist. She has worked with the Colombian government for many years in sustainable development and education.

Marion Howard, professor emerita at Brandeis University, taught sustainable development for fifteen years and is an active practitioner working with community-based conservation.

Esther Kamau, a PhD student at the University of Massachusetts, Boston, has over ten years of experience in the humanitarian and development fields in Kenya and East Africa.

Lu Lei has been a researcher at Renmin University of China. He also worked as an assistant resident representative at UNDP in Beijing and country director for TPAF.

Agustin Madrigal Bulnes is a geologist and cofounder and director of Salvemos al Rio Laja, AC. Since 2006, he has led Mexico's Watersheds and Cities program.

Rixcie Newball is an economist specializing in environmental economics; he heads the Seaflower Alliance in San Andres, a Colombian program of the Office of the President.

Elkanah Odembo, founding director of Nairobi-based Ufadhili Trust, has held leadership roles in many NGOs. He served as Kenya's ambassador to France and the United States.

Raymond Offenheiser, director of the Keough School of Global Affairs, distinguished professor of the practice at Notre Dame, was president of Oxfam America for over twenty years.

Andrea Savage Tejada is a practitioner working in conservation finance, especially in Latin America, applying economic tools for conservation and community well-being.

Laurence Simon, professor and director of the Center for Global Development and Sustainability at Brandeis University, founded and led its SID program (1993–2014).

Christian Velasquez Donaldson is policy adviser on International Financial Institutions (IFIs) at Oxfam International and is currently based in Washington, DC.

Index

A4ID. *See* Advocates for International Development
Abed, Sir Fazle Hasan, 54
ABT Associates, 91
Accountability, 16, 128, 236; challenges with, 139–140; focus on, 159; of INGOs, 127; institutionalized, 18; lack of, 76; as mutual, 45n2, 238–239; Oxfam International and, 132–134; transparency and, 19, 23, 114, 244–245
Accra Agenda for Action (2008), 13, 241
ACEP. *See* African Center for Energy Policy
Action Against Hunger USA, 6
ActionAid, 91, 186
Adaptive management, 35
Addis Ababa, 126
Adelman, Irma, 17
Advocates for International Development (A4ID), 13
AfCFTA. *See* African Continental Free Trade Agreement
Afforestation, 167
Africa, 56; entrepreneurship in, 96, 100; human well-being in, 17; innovation in, 100; leadership in, 99, 102, 104; southern, 121; sub-Saharan, 99; visible needs of, 95. *See also* South Africa
African Center for Energy Policy (ACEP), 136

African Continental Free Trade Agreement (AfCFTA), 191
African NGOs, 185–195
African Union (AU), 136, 191, 195
Africans, 3; capacity, 233–234; local challenges addressed by, 106; pride of, 102; students, 57; trust earned by, 98
AfroBarometer, 186
Aga Khan Foundation, 54
Agenda 21, 27, 37, 241
Agenda for Sustainable Development, 2030, 6, 27, 44, 156, 241
Aid, 15; corruption, governance and, 22–23; power and aid, 34; demeaning terms and aid, 34; dependence on, 243; effectiveness of, 34–35, 233; fragmentation of, 33; industrialization of, 20
Aid-delivery system, 35
Alcoholism, 79
Alder, Jackie, 123
Alignment, 45n2
Alkire-Foster method, 230
Allende Reservoir, 171, 183
Amazon basin, 151
American Jewish World Service, 52
American University, 83
AmidEast, 53
Amnesty International, 186
ANH. *See* National Agency of Hydrocarbons
Anti-Corruption Conference, 22

275

Murag'a county, 165
MVP. *See* Millennium Villages Project

Narmada River, 151
National Agency of Hydrocarbons, Colombia (ANH), 210–211
National Climate Change Action Plan, 167
National execution (NEX), 197–200, 203–205, 207–208
National Public Radio (NPR), 62
Nationalism, 127
The Nature Conservancy, 114, 122
Neocolonialism, 18, 90
Neoliberalism, 8
Nevis, 122
New Development Bank, 153
New School for Social Research, 52
NEX. *See* National execution
NGO Act of 1990, 190
Ngoile, Magnus, 115
NGOs. *See* Nongovernmental organizations
Niger, 86–88
Nigeria, 192, 229
Nongovernmental organizations (NGOs), 4, 54, 69, 111; contract bidding by, 88; engagement of, 14; as local, 236; for poverty-alleviation programs, 73; role of, and academia, 117–120. *See also* African NGOs
NORAD. *See* Norwegian Agency for Development Cooperation
North, 1, 7; dominance of, 16–19, 229–230; as model, 93; power struggles between South and, 18, 32; reliance on, 241; resources in, 19; as reversing attitudes, 245; roles of South and, 227–228; values of, 29
Northern hegemony, 39
Norwegian Agency for Development Cooperation (NORAD), 74, 75
Northwestern University, 84
Novartis Foundation for Social Development, 74
NPR. *See* National Public Radio

Obama, Barack, 137
OCAS. *See* Citizens Water and Sanitation Council; Citizen's Water and Sanitation Council
Oceans, 109–112
ODA. *See* Official development assistance

OECD. *See* Organization for Economic Cooperation and Development
Official development assistance (ODA), 10, 23
Oil for Agriculture, 136
One Acre Fund, 6
One Belt One Road. *See* Chinese Silk Road initiative
One Foundation, 203–204
Open Society Foundations, 53
Oppression, 52, 231
Organisation for Economic Co-operation and Development (OECD), 12, 21, 199
Osher Lifelong Learning Institute at Brandeis (BOLLI), 54
Our Common Future, 28, 60
Overbrook Foundation, 172
Oxfam America, 125, 141n1
Oxfam Great Britain, 131, 141n1
Oxfam International, 3, 12, 54, 125, 221–224; Congress support for, 137; rights-based approach of, 133; self-evaluation of, 128–129; strategies of, 132; voice of, 130
Oxfam Research Network, 132

Panday, Devendra Raj, 11, 15, 20
Pandemics, 25
Paris Agreement on climate change (2015), 126, 154–155, 191
Paris Declaration on Aid Effectiveness (2005), 13, 21–22, 33, 45n2, 89
Participation, 21; devolution and, 161–163; engaging, 245n1; levels of, 81; meaningful, 27, 36–39; public, 168; structures of, 160; sustainability and, 37–39
Paternalism, 33
PATF. *See* Poverty alleviation task force
Patterson, Don, 172
Payments for ecosystem services (PES), 119
PBC. *See* People's Bank of China
PDA. *See* Population and Community Development Association
PDIA. *See* Problem Driven Iterative Adaptation
Peace building, 25, 75
Peace Corps, 89–90
People's Bank of China (PBC), 201
Persian Empire, 64
Peru, 134–135

About the Book

Practicing Development bridges the gap between academia and the world of practice to address challenges and propose concrete steps toward more equitable, effective, and sustainable development.

The authors draw from their on-the-ground experiences as they discuss what "development" is, how to attain it, and what their findings mean for the funding and practice of development efforts. Often challenging conventional wisdom, they provide a range of concrete examples of innovation, responsiveness, and sustainability—and perhaps most important, explore how practitioners might be better educated to achieve positive change.

Susan H. Holcombe is professor emerita of the practice and **Marion Howard** is professor emerita at Brandeis University's Heller School for Social Policy and Management.